IMAGES
of America

HIGHLANDS

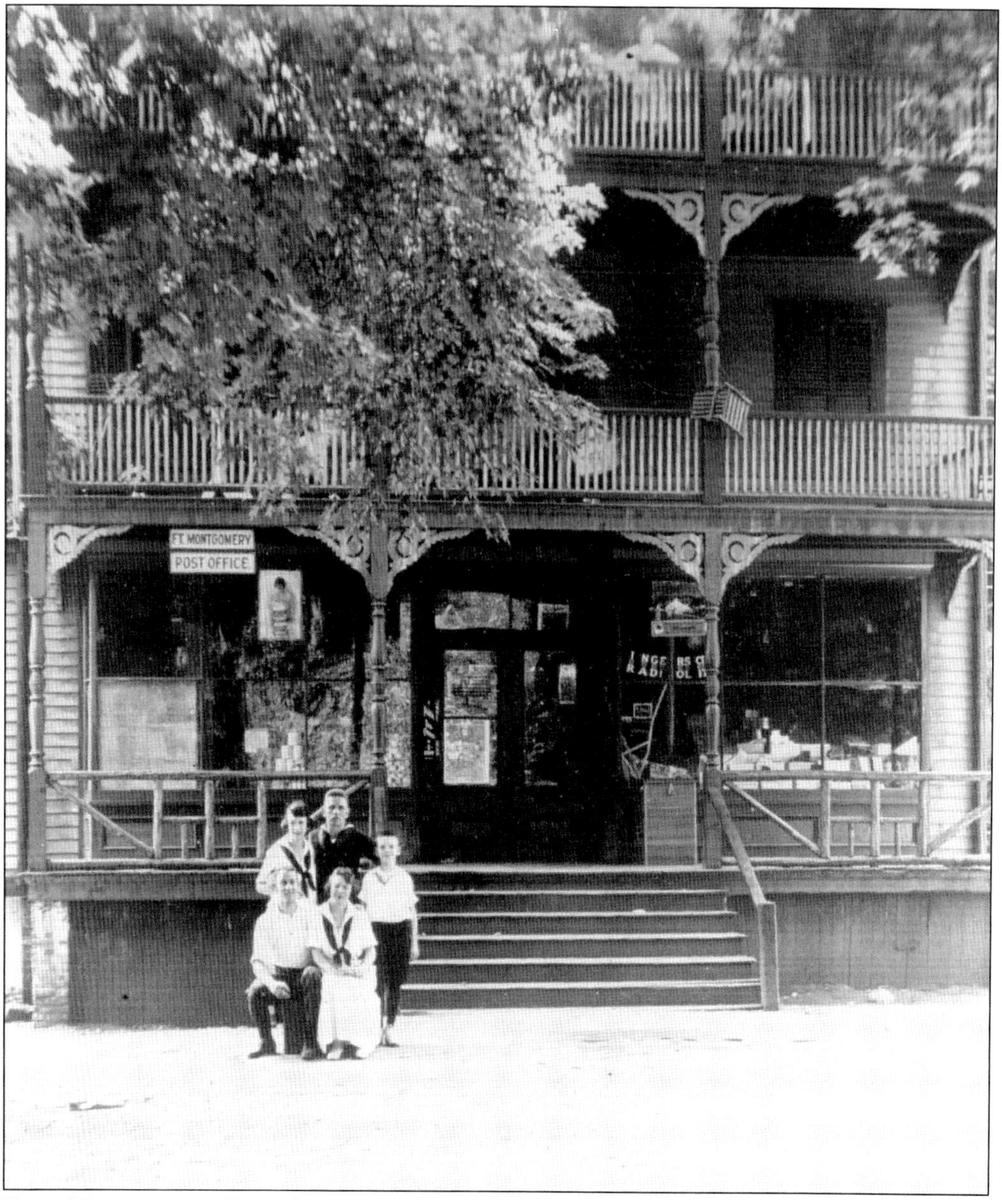

FORT MONTGOMERY POST OFFICE. A century ago, this three-story Victorian structure housed the Fort Montgomery Post Office and a general store operated by postmaster Clarence Weyant. Immediately in front, a group of five gathers on "Fourth of July, 1919." The store sold food, necessities, and penny candy. Its location near the railroad station and dock made it a popular spot with tourists as well as residents. (THHS Archives.)

On the cover: Please see page 72. (PIPC Archives.)

IMAGES
of America

HIGHLANDS

Ronnie Clark Coffey

ARCADIA
PUBLISHING

ISBN 978-0-7385-4647-6

Published by Arcadia Publishing
Charleston, South Carolina

Printed in the United States of America

Library of Congress Catalog Card Number: 2006928538

For all general information contact Arcadia Publishing at:
Telephone 843-853-2070
Fax 843-853-0044
E-mail sales@arcadiapublishing.com
For customer service and orders:
Toll-Free 1-888-313-2665

Visit us on the Internet at www.arcadiapublishing.com

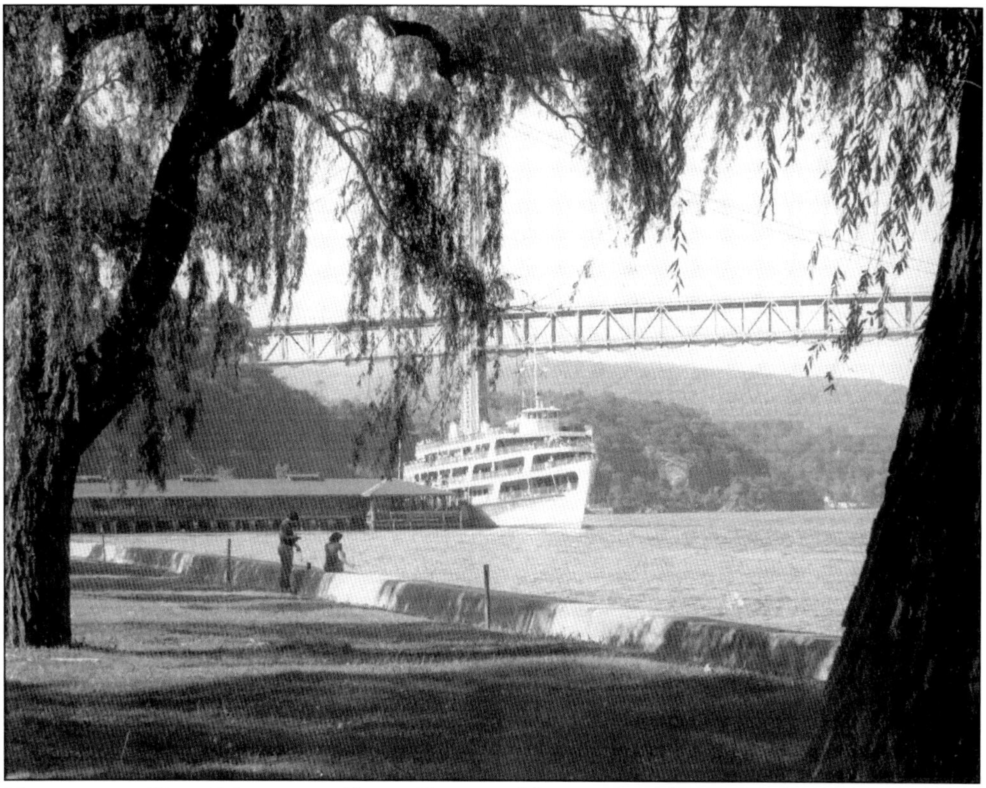

***DAYLINER* AT BEAR MOUNTAIN.** Framed by graceful riverside willow trees, the *Dayliner* waits at Bear Mountain Dock for New York City–bound passengers. Noted for their scenic grandeur, the Highlands of the Hudson River are an ideal destination for a day trip. For the residents of the Town of Highlands, this lovely place where mountains meet river is home. (PIPC Archives.)

Contents

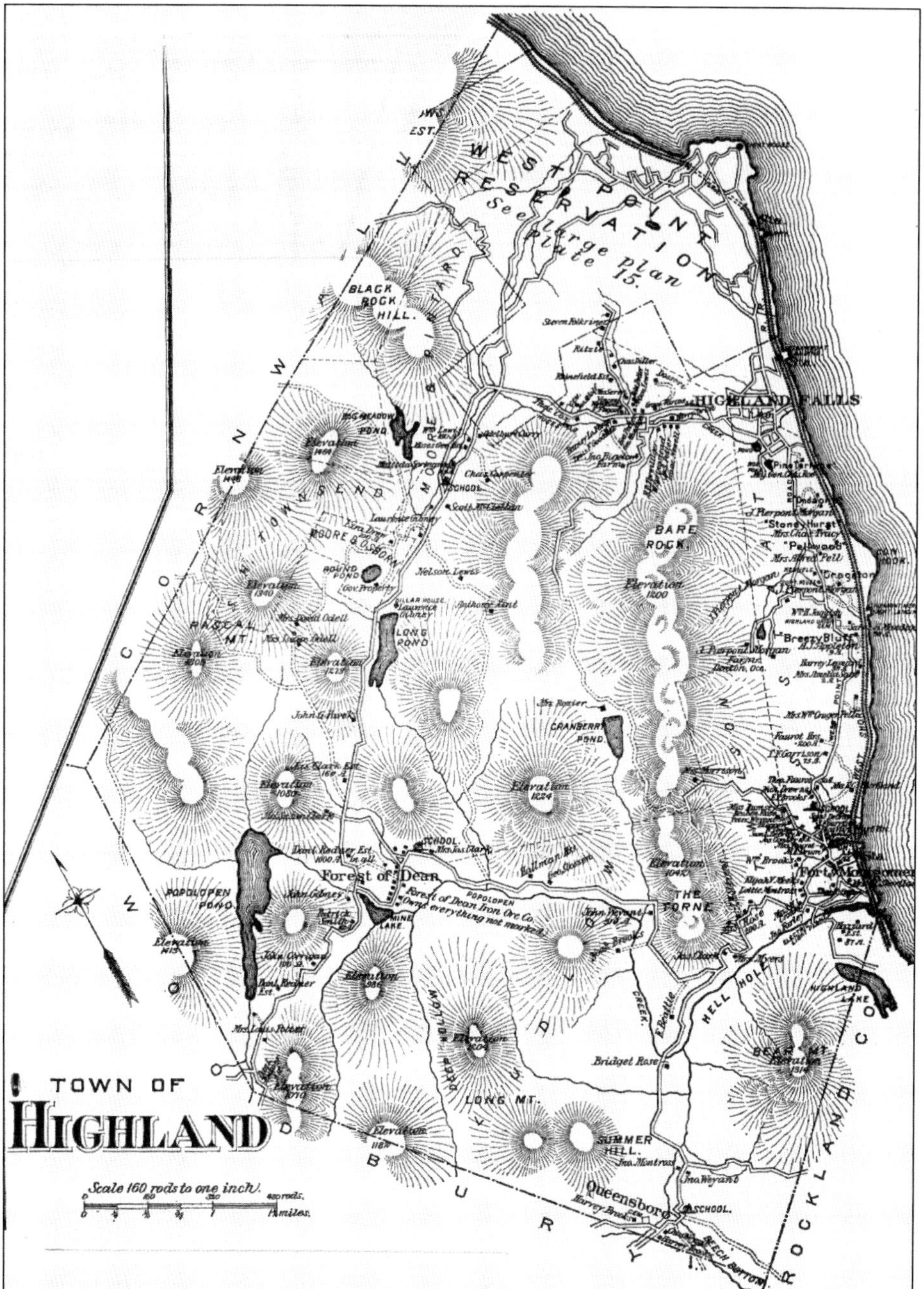

TOWN MAP. From north to south, the historic Town of Highlands is comprised of West Point, Highland Falls, Fort Montgomery, and part of Bear Mountain State Park. Within its boundaries are the United States Military Academy, Black Rock Forest Preserve, a segment of the Appalachian Trail, numerous lakes, streams, mountains, and the majestic shoreline of the Hudson River. (Sidamon-Eristoff Collection.)

INTRODUCTION

In the Highlands, the powerful forces of nature are ever-present. It is a place that affects you emotionally, opens the senses, and connects you with the ground on which you stand.

—Frances F. Dunwell, *The Hudson River Highlands*

Even Henry Hudson was impressed. On his famous exploration voyage, the ship's officer, Robert Juet, described the reason Hudson anchored the Half Moon in the river on September 30, 1609: "The high land hath many Points, and a narrow channel, and hath many eddie winds." Thus, awed by scenery and weather, a writer entered the Hudson Highlands into recorded history.

Before the arrival of Europeans, the land had been a bountiful home to tribes of Native Americans, particularly the Munsee-speaking Lenape Indians, later known as the Delaware. Utilizing the resources of forest, streams, lakes and river, they lived in well-organized villages and used rock shelters as temporary residences for hunting and fishing trips. They gathered oysters a foot wide from the vast reaches of the river and brought them home to feast. Skeletons of sturgeon over five feet long have been unearthed in their shelters. From the meticulous study of artifacts, archeologists have determined that Native Americans had thrived in the region at least 10,000 years before the first sailing ship appeared. From that moment, life along the tidal waterway that the Lenape called "the river that flows two ways" was never the same.

The Dutch scorned the rocky soil of the Highlands in favor of the more fertile areas around Manhattan and Albany. The English, however, after their defeat of the Dutch, encouraged settlement to strengthen their hold on New York. In the early 1700s, the British Crown gave land grants along the river and so began a new chapter in the Hudson Valley. The tract given to Samuel Staats would become Fort Montgomery. The parcel given to Gabriel and William Ludlow would become Buttermilk Falls. The grant to Charles Congreve would become West Point.

In the beginning, the population was sparse. The first major industry was iron mining west of the river at a settlement named Forest of Dean, also the name of an ancient mining region in England. The rich ore became famous for its high quality. The large land grants changed owners and were divided by stone walls, sold, and then resold. Farming and cordwood cutting were other early industries. By 1777, many of the settlers, catching the Revolutionary fever, helped build and maintain Fort Montgomery on the north side of Popolopen Creek and Fort Clinton on the south side. Anticipating a British attack up the Hudson, they also installed a log boom with a massive chain laid on top of it from Fort Montgomery to Anthony's Nose. Seeking to control the Hudson River, the British attacked on October 6, 1777. They captured both forts and then dismantled the chain. In 1778, a second chain was placed between West Point and Constitution Island, but the British did not come this way again. Meanwhile, West Point was deemed the ideal location for a military academy. Though it had been George Washington's dream, the academy was not established until 1802, under Pres. Thomas Jefferson.

In the 1790s, a gristmill was built at the foot of Buttermilk Falls. Later sold to David Parry, it became the focal point of a village. The nearby Swim's Tavern gave the name Swimtown to the area south of the mill. At the same time, a Frenchman named Eugene Lucet opened a gristmill five miles south on Popolopen Creek. The creek was deep at its mouth and could accommodate vessels of 50 tons. Three docks, three houses, and a slitting mill to manufacture nails also sprang up along the creek. Separate post offices were established in the mid-1800s for Fort Montgomery and Buttermilk Falls, which later changed its name to Highland Falls. Separate West Shore Railroad stations soon followed. Simultaneously, tourism at West Point became fashionable, leading to the growth of the hospitality industry in Highland Falls and Fort Montgomery.

As urban overcrowding increased in New York City, the Highlands became a popular destination for people seeking the peace and beauty of nature. Hikers and campers were common sights in the warm weather. Travelers came by rail, riverboat, and over land, which led to the improvement of roads and the building of bridges. Several wealthy visitors purchased country estates along the Hudson, among them John Bigelow, J. P. Morgan, Alfred Pell, and Charles Tracy.

By 1900, the Palisades Interstate Park Commission had begun a massive environmental protection project to preserve the shore of the Hudson from excavation, trap rock mining, and overbuilding. In 1910, the commission established Bear Mountain State Park, which became an immediate success, rivaling the most popular national parks. The widespread use of the automobile and the consequent building of the Bear Mountain Bridge lured tourists to the Highlands but gradually led to the obsolescence of the West Shore Railroad. Economic and sociological changes were occurring as well. Expansion of the United States Military Academy increased the student body and the corresponding need for more construction and support personnel. Immigrants from Alsace-Lorraine, Czechoslovakia, Ireland, Italy, Germany, Greece, and other countries helped fill the need with their skills. African American cavalrymen, known as Buffalo Soldiers, were stationed at West Point and many lived in Highland Falls with their families.

All this time, the number of schools, churches, businesses, and homes increased. Because of the many career opportunities at West Point, the federal government was the main employer of the Town of Highlands; however, it was not the only one. Industries included factories for manufacturing shirtwaists and razor strops, flower growing, soda bottling, ice harvesting, milling, fuel extracting, iron mining, and farming. West of Highland Falls, dairy farms lined the road to Central Valley at Stony Lonesome and along Route 293. In 1942, the federal government assumed ownership of much of this land to increase training facilities for the army. Although all understood the noble purpose, the loss of old homesteads still left some families heartbroken.

Like the long gray line of cadets past and present, residents of the Town of Highlands have served their country proudly and with the same devotion as the first Revolutionary soldiers, both in war and in peace. At no time was this pride more evident than in 1981, when citizens welcomed home the American hostages who had been held in Iran. The outpouring of warmth and patriotic spirit gave the town the nickname it so appropriately bears today: "Hometown, USA."

The history of the Town of Highlands outlined above in words is now presented in visuals. The photographic image offers a compelling way to view history—through the details. The amateur and professional photographs compiled here come from a variety of sources. They were all saved by their owners. Some were framed and displayed proudly for many years or pasted carefully into black-paged albums. Others, almost forgotten, were resurrected from dusty attics, musty files, cigar boxes, and baby books for this purpose. Some were identified on back or front with all the names correctly spelled and all the dates correctly written. The identifications of others relied on the memories of family and friends and were dated by clothing or age of the youngest cousin.

Whatever the provenance, these images now give us the opportunity to see the past and to enter it, time and time again.

—Ronnie Clark Coffey

One

Revolutionary Road

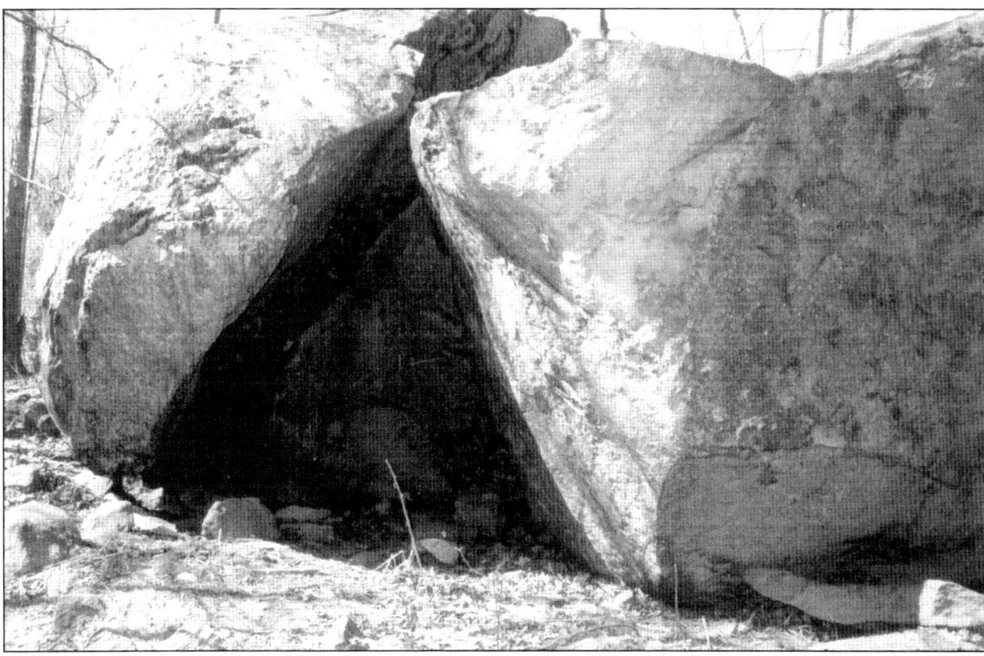

Rock Shelter. Human habitation in the Hudson River Valley can be dated back over 10,000 years. Archaeologists have excavated rock shelters such as this one in Fort Montgomery that were used as hunting and fishing camps. The predominance of spear points and arrowheads indicate that they were used primarily by men. Well-preserved pipes and pots, bones of large sturgeon, and oyster shells from the Tappan Zee have all been unearthed in Highlands rock shelters. (Scott Collection.)

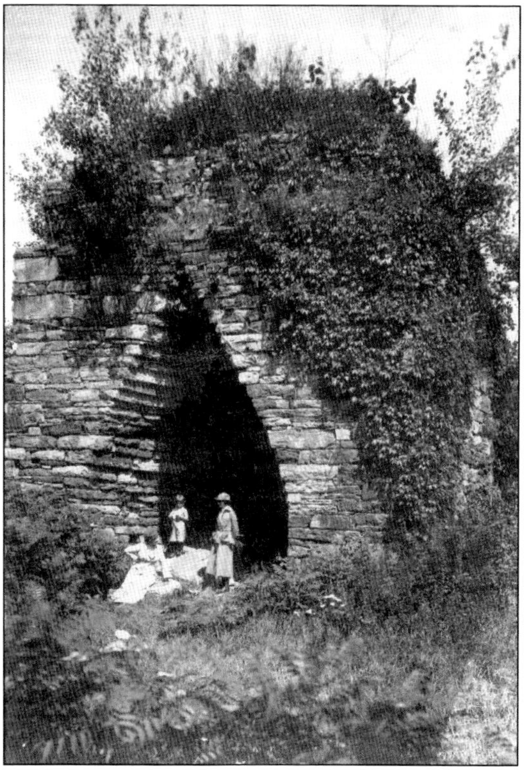

QUEENSBORO FURNACE. One of the earliest industries in the Highlands was iron mining. Rich veins of ore had been discovered at several locations. After being mined and processed, iron was brought to a forge such as this one near Mine Road, Fort Montgomery, where it could be melted down into "pig iron" and then shaped into bars for shipment. This Revolutionary War–period forge was photographed in 1910. (PIPC Archives.)

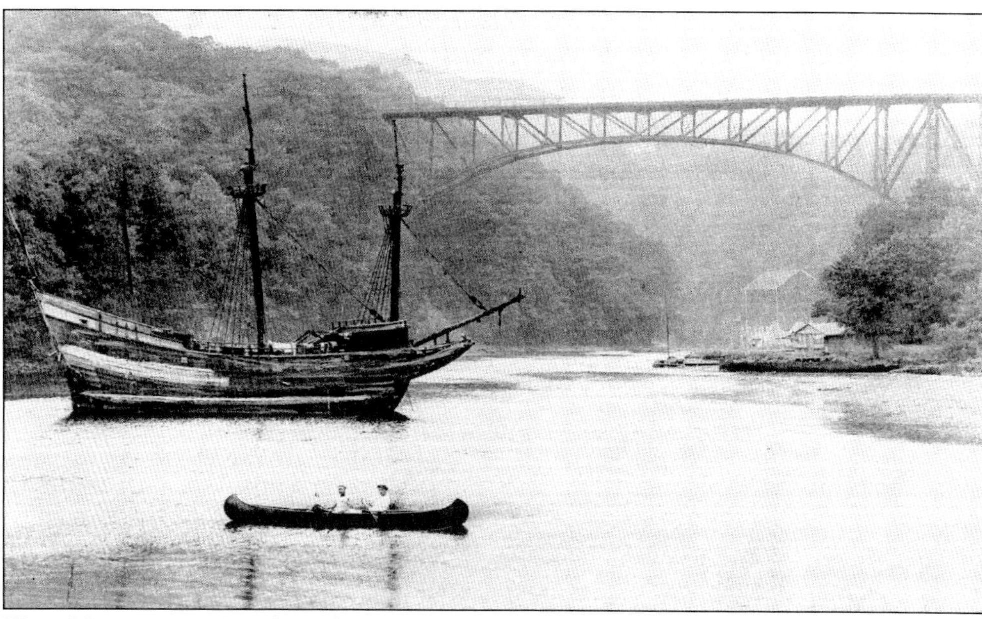

HALF MOON, 1911. A replica of Henry Hudson's *Half Moon* was anchored at Popolopen Creek following the Hudson-Fulton Celebration of 1909, in commemoration of the 1609 exploration of the river. Hudson, an Englishman, was hired by the Dutch to find a passage through North America. Following the advice of his friend Capt. John Smith, Hudson explored a "sea" near New England, going as far as Albany. (Scott Collection.)

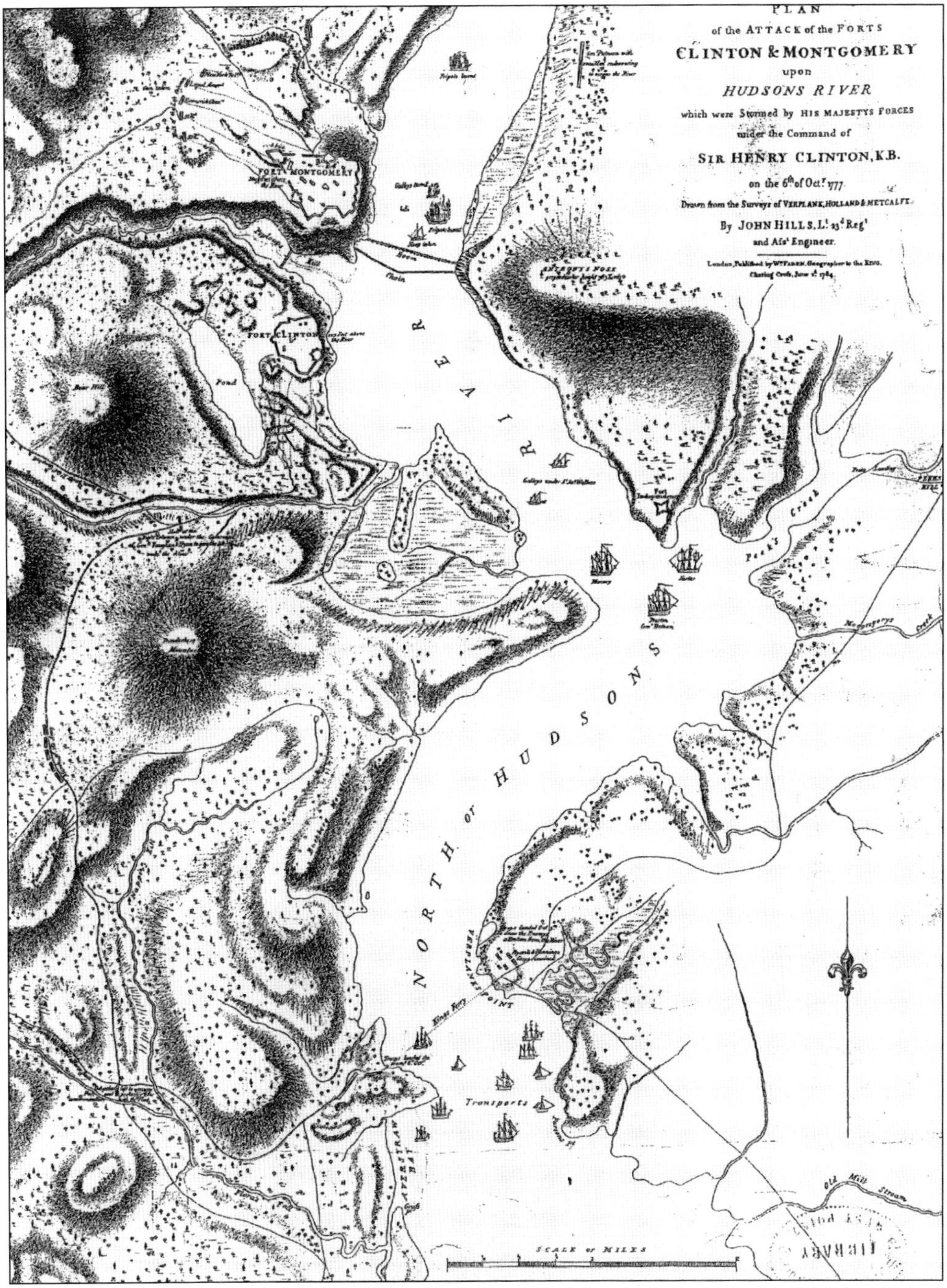

Map of British Attack. At the dawn of the American Revolution, the Highlands had tremendous military importance. The British intended to "divide and conquer." Commanded by Sir Henry Clinton, the army expected to separate the northern colonies from the southern by controlling communication and transportation on, as well as across, the Hudson River. The American plan was to block passage of the British up the Hudson. (USMA Library.)

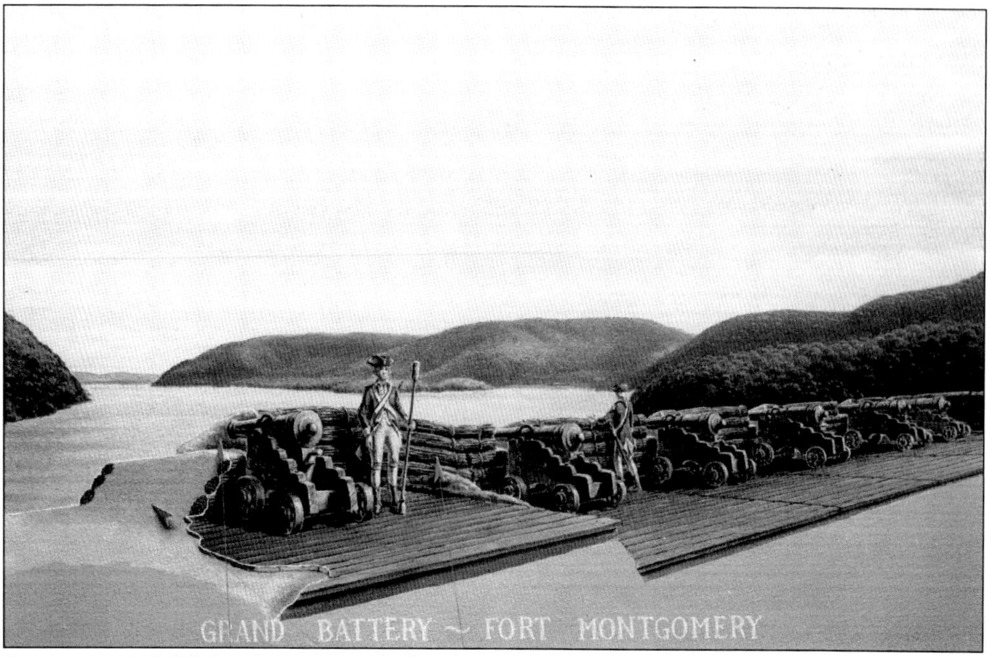

BATTERY, 1776. Under the command of Col. James Clinton, American troops built fortifications at Fort Montgomery on the north side of Popolopen Creek and Fort Clinton on the south side. Fort Montgomery was named for General Montgomery, a fallen hero of the Battle of Quebec. Fort Clinton was named for Colonel Clinton's brother George, the governor of New York. (PIPC Archives.)

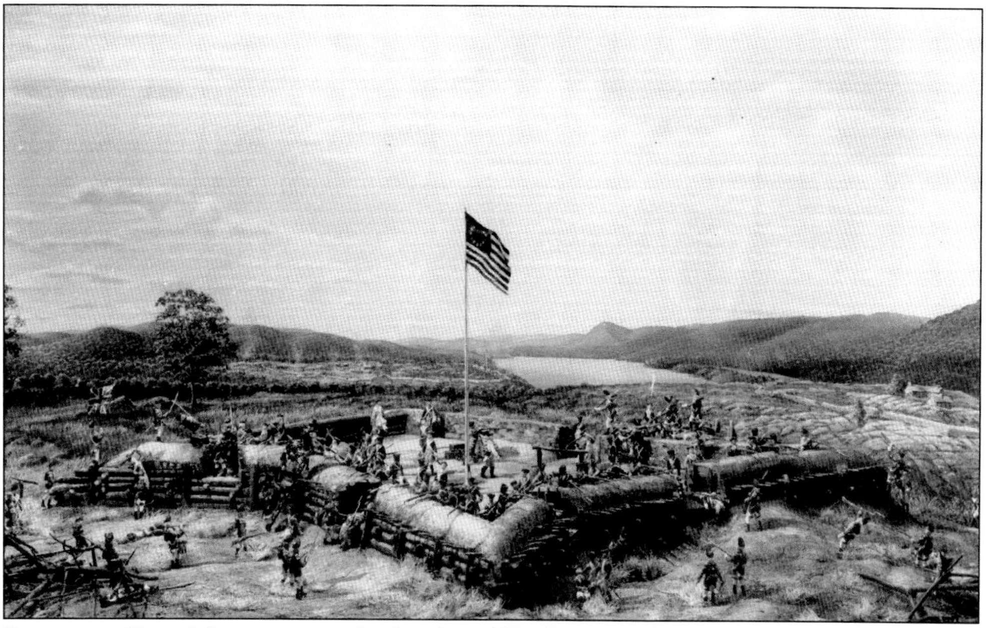

BATTLE OF FORT MONTGOMERY. In October 1777, the critical moment came. On the heights above the Hudson, an American force of 600 volunteer farmers and woodcutters met a trained, professional army of about 3,000 British and Hessian soldiers. After a full day of vicious fighting, the Americans finally succumbed. Historian Robert Binneweiss calls it "one of the most gallant stands in the annals of U.S. military history." (PIPC Archives.)

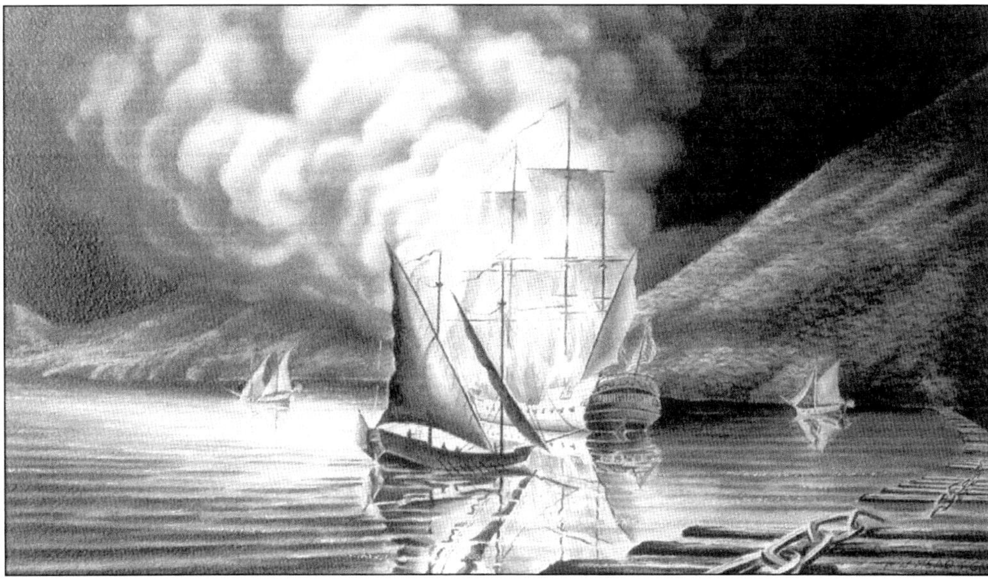

Chain and Ships. Defenses at Fort Montgomery included a massive chain stretched across the river to keep the British from sailing north. As seen here, the chain was supported by log rafts to keep it afloat. The Americans had positioned five ships to guard the chain. As the outcome of the battle became evident, the patriots burned their ships to prevent their capture. A witness described them as "pyramids of fire." (PIPC Archives.)

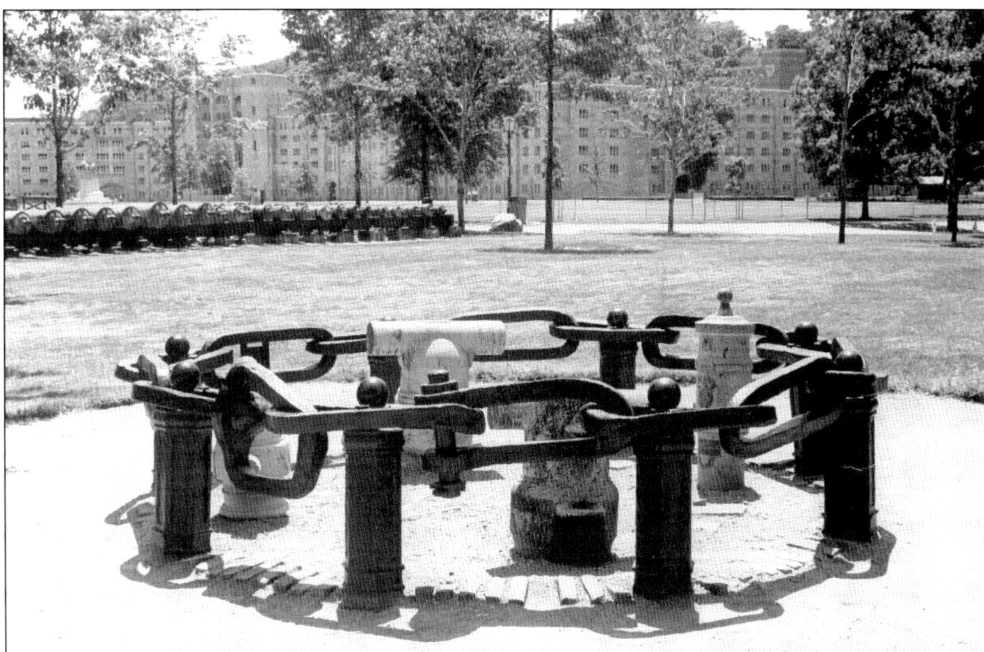

The Great Chain. The links displayed here at West Point are from a larger chain stretched across the Hudson between West Point and Constitution Island in 1778. This "Great Chain" was used until the end of the Revolutionary War but was never tested. Despite the capture of Forts Montgomery and Clinton, the British failed to control the Hudson and the war moved south. (U.S. Army photograph, Bosch Collection.)

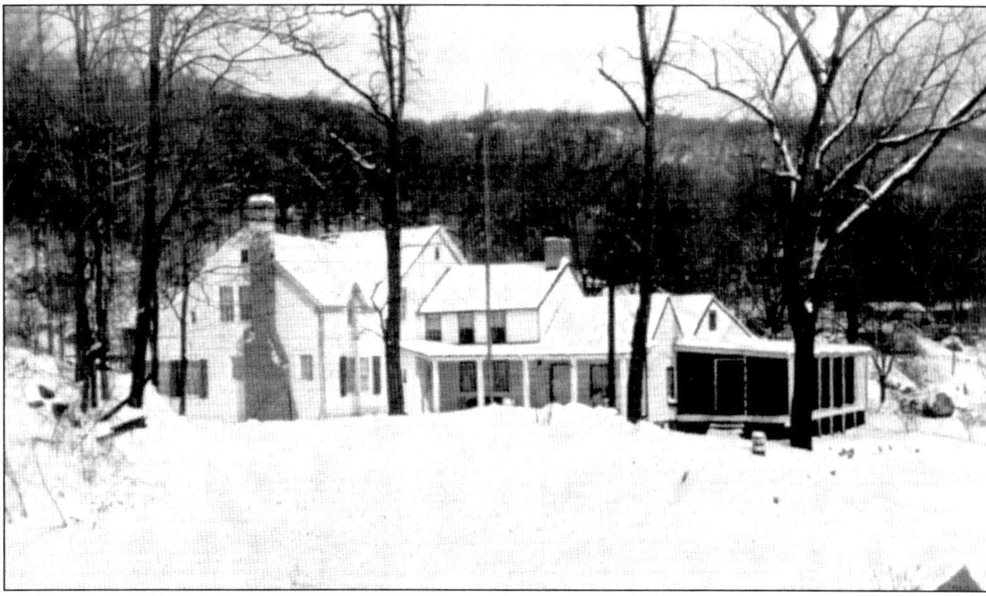

Garrison Home. This house on Route 9W was the home of Isaac Garrison, a cannoneer captured at the Battle of Fort Montgomery. Revolutionary heroine Molly Corbin lived for a time at the Garrison Homestead in Fort Montgomery after the war. "Captain Molly" was wounded at Fort Washington while she took the place of her husband, an artilleryman, who was killed while preparing his cannon for firing. A monument marks her grave at the West Point Cemetery. (Scott Collection.)

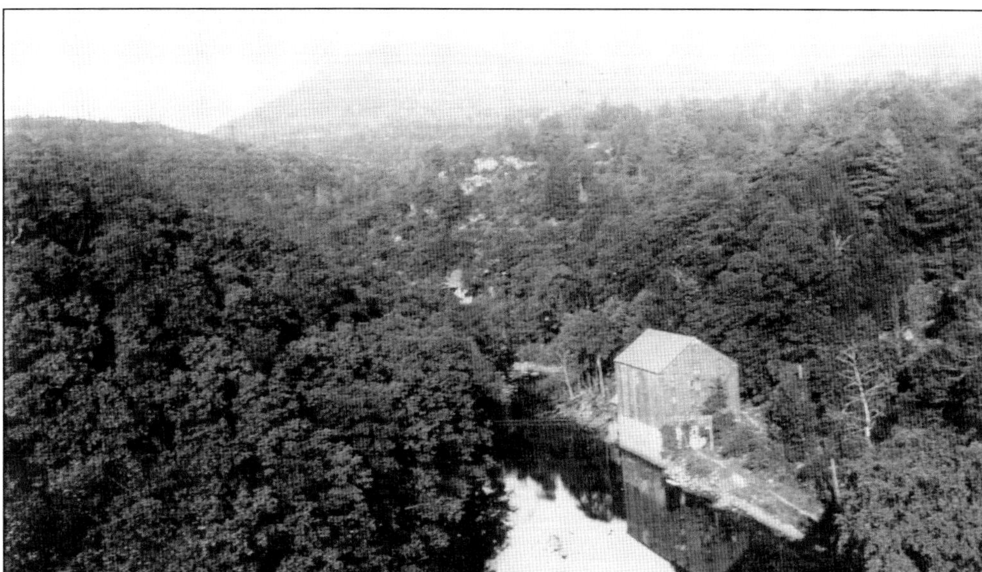

Lucet Mill, c. 1790. After the Revolutionary War, the number of settlers in the Highlands slowly increased. During the late 18th century, Eugene Lucet built a gristmill on the north shore of the Popolopen Creek. It was well situated because the creek was navigable for vessels up to 50 tons. Soon the area had three docks, three dwellings, a store, a sawmill, and a slitting mill for the manufacture of nails. (Gunza Collection.)

Two

Early Days

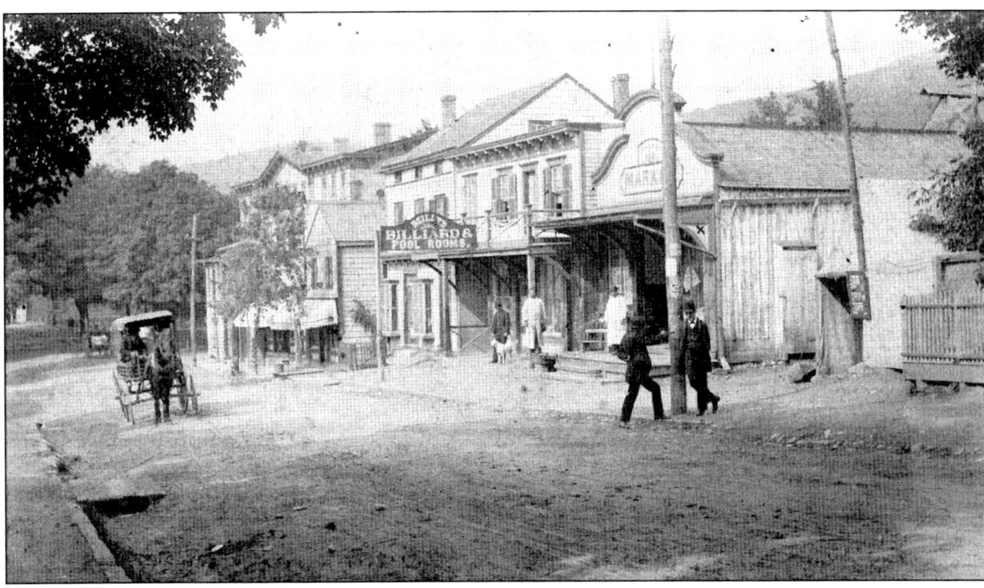

Street Scene, c. 1900. Bystanders pause to watch a buggy traveling north on Main Street, Highland Falls, as it passes a cluster of wood-frame buildings. Visible farthest down the unpaved road is the long, high roof of the Stephens Hotel, followed by the brick facade of the Kopald house. The building to the right of the billiard parlor sign has been known more recently as Andy's Restaurant. (Parry Collection.)

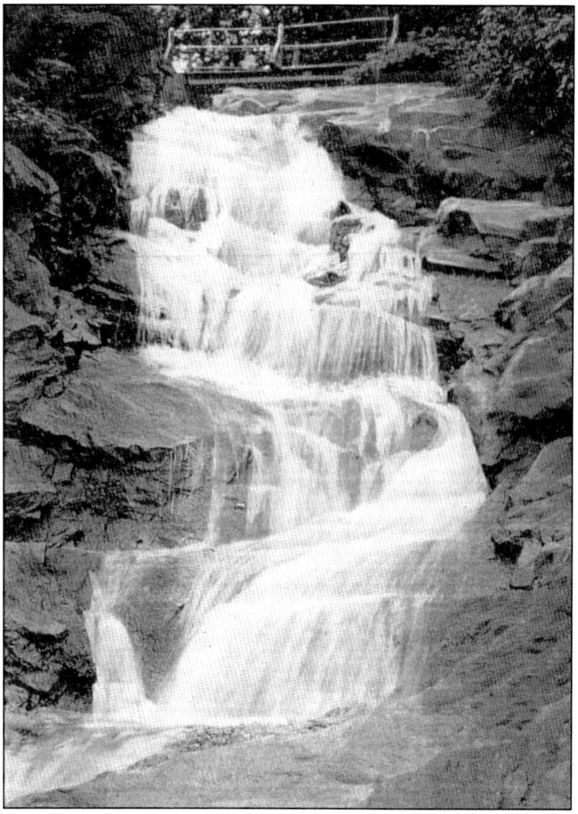

BUTTERMILK FALLS. The village of Highland Falls was originally called Buttermilk Falls. To early settlers, this frothy stream spilling down the mountain resembled buttermilk. During the late 1800s, the roaring waterfall was a tourist attraction. Although much of the water was eventually diverted, the flowing brook can still be enjoyed from the bridge on Main Street. (Gunza Collection.)

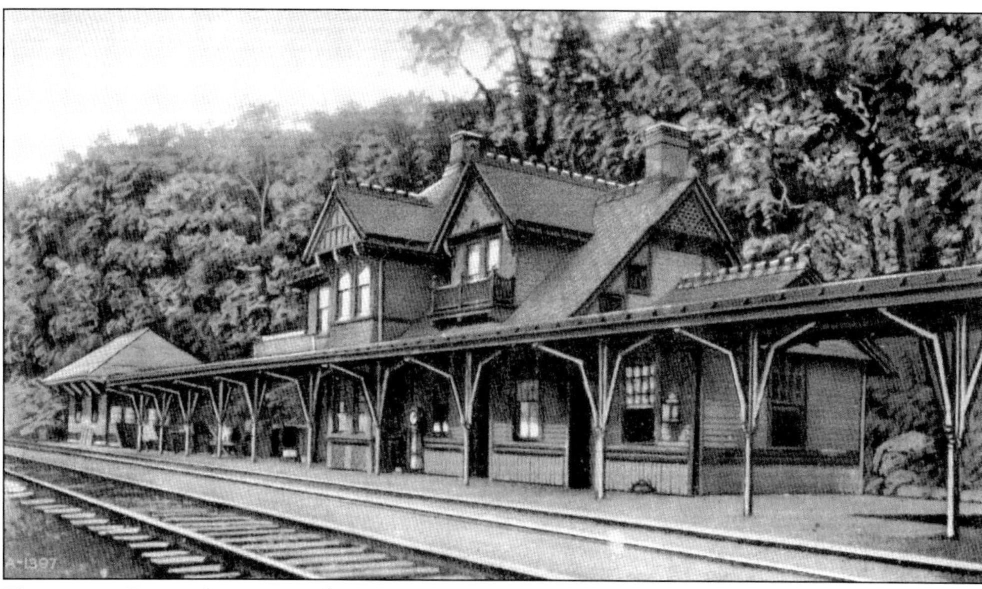

HIGHLAND FALLS STATION. The New York, West Shore, and Buffalo Railroad was formed in 1881. Originally conceived as a rival passenger line to the New York Central, the West Shore evolved into a freight line. This vintage postcard of the railroad station shows the homelike Victorian style in vogue in 1882. One of a handful of West Shore depots still standing, the Highland Falls station survives as a private home and marina. (Gunza Collection.)

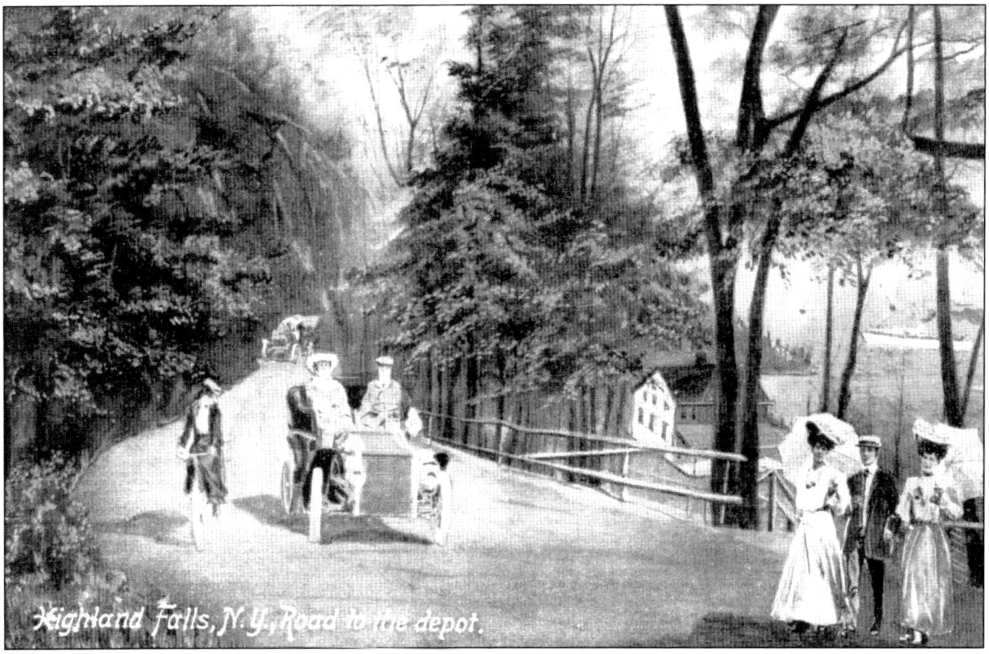

STATION ROAD. The winding path from Main Street to the village train station was called Depot Road, now known as Station Road. The steep incline meanders through dense woods. It was the only road from the steamboat dock and the station up to town. As seen in this c.1911 postcard, it was a well-traveled thoroughfare for a Sunday drive or a casual stroll. (Gunza Collection.)

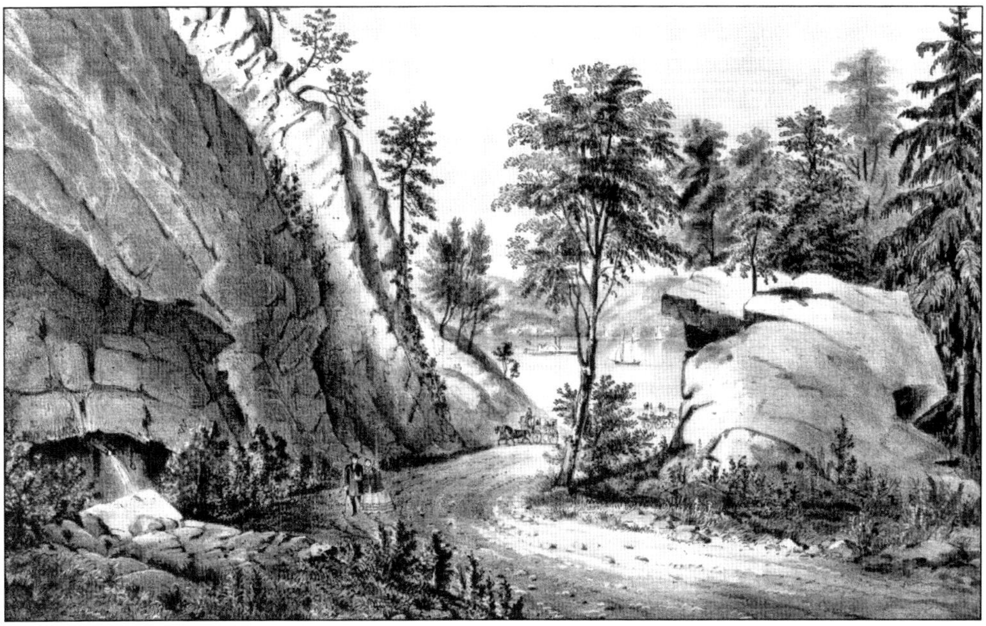

MOUNTAIN SPRING. This 1862 lithograph was one of over 7,000 produced by the printing firm of Currier and Ives during its 73-year history. It was drawn by Fanny F. Palmer, one of the best-known artists in the company's employ. An accomplished painter, she captured the tranquil beauty of the Depot Road with its rocky outcroppings. The spring beneath the cliff face still exists. (Museum of the City of New York.)

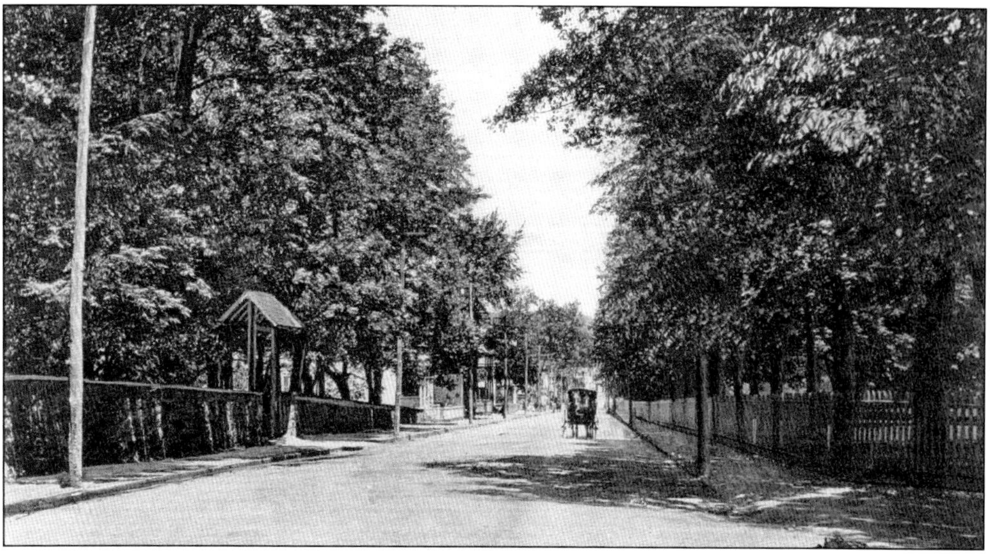

MAIN STREET. Looking north on Main Street, this quaint view from the early 1900s shows the single road through Highland Falls with the church grounds of Holy Innocents on the left and the fenced gardens of Ladycliff on the right. Buggies like the one pictured were available from Bosch's, Weyant's, and Pierce's Liveries. The writer of the postcard expresses that she had a "pleasant time" in the Highlands. (Gunza Collection.)

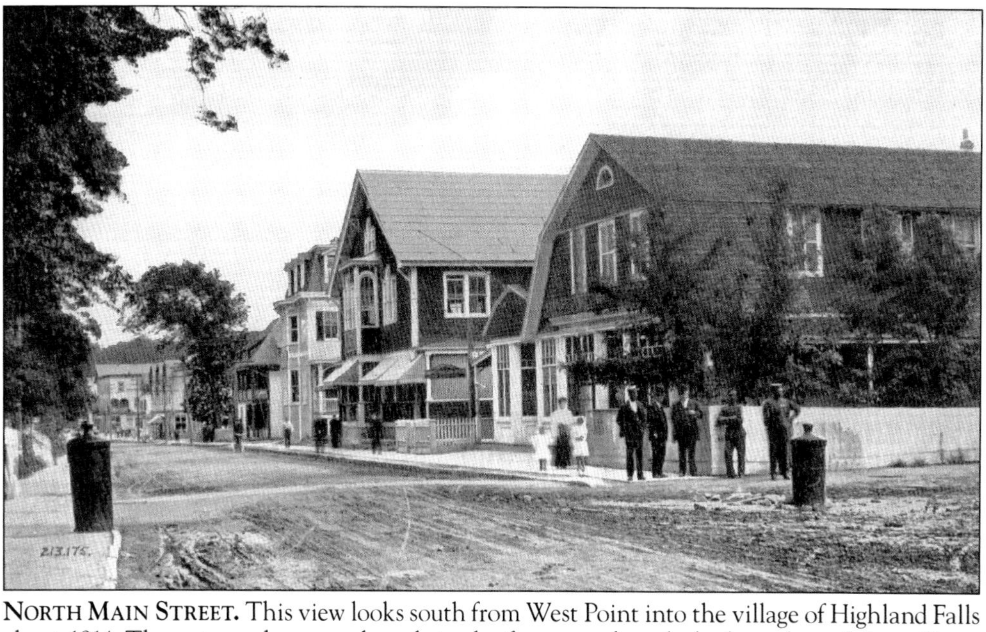

NORTH MAIN STREET. This view looks south from West Point into the village of Highland Falls about 1914. The upturned cannon barrels in the foreground mark the boundary of the military academy. On the right, several passersby linger on the corner. Although many residents owned chickens, goats, ducks, cattle, and sheep, a 1908 ordinance forbade residents from allowing animals to roam at large on village streets. (Gunza Collection.)

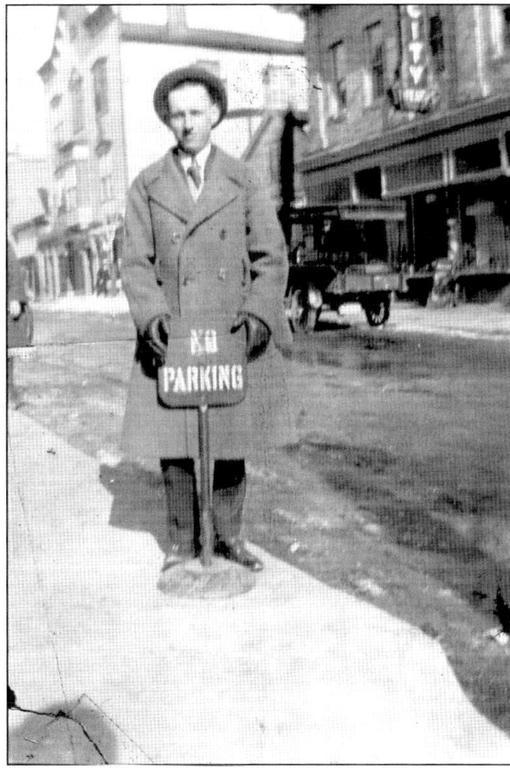

VILLAGE CENTER. Posing behind a stenciled No Parking sign is Edwin McCormick of Highland Falls. Main Street is still unpaved in this c. 1918 view. To the left is the peaked roof of the building now known as Hoffman's Hardware. To the right is the City Theatre. Barely visible behind McCormick is the Highland Falls Library. (McCormick Collection.)

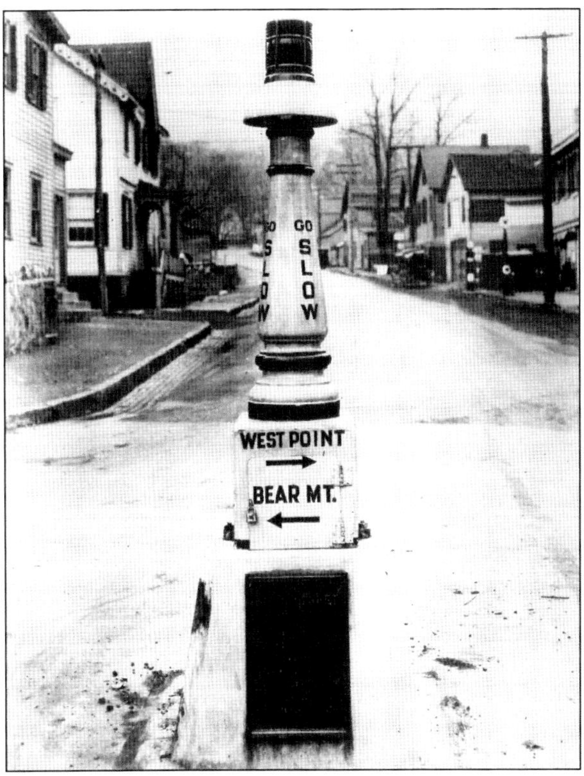

TRAFFIC SIGNAL. This traffic signal, at the corner of Main Street and Mountain Avenue, stood in its Highland Falls location for five decades. Village president Chester Weyant erected it when Main Street was paved in 1924. (Gunza Collection.)

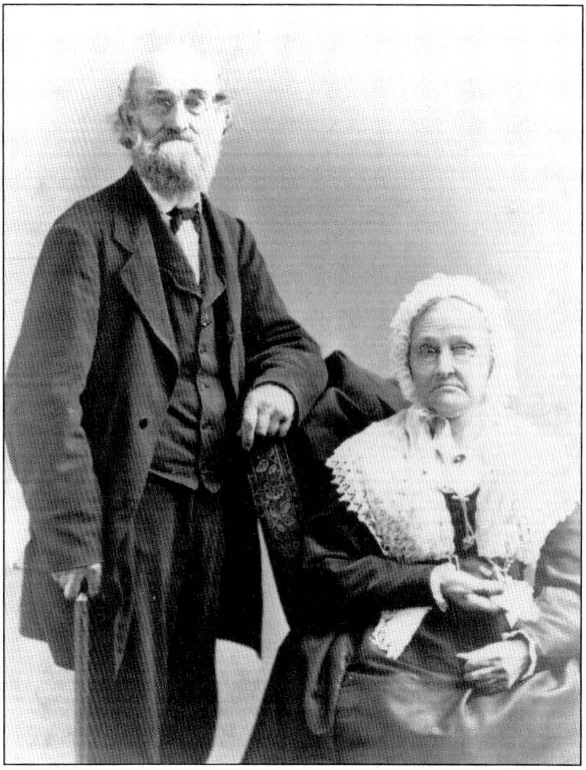

DAVID AND MARY PARRY. Passed from father to son for six generations, the oldest continually owned business in Highland Falls is that of the Parry family. In 1838, David Parry, pictured here with his wife, Mary, moved to Highland Falls from Pennsylvania and bought a mill for grinding flour. Keeping up with the changing times, the family expanded its flour and feed trade over the years to include lumber, straw, hay, coal, and fuel oil. (USMA Library.)

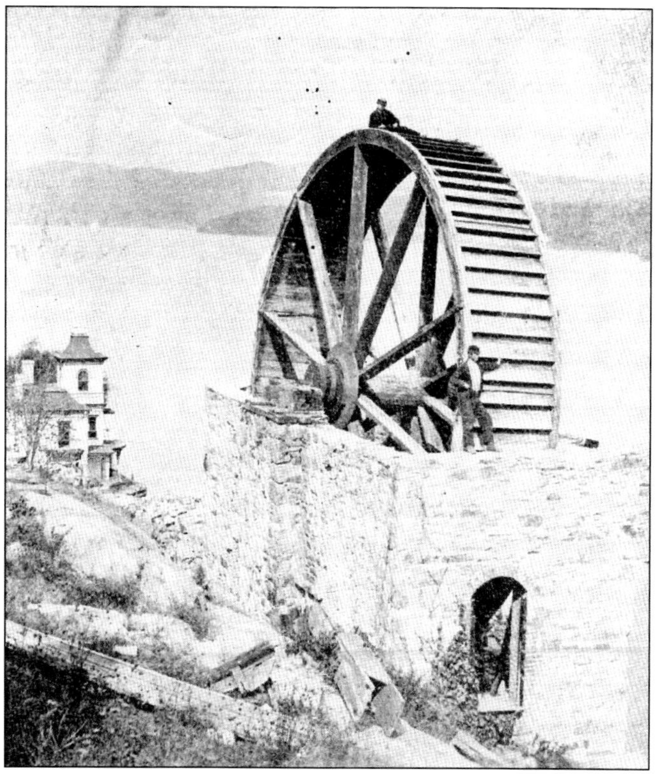

PARRY'S MILL. In 1774, David Lydig purchased a mill site at the base of Buttermilk Falls and built a gristmill to grind corn, rye, and wheat. He sold it in 1838 to David Parry, who expanded the mill. Its proximity to the river facilitated delivery and shipment by boat. The picturesque view from the river and toward the mill was a favorite subject for Hudson River artists. (THHS Archives.)

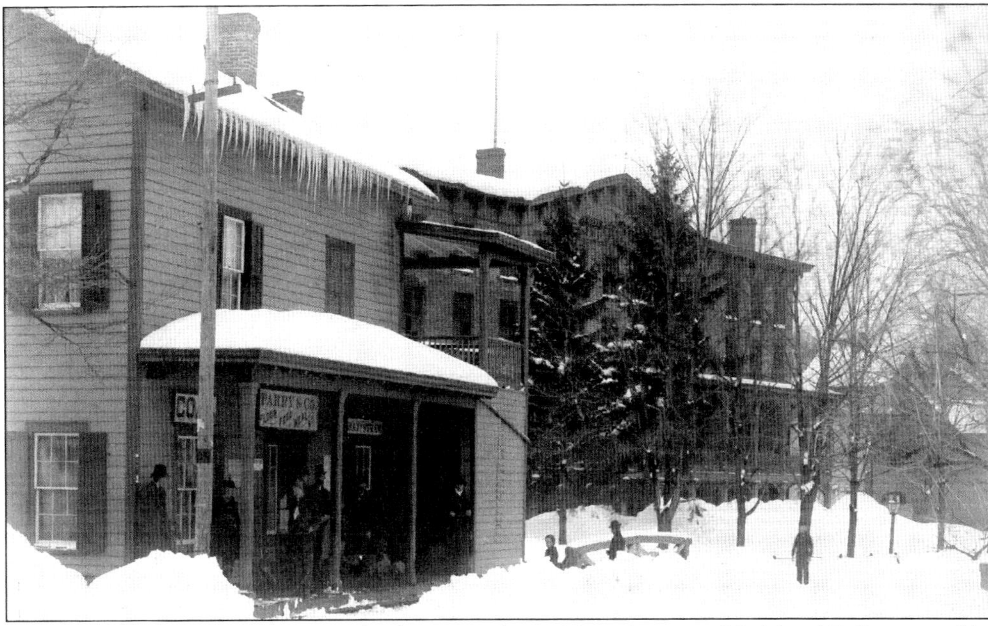

BLIZZARD OF 1888. Looking north, this view shows Main Street in Highland Falls covered by the legendary blizzard of 1888. The building at left, with its quaint second-story porch, still exists although it no longer houses the Parry Company. In the center is the Stephens Hotel, a center of town social life in the early 1900s. In 1924, the structure was converted into the Storm King Apartments; it was demolished in 1976. (THHS Archives.)

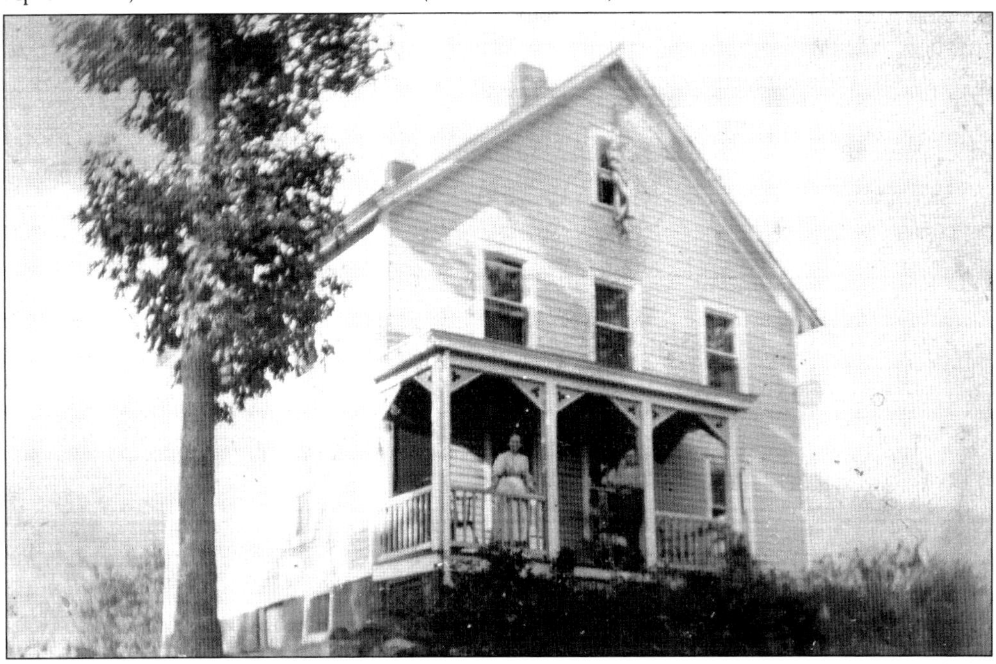

VAN VOORHIS HOMESTEAD. The Van Voorhis family home, at 97 Mountain Avenue, is much the same today as it was in 1909, when Georgia and her son Arthur stood on the porch. A separate kitchen building was situated behind the house. Like many local families, the Van Voorhises moved from a more rural dwelling into the town proper in the 1840s. (Storms Collection.)

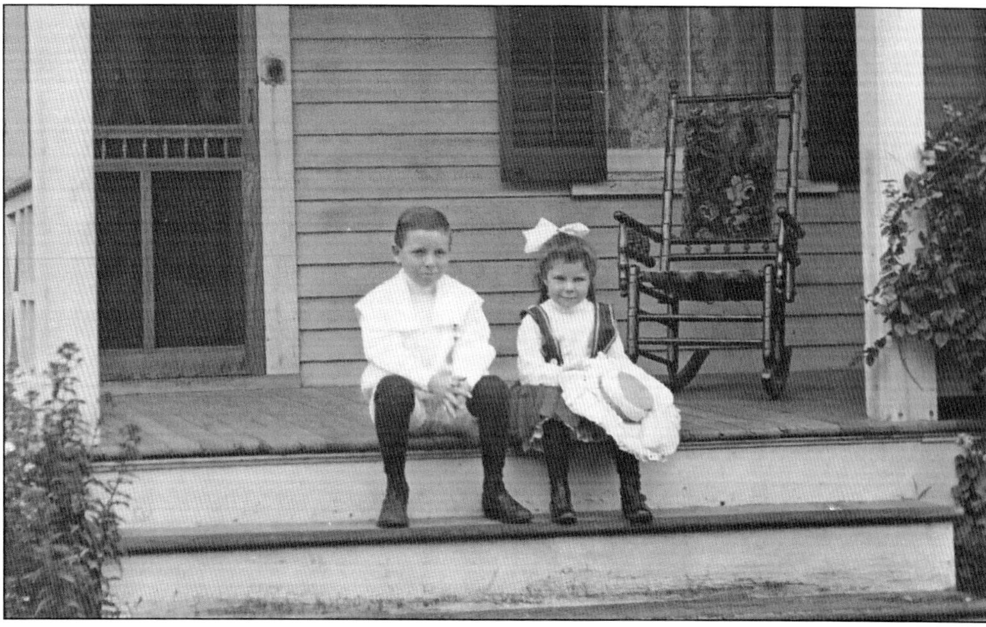

FRANKLYN AND HESTER FICKEN, C. 1930. Dressed in their Sunday best, Franklyn and Hester Ficken sit on their front porch. The Ficken family occupied a homestead with a large farmhouse in Stony Lonesome, at the crest of Mountain Avenue in Highland Falls. The land was purchased under eminent domain by the federal government around 1942 and is now the site of the Stony Lonesome entrance to the United States Military Academy. (Yagel Collection.)

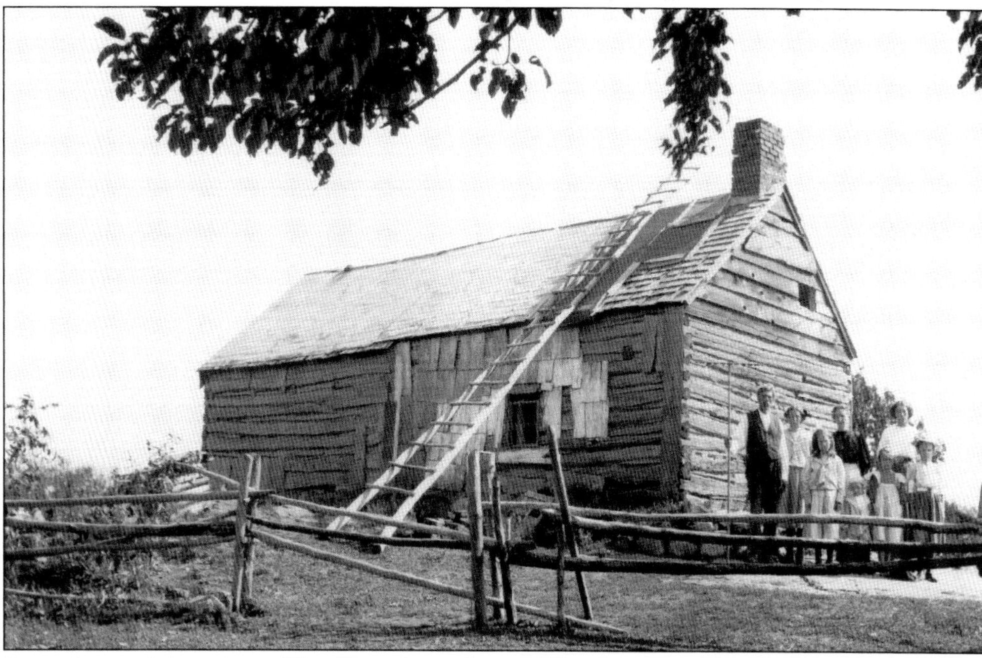

ROSE CABIN. The cabin of farmer and woodcutter John Rose was already a century old when this photograph was taken in 1910. Two rooms and an attic housed the family in a mountain location west of Long Pond. As coal replaced wood for fuel, the need for cordwood cutting diminished. Rose was part of the last generation of Highlands woodsmen. (PIPC Archives.)

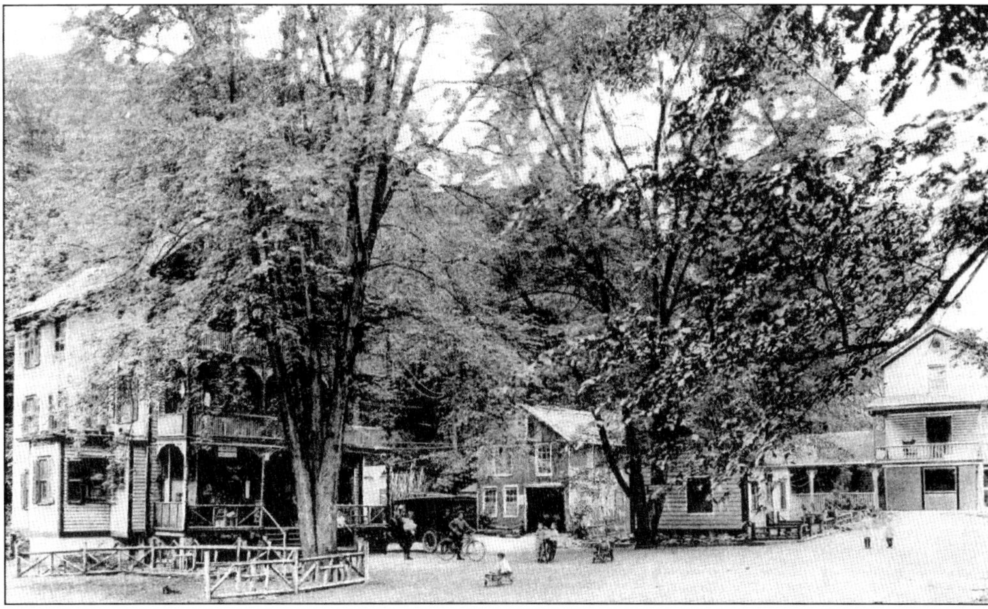

Fort Montgomery. During the 1800s and early 1900s, Fort Montgomery was a small rural hamlet, as shown in this vintage postcard. The center of the village was at the riverside end of Mine Dock Road. A store, post office, and farmhouses are visible in this view. Fort Montgomery was the site of the ore dock for the local mines. Steamboats stopped to pick up the iron ore and to deliver coal and other necessities. (Gunza Collection.)

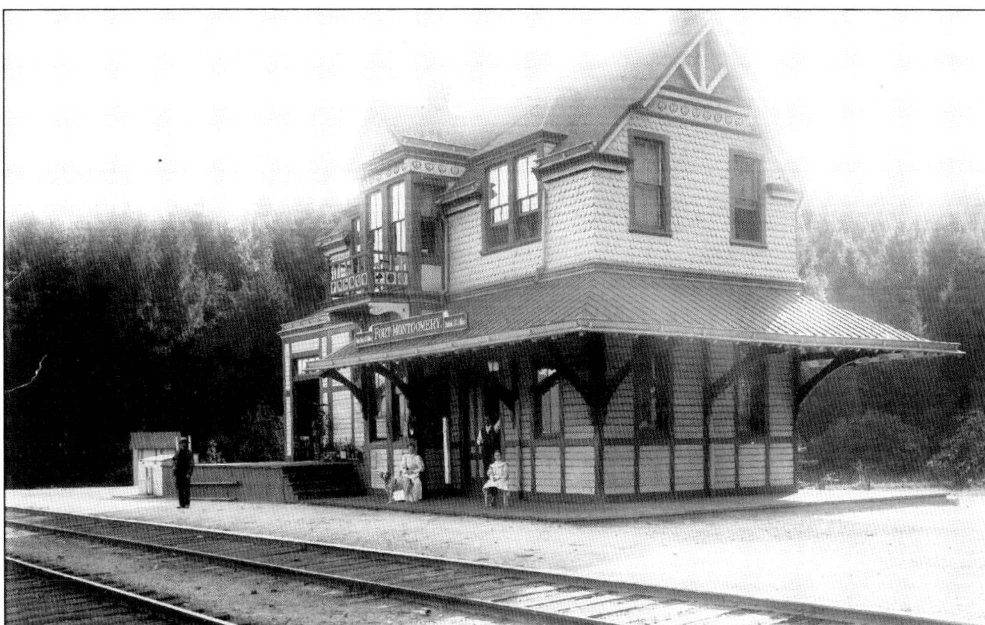

Fort Montgomery Station. The West Shore Railroad extended 425 miles from Weehawken, New Jersey, to Buffalo, New York. Construction of this railroad, with its many tunnels and bridges, was a massive project. Great care was taken in building the stations along the route, as they were architectural beauties that enhanced the spectacular scenery of the road. The sign on the Fort Montgomery station reads, "New York 43 miles. Buffalo 383 miles." (THHS Archives.)

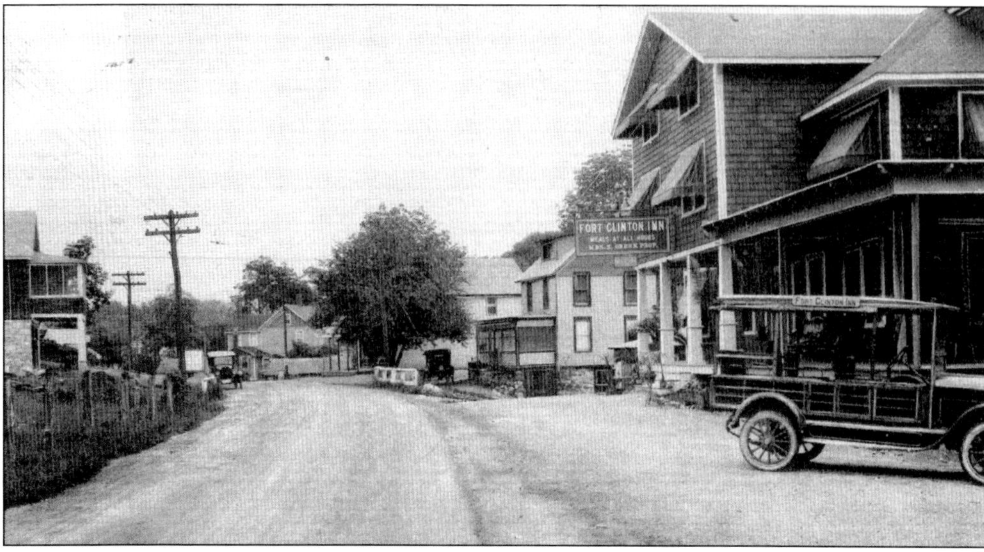

FORT CLINTON INN, C. 1929. The Fort Clinton Inn in Fort Montgomery offered "meals at all hours" as well as transportation to the Fort Montgomery railroad station in its handsome jitney. The inn later shared the building with an A&P Supermarket. The road pictured here, old Route 9W, was once the only north-south highway through the Highlands. The wider, more direct Route 9W was constructed about 1935. (Gunza Collection.)

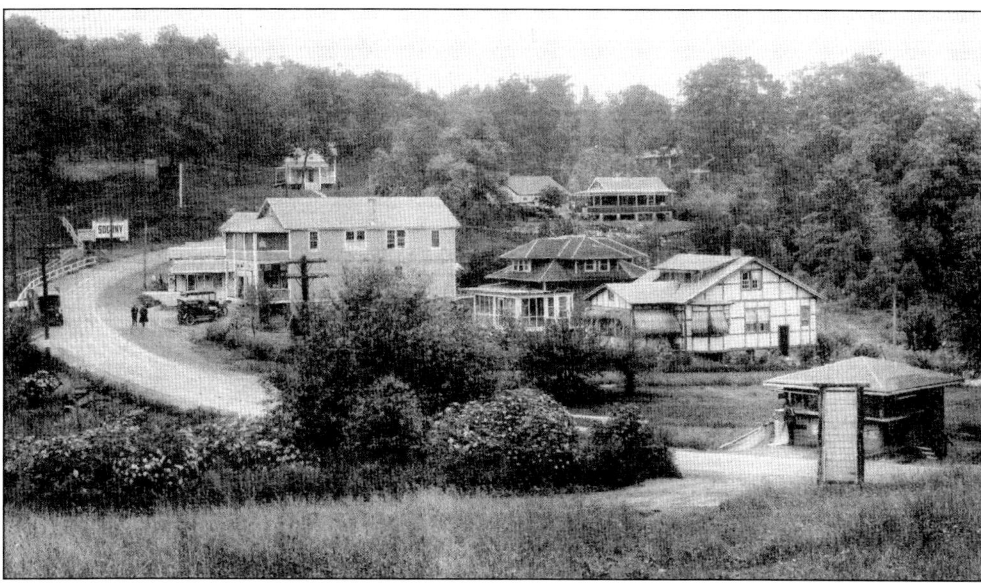

STATE ROAD, FORT MONTGOMERY, 1930. *Scarborough's Automobile Tour Book of 1916* gave these directions from Stony Point north: "Stone and dirt road. . . . Slow. Narrow road. . . . **Fort Montgomery.** Turn left and go up hill. Slow. Sharp curves. Bridge. Bear to right of watering trough onto Main Street. **Highland Falls.** Straight ahead. Go through gateway to **West Point.** Artillery parade grounds on left." (Gunza Collection.)

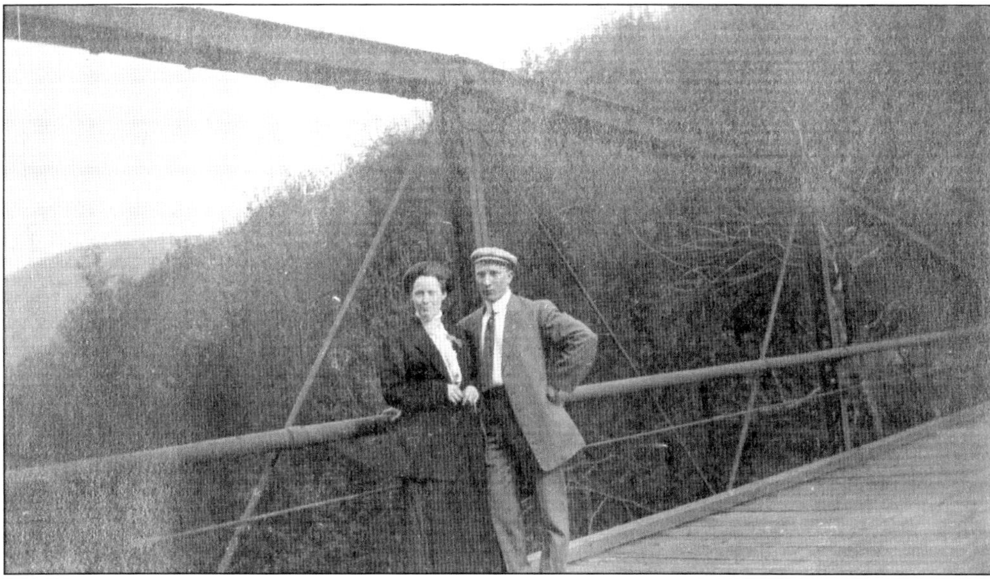

OLD POPOLOPEN BRIDGE. Highlands visitors Daisy and Ed Scully wrote the following note on this 1910 postcard: "This was taken two weeks ago up at Camp. We went up for the day. This is taken on the bridge over the falls." They also mention spending the previous evening watching for Haley's Comet. Note that the bridge road was made of wooden slats. Within a few years, a new span would be built. (Burley Collection.)

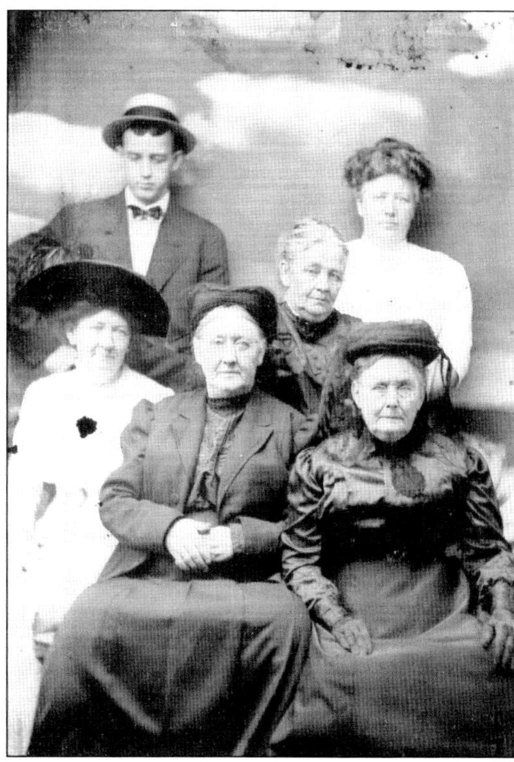

ANCESTORS, 1912. Among the group in this family portrait are the ancestors of two well-known local families. On the right in the first row is Catherine Keenan Wise, a grandmother of the Baker and Davis families. Behind her to the left is Mary Brennan Shelley, an ancestor of the Rafferty family. Two of the women, recently widowed at the time, wear black mourning attire from veiled head to toe. Wise even wears black gloves. (Baker Collection.)

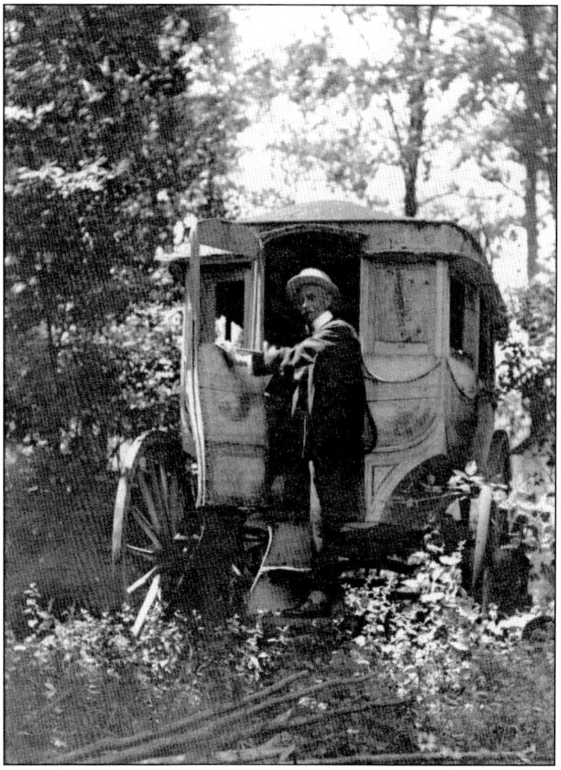

Traveling Salesman. Part of a bygone era, the gentleman seen here in front of his coach wagon was an itinerant peddler and artist who traveled through the Town of Highlands and its vicinity in the early 1900s. Known as "Quinlan," he sold pots and pans, sundries, herbs, and medicines. He eventually settled in Fort Montgomery. (Scott Collection.)

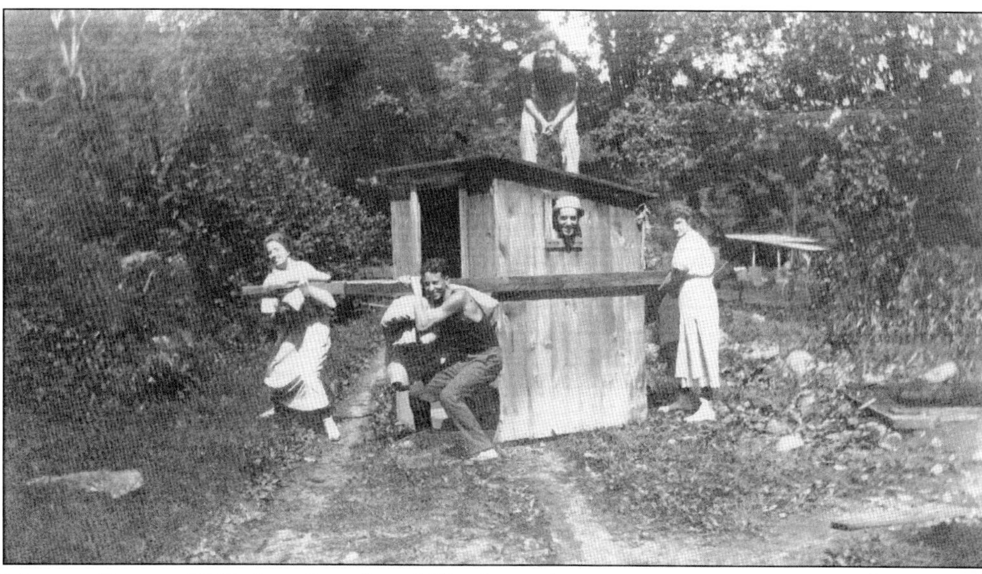

Moving Day, c. 1920. A reality of rural life, the outhouse was a necessity on every homestead. Placed over a pit four feet square and five feet deep, an outhouse was moved to a new spot when the pit was almost full. The old location would be filled in with earth. In this photograph, Fort Montgomery's Julia Cobey, left, and four other friends have nailed boards to the structure for easy transportation. (Scott Collection.)

Three

GATEWAY TO WEST POINT

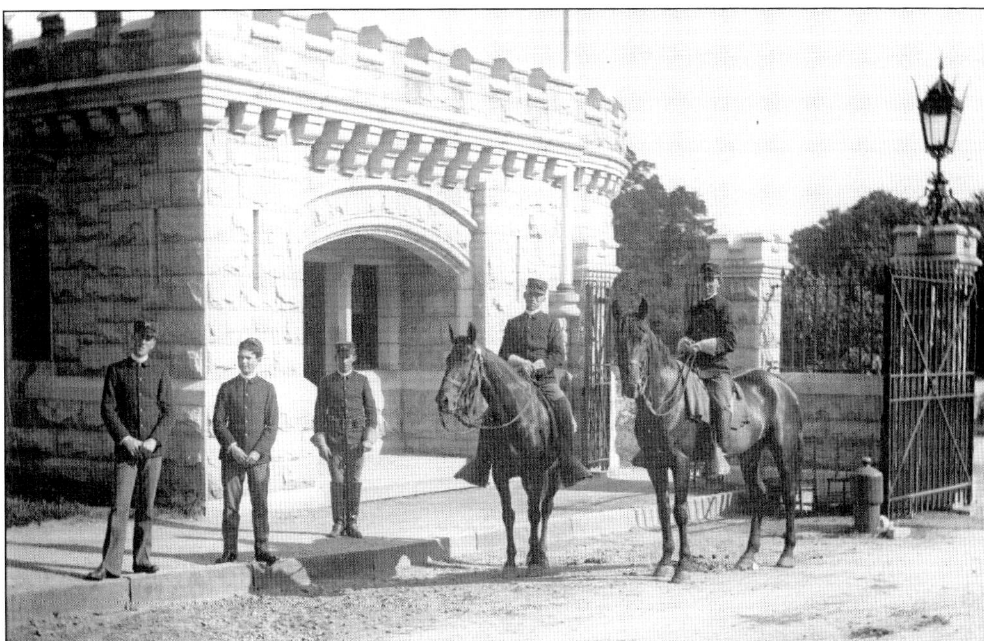

SOUTH GATE, 1902. Although its location and architecture have changed with time, the South Gate has always been the main entrance to West Point. People have passed through it to serve their country, teach, work, visit, observe a ceremony, or view a sporting event. The traveler must pass through Fort Montgomery and Highland Falls, making each one a gateway to West Point. Thus, the surrounding areas developed a hospitality industry, providing visitors with places to rest, eat, and shop. (USMA Library.)

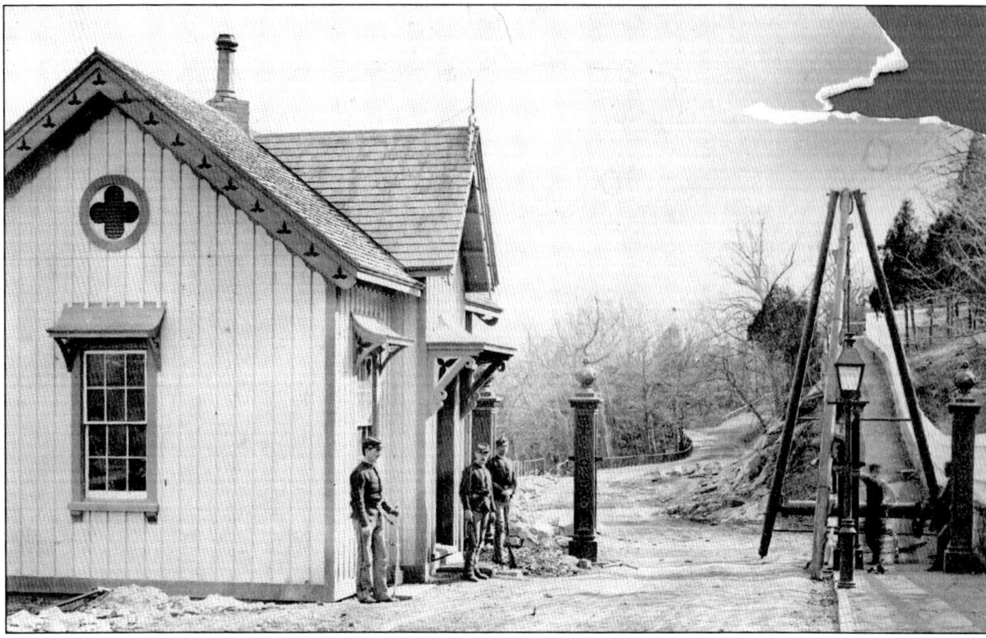

SOUTH GATE c. 1865. Three soldiers stand guard at the South Gate in this Civil War–era photograph. Construction is in progress as support posts await the installation of gates. Two young boys linger on the sidewalk at right. (USMA Library.)

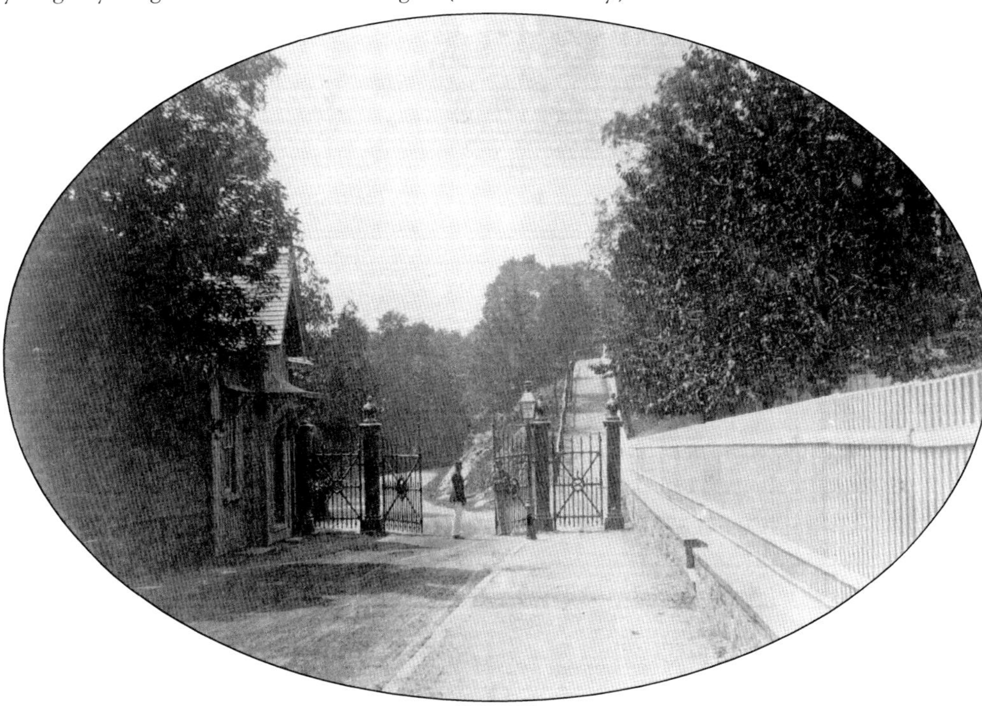

SOUTH GATE, c. 1880. Looking south, this 1880s view of the gate depicts an inclined path still in use today. The village of Highland Falls is one mile farther down the unpaved road, through the dense woods. The elegant black iron gates shown here were later moved to the West Point Cemetery, where they remain today on more solemn guard duty. (USMA Library.)

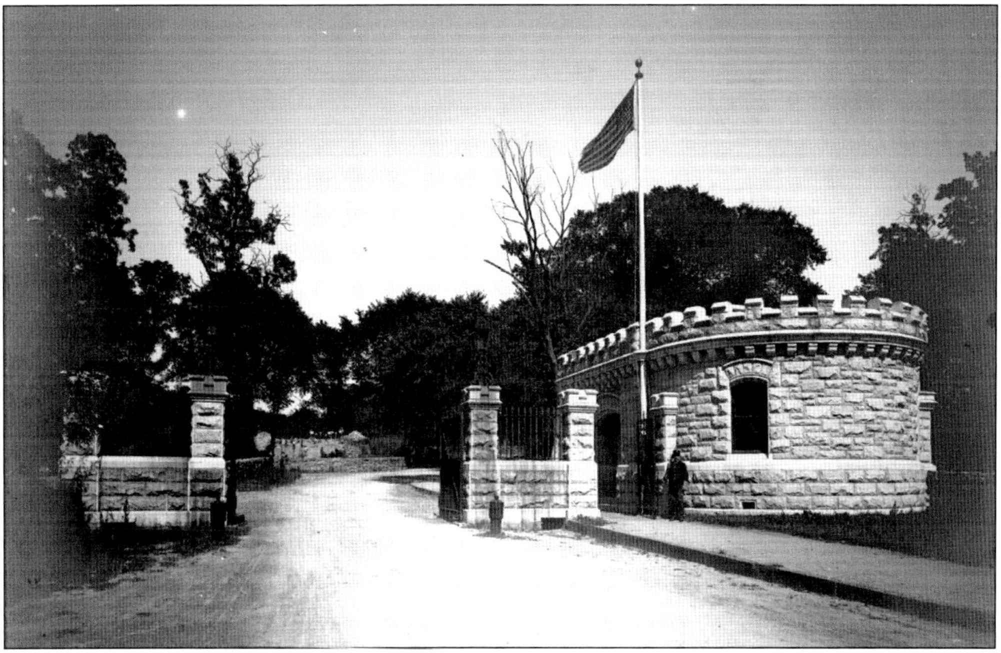

SOUTH GATE, 1902. From the Highland Falls side, the 1902 South Gate appeared like a small castle. The imposing stone building was designed by Richard Morris Hunt. Impressive stone pillars framed the southern approach road to the academy. Along that road were a variety of inns, hotels, restaurants, and stores to accommodate the growing demand of tourists. (USMA Library.)

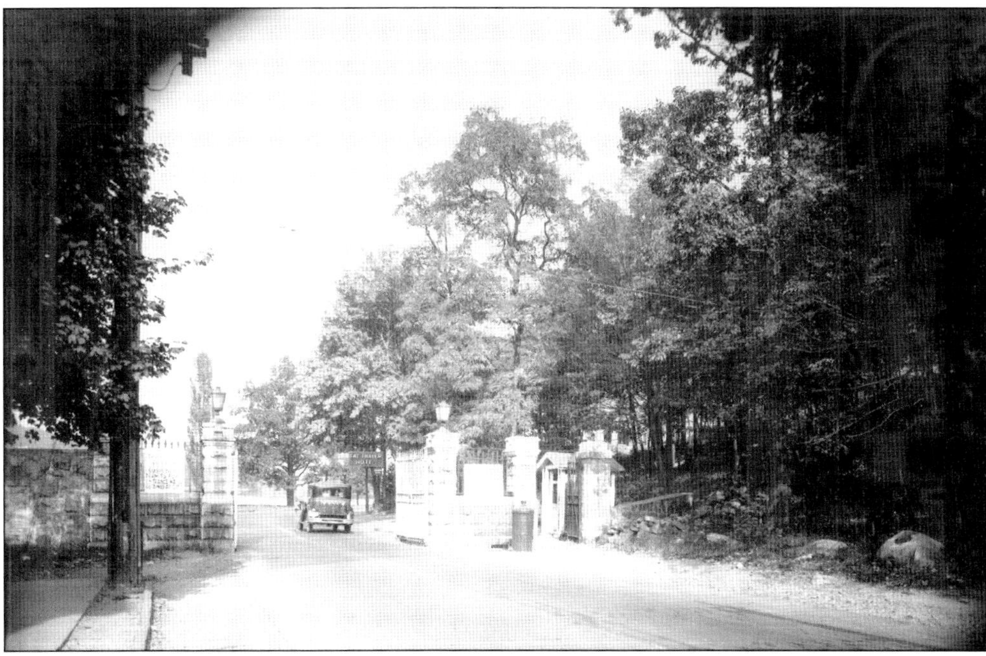

SOUTH GATE, C. 1919. The stone pillars remained at the entrance to West Point in the early 20th century. For automobiles in the early 1900s, the South Gate was the only gate, as there was no northern road leading off the post, nor were there any bridges across the Hudson. There was, however, a ferry to Garrison accessible from the West Point dock. (USMA Library.)

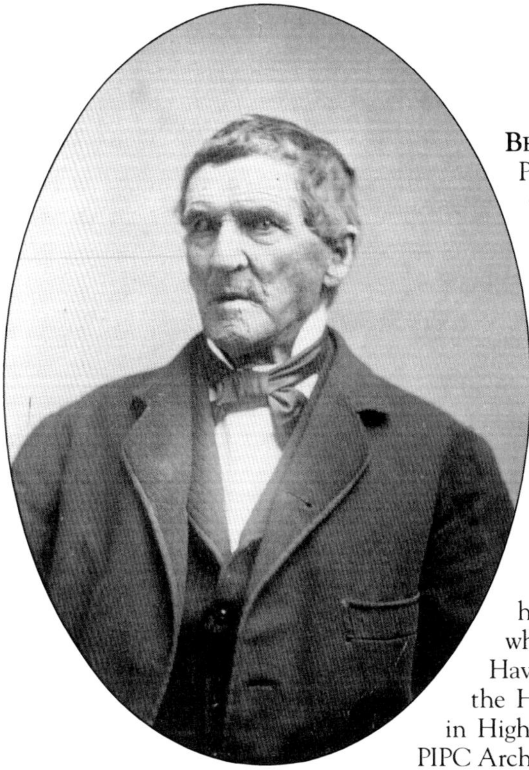

BENNY HAVENS. In the early days of West Point, local entrepreneur Benny Havens kept a "retreat" on the post where cadets could purchase alcoholic beverages. Banished from the grounds in 1824, he opened an establishment beneath a cliff near Buttermilk Falls, shown below. His pub, famous for buckwheat cakes and rum drinks, became popular with cadets who secretly left academy grounds and traveled on foot, by boat, or over ice to enjoy the refreshments. Among his clients were Jefferson Davis, George Pickett, George Custer, and Edgar Allan Poe. Although notorious for serving alcohol, Benny Havens provided a place where cadets enjoyed home-cooked meals and could relax for a while. Soldiers frequently sang the song "Benny Havens, Oh" as they sailed past the inn along the Hudson. Havens died in 1877 and is buried in Highland Falls. (Above, USMA Library; below, PIPC Archives.)

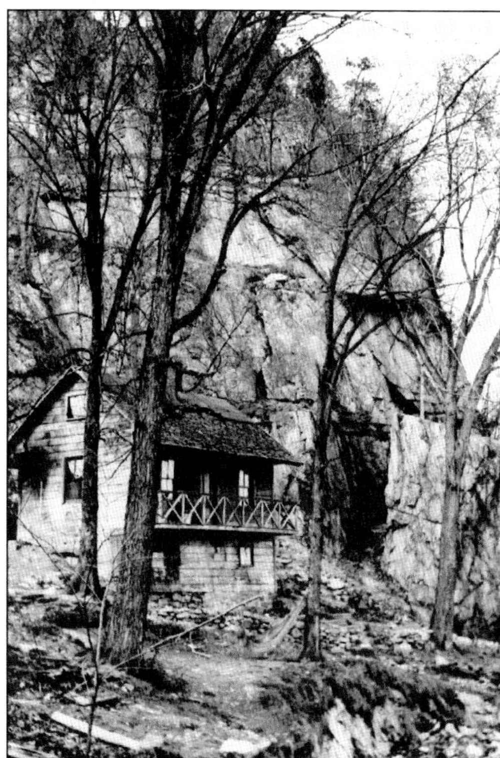

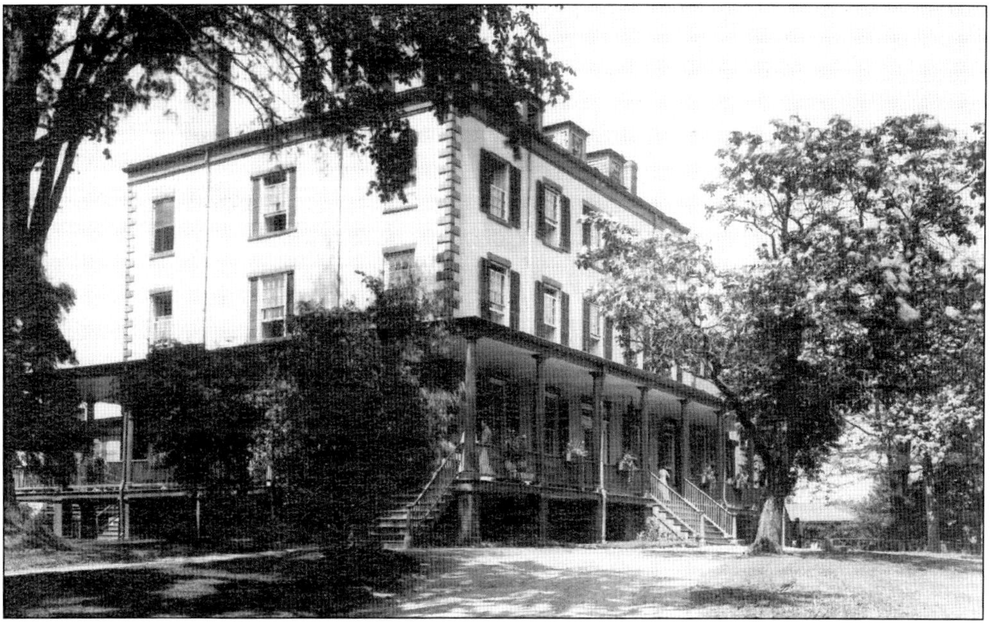

WEST POINT HOTEL. In response to a need for accommodations for official visitors, the West Point Hotel was built in 1829 at a cost of $18,000. Overlooking the Hudson at Trophy Point, the hotel became a favorite of cadet families and friends. It advertised itself as "a substantial place of rest and fair feeding," serving the public until the 1920s. Among its notable guests were Pres. Abraham Lincoln, Ulysses S. Grant, and Charles Dickens. (Gunza Collection.)

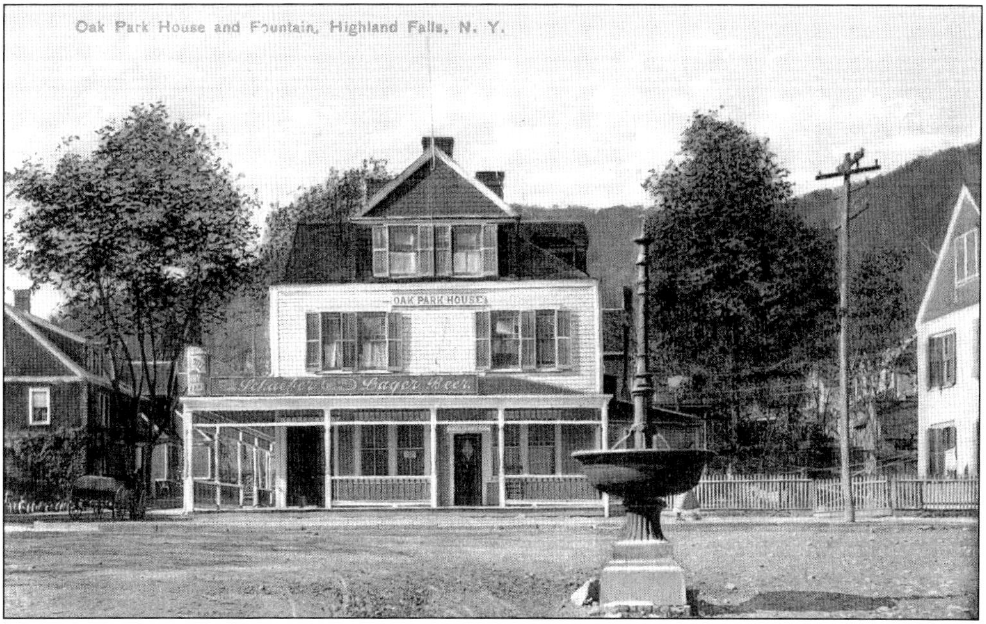

OAK PARK HOUSE, 1911. During the late 19th century, thousands of visitors sought summer accommodations in the Highlands. The Oak Park House, on the corner of Main Street and Drew Avenue, welcomed "transient and permanent boarders." Dinner was served from noon to 2:00 p.m. under the auspices of the manager, Kate Darcy. Today it is the Christiana Hotel. (Gunza Collection.)

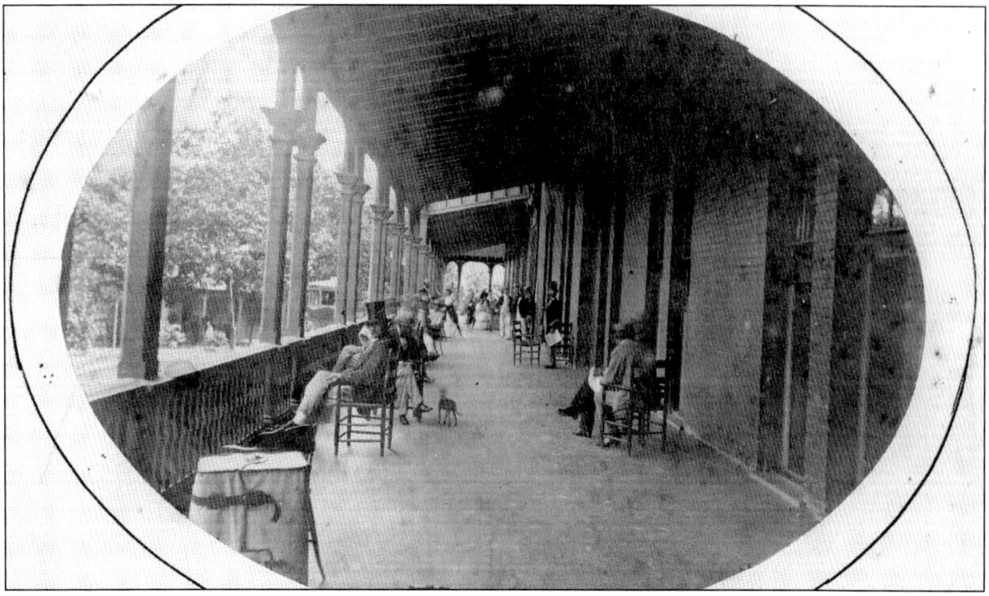

COZZENS' HOTEL, C. 1865. During the 19th century, the scenic Hudson Valley became a destination for vacationing city-dwellers. Cozzens' Hotel opened in 1849 and became the most fashionable summer resort in the Highlands. Visitors enjoyed its wide front porch, the river view rooms and elegant furnishings, the roar of Buttermilk Falls, and the congenial host, William Cozzens. Famous guests included President Lincoln, Gen. Winfield Scott, and Edward, the Prince of Wales. (USMA Library.)

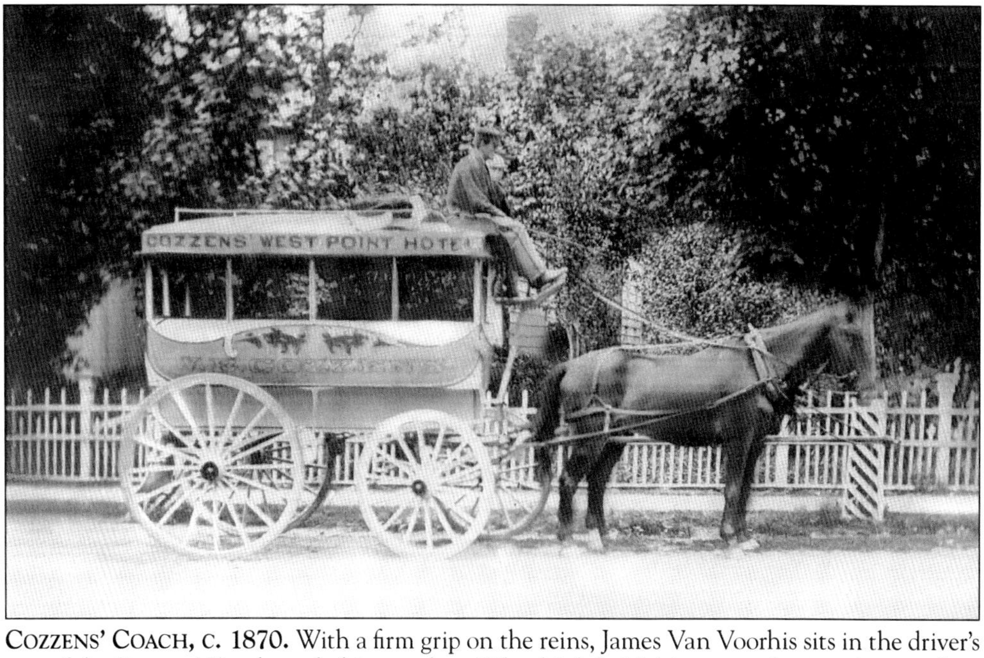

COZZENS' COACH, C. 1870. With a firm grip on the reins, James Van Voorhis sits in the driver's seat of the Cozzens' Hotel coach, his grandson Gil to his left. Making several trips a day, coaches, wagonettes, and omnibuses shuttled patrons between the steamboat dock or railroad station and the luxurious Highland Falls retreat. Later called Cranston's, the hotel featured steam heat, elevators, and an orchestra giving daily concerts. (Storms Collection.)

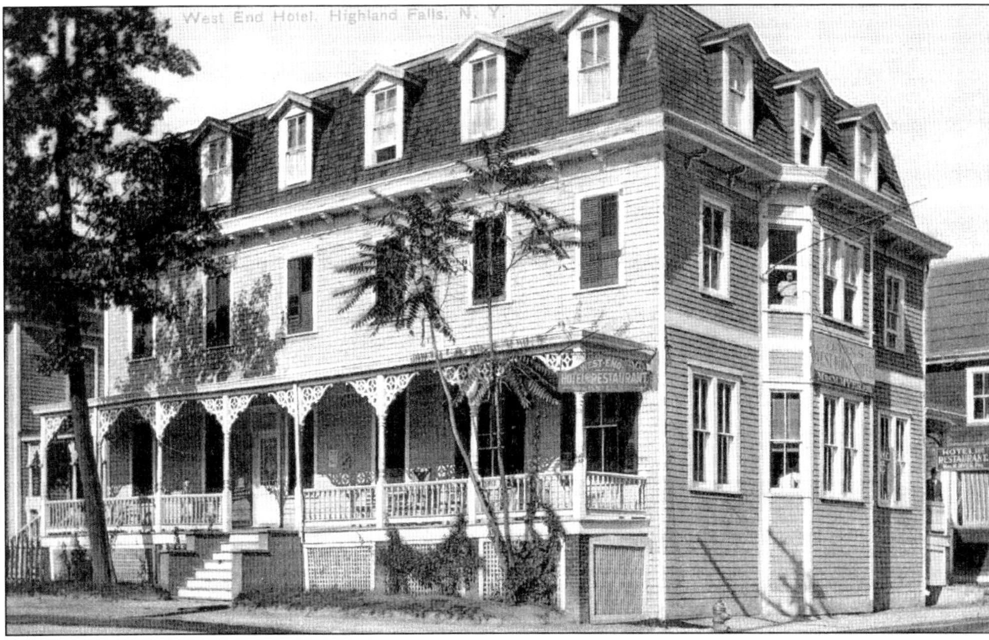

WEST END HOTEL, 1914. Shadows of its elegant scrollwork are cast on the porch of the West End Hotel by the afternoon sun. Owned by the O'Flynn family, the lovely hotel and its public restaurant were managed by Mrs. M. Myer. Perhaps it is she who looks out from the right second-story window. The building faced Homestead Avenue on the corner of Main Street in Highland Falls until it burned, about 1918. (Gunza Collection.)

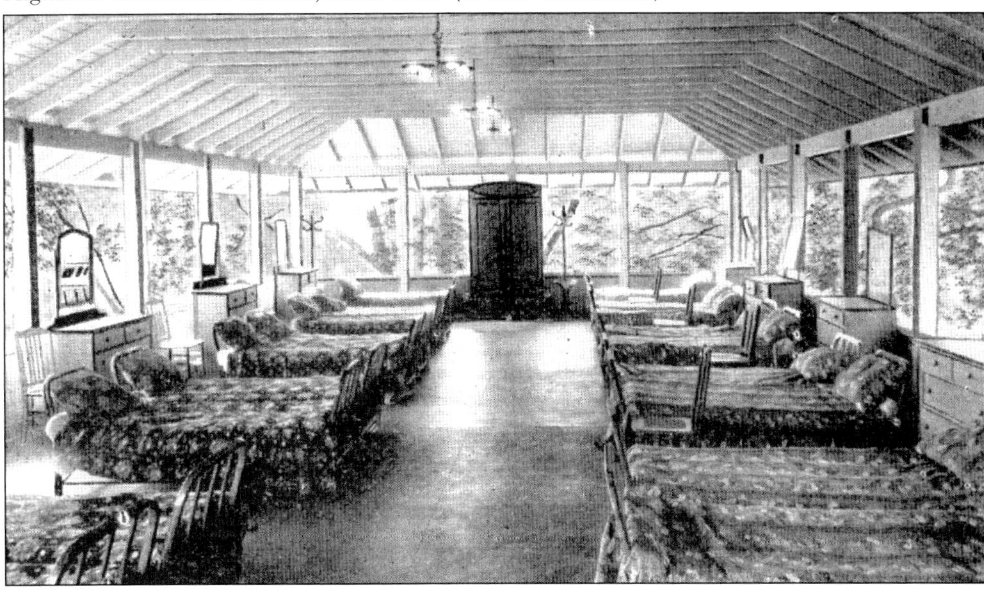

SCHILDKRAUT'S HOTEL, C. 1926. Billing itself as "America's most picturesque resort," Schildkraut's Pine Terrace Park Hotel in Highland Falls overlooked the Hudson just south of town. The hotel featured a vegetarian restaurant, sitting rooms, lounges, a ballroom, and porches with impressive views of the river and mountains. The Roof Garden, pictured here, offered the healthful option of open-air sleeping. The building exists as the Peregrine Hall Apartments. (Gunza Collection.)

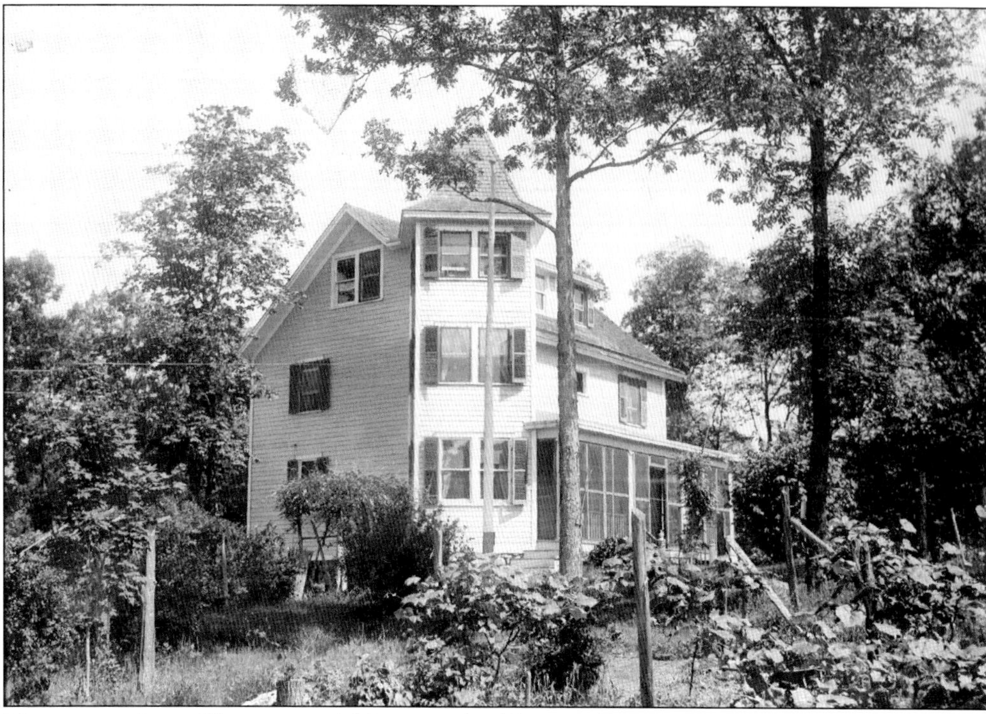

Mountain Inn. This turreted Victorian building in Fort Montgomery and a companion outbuilding were known as the Mountain Inn. During the early 1900s, visitors slept in the three-story main house, seen above. They took their meals a short distance away in a comfortable dining room, seen below. At the end of a gracefully curving private road, patrons enjoyed a secluded woodland setting with a spectacular river view. After many years as a private home, the main house is once again an inn, the Victorian River View. The same family has owned this property for five generations. (Above, Scott Collection; below, Gunza Collection.)

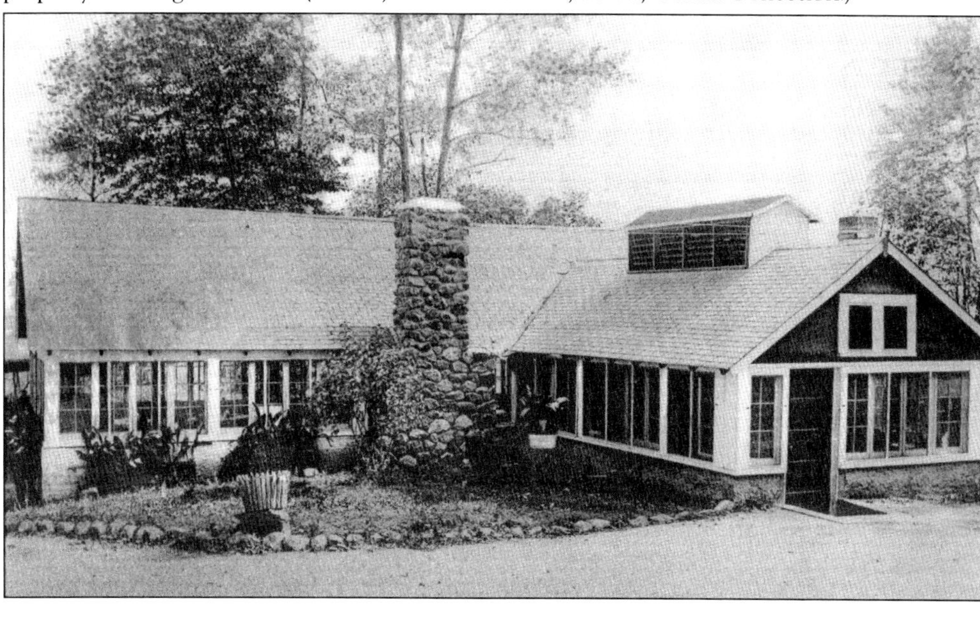

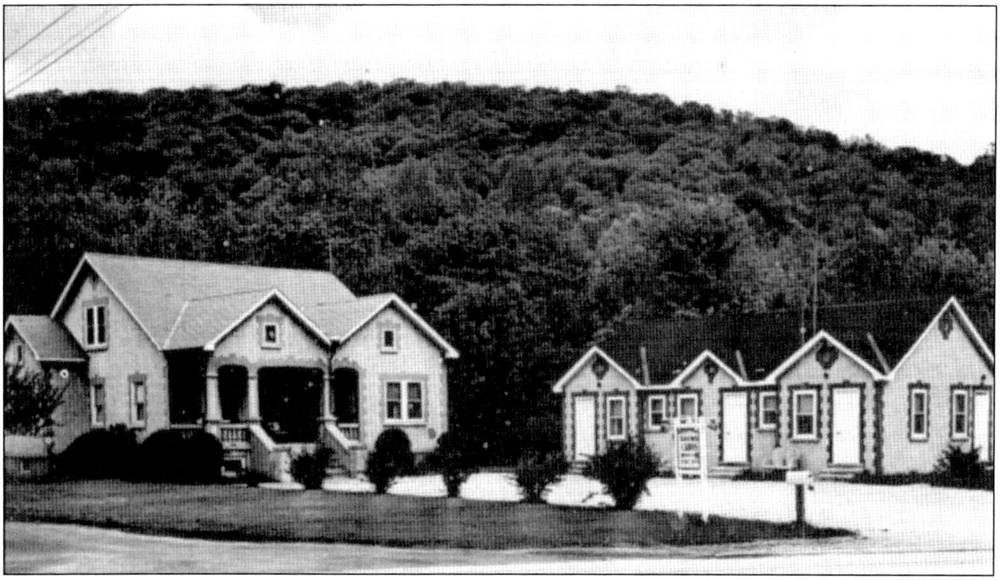

BEAR MOUNTAIN CABINS, 1958. At the corner of Franklin Street and Route 9W in Fort Montgomery stand the Bear Mountain Cabins. This 1958 postcard advertises "new and modern cabins, cross ventilation, private showers, innerspring mattresses and free parking." Nearly 50 years later, the charming cabins are still accommodating visitors to the Highlands. (Gunza Collection.)

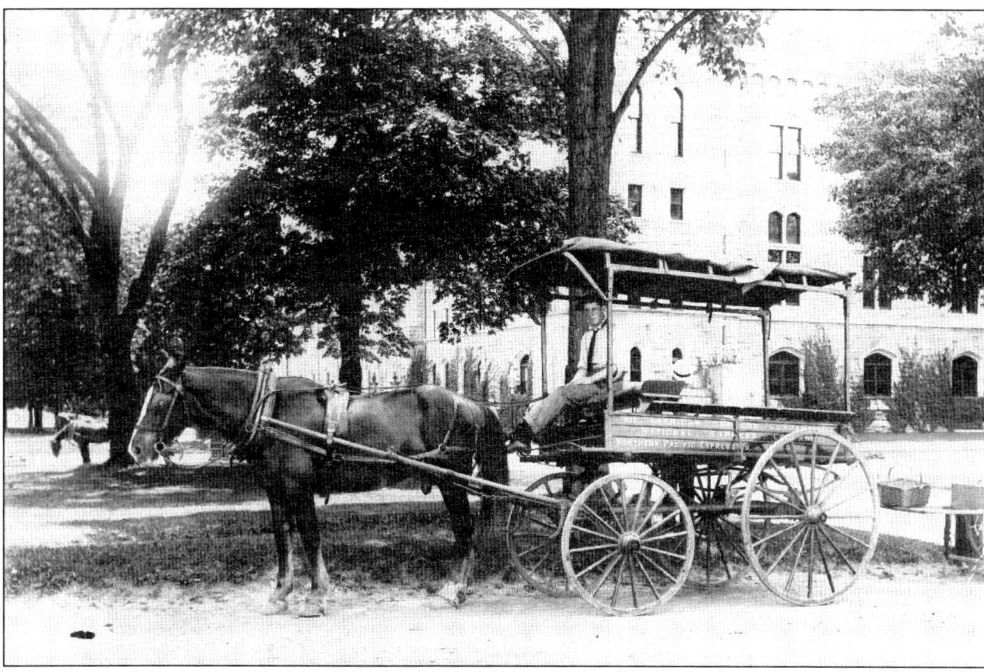

DELIVERY WAGON, 1885. Established in 1850, the American Express Company became a successful delivery service known for reliability. At the time, the U.S. Postal Service was slow, expensive, and not inclined to deliver packages. In contrast, American Express specialized in small parcels and money orders. Local residents were hired to drive the delivery wagon, shown here, stopped near the cadet barracks at West Point. (Graber Collection.)

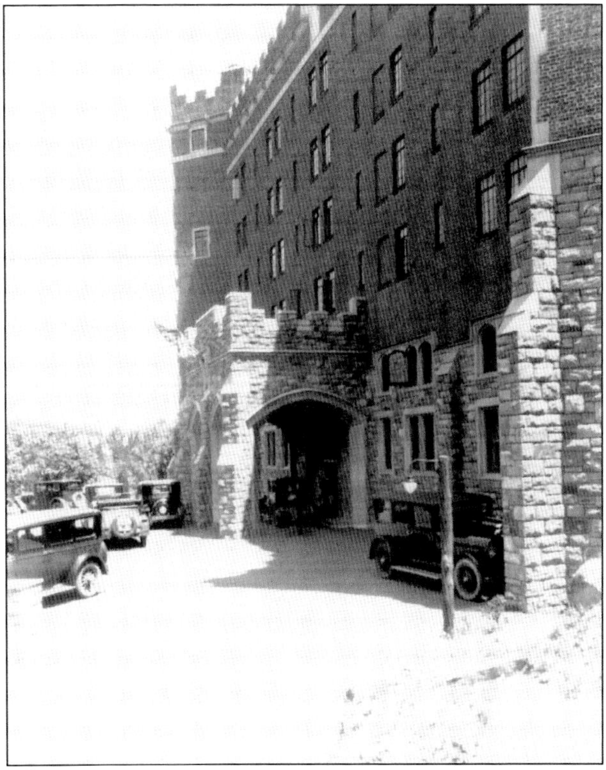

HOTEL THAYER. The newly opened Hotel Thayer, the only privately owned hotel on the grounds of West Point, welcomed its first patrons in 1928. It is named for Col. Sylvanus Thayer, superintendent of the military academy from 1817 to 1833. In 1980, a new wing was added to the southwest side of the building, but the entrance remains the same, busy with eager visitors checking in and out. (USMA Archives.)

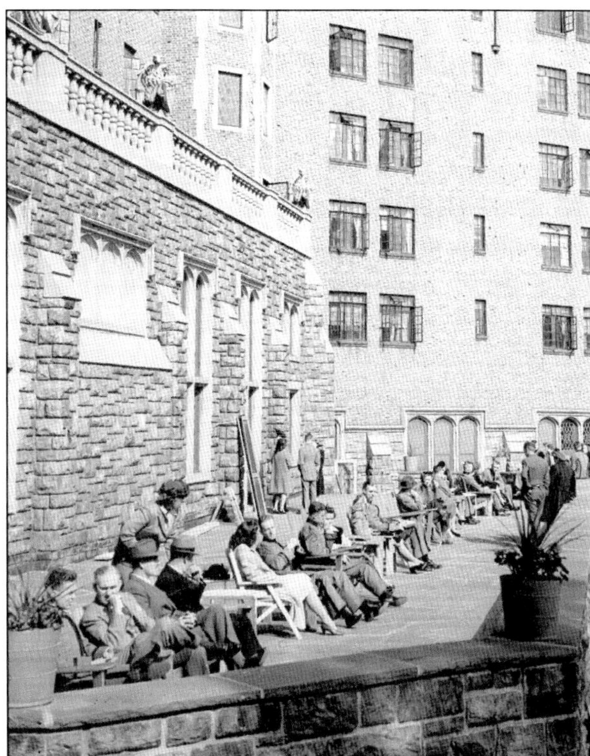

REAR DECK, HOTEL THAYER. Patrons enjoy some sunshine on the rear deck of the Hotel Thayer around 1949. Listed on the National Register of Historic Places, the hotel has hosted a variety of notables including Pres. John F. Kennedy, Pres. Dwight D. Eisenhower, Gen. Douglas MacArthur, Gregory Peck, Luciano Pavarotti, and the Ladycliff College Alumni Association. (USMA Library.)

HOTEL THAYER, RIVERSIDE. From the rear windows and terrace of the Gothic-style granite hotel there is a dramatic view of the Hudson River and Breakneck Mountain to the east. To the north one can see historic Constitution Island, a Revolutionary War fortification and home of the Warner sisters. In every direction, guests can enjoy the peaceful grandeur of the Highlands. (USMA Library.)

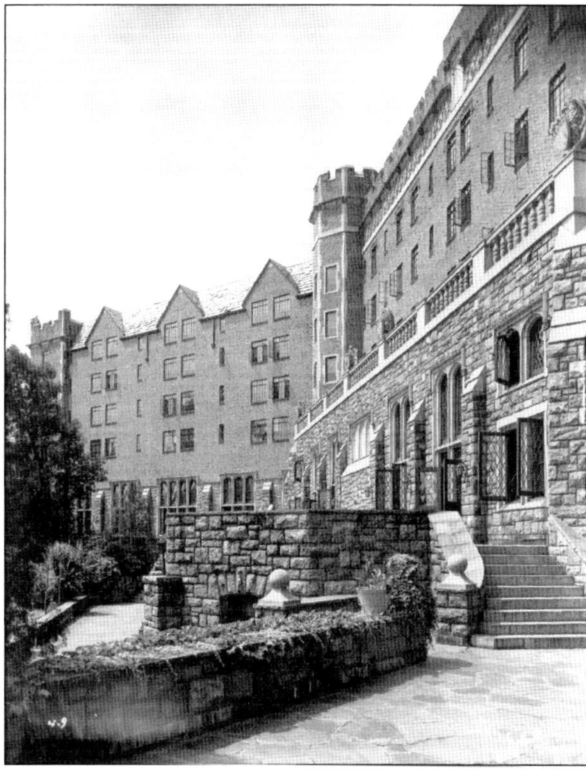

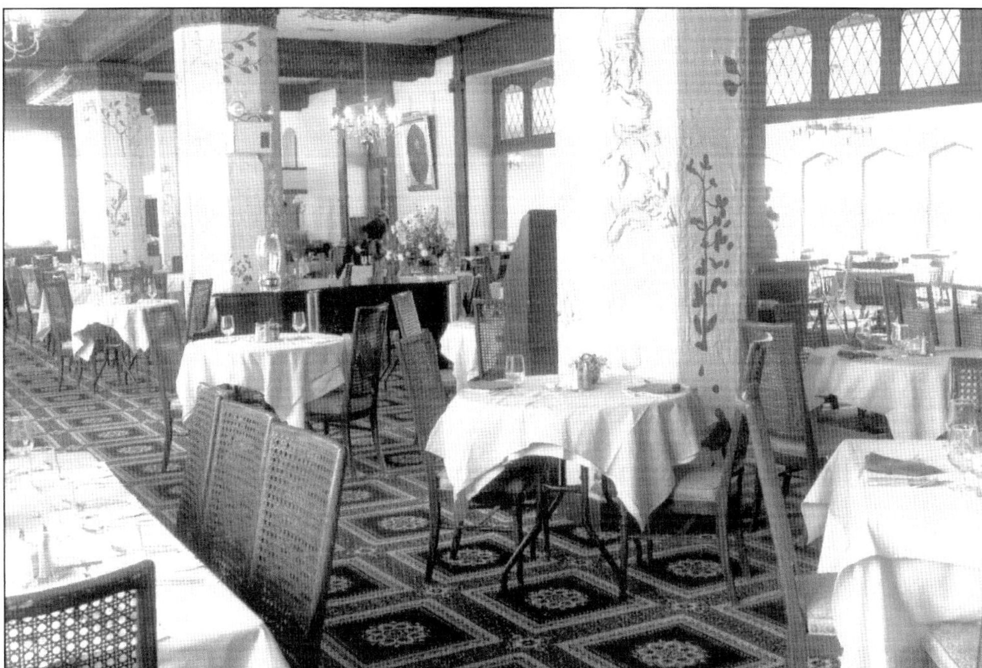

DINING ROOM. Although renovations have occurred over the years, the Victorian elegance of the Hotel Thayer's dining room has been preserved. This 1972 image is timeless. Sunday brunch at the Hotel Thayer is a popular tradition with locals and visitors alike. (USMA Library.)

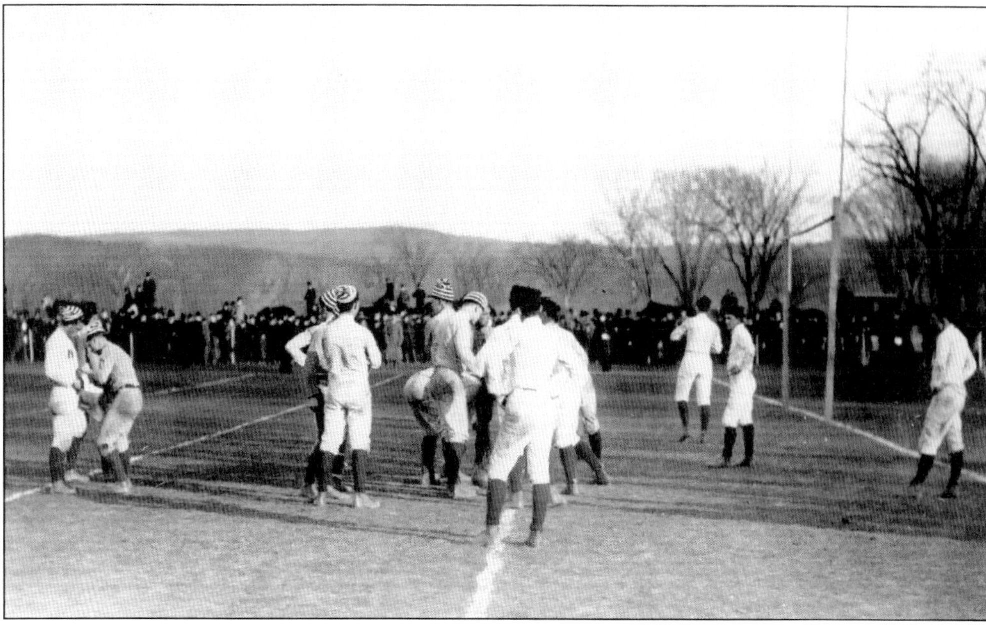

First Army-Navy Game, 1890. Army football has brought many visitors to the Highlands. It began in 1890, when the naval academy challenged the military academy to the first official football game played at West Point. The Army team was coached and captained by one of its players, Dennis Michie. Wearing knitted skating caps as their only head gear, the teams ready themselves for the next play. That year, Navy defeated Army 24-0. (USMA Library.)

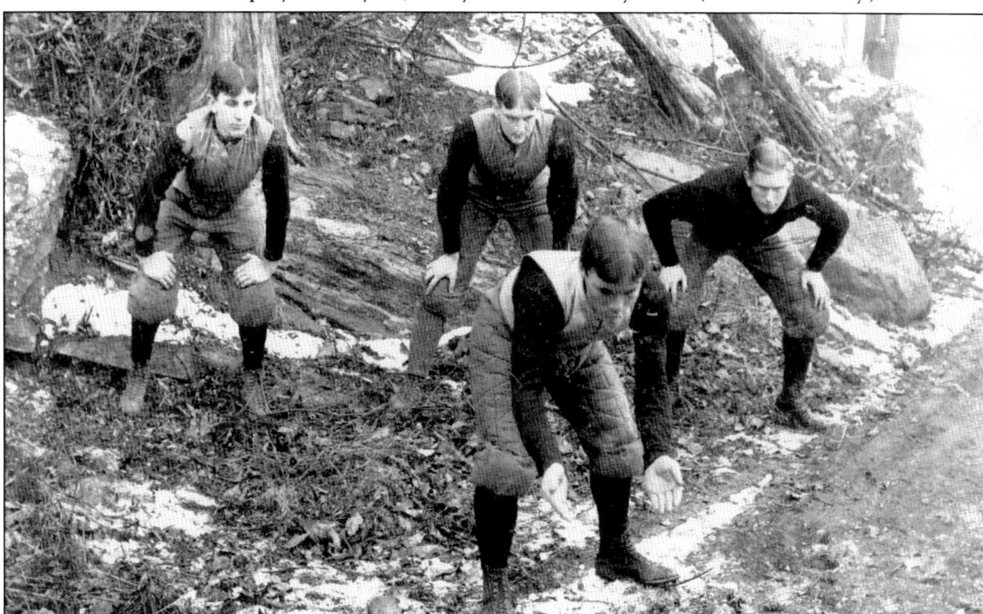

Army Backfield, 1898. Dressed in tightly laced canvas vests and padded pants, the Army backfield poses during a practice for the 1898 season. Their schedule that fall included games with Tufts, Wesleyan, Harvard, Yale, Lehigh, and Princeton. Other frequent opponents in the early years were Dartmouth, Brown, Union, and Navy. Visiting teams and football fans were accommodated at the hotels and guesthouses of Highland Falls and Fort Montgomery. (USMA Library.)

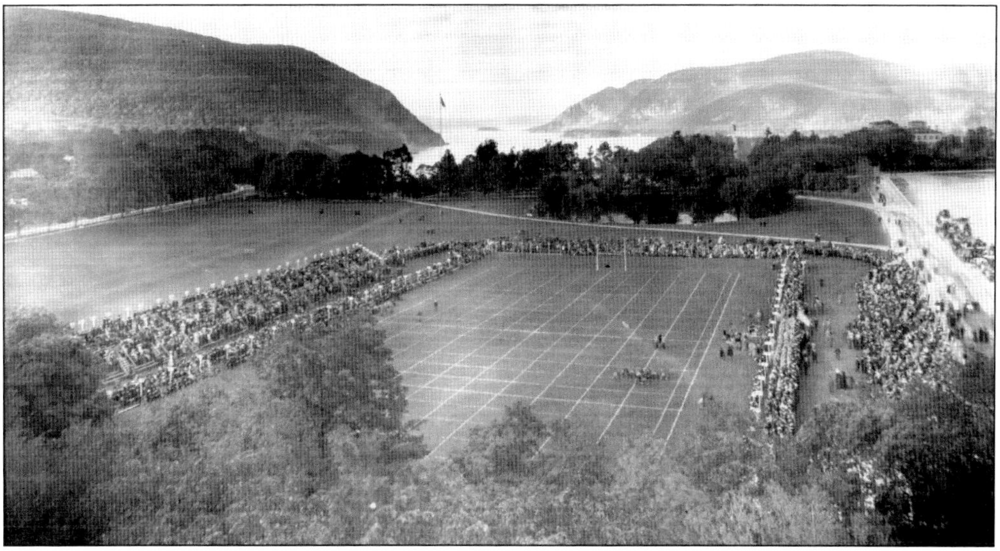

ARMY-YALE, 1907. Army Football continued to grow in popularity, as indicated by a crowded Cullum Field seen here in its majestic Highland setting. By the early 1900s, demand for seating exceeded supply. A plan was implemented to issue three tickets in a season to subscribers, who paid $5 each. Eventually a new stadium was built, named after the team's first captain, Dennis Michie. (USMA Library.)

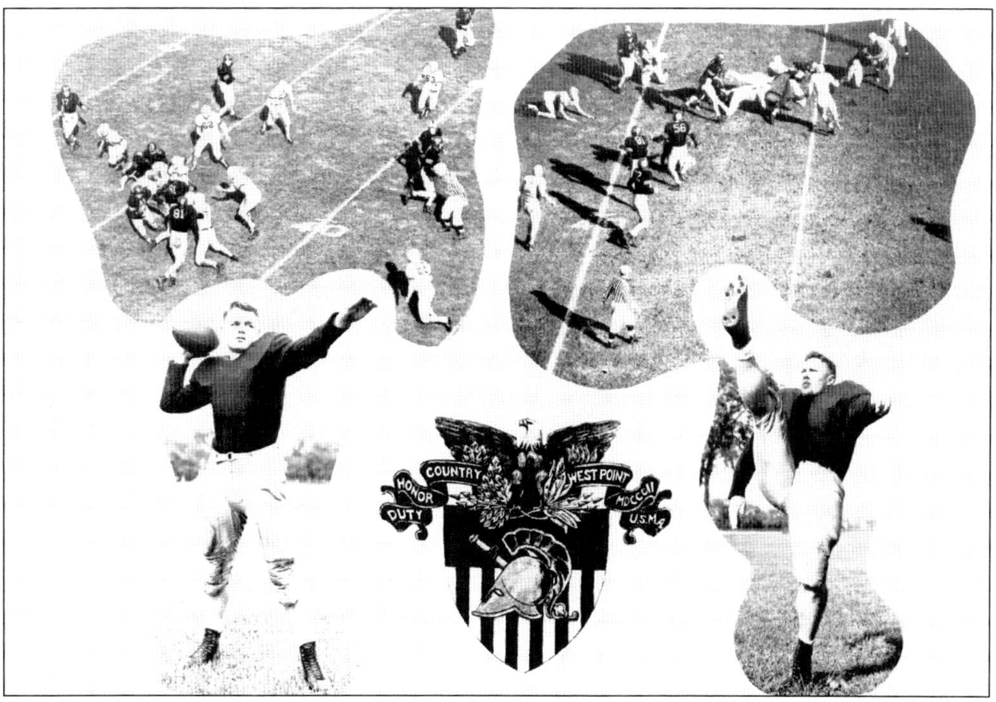

DAVIS AND BLANCHARD. Two legendary athletes, Glenn Davis, left, and Felix "Doc" Blanchard, played for the Army Football team from 1944 to 1946. Both All-American and Heisman Trophy winners, they led Army to a 27-0-1 record and two national championships during the three years they were in school together. During those war years, interest in service academy football was high among soldiers abroad and those on the home front. (USMA Library.)

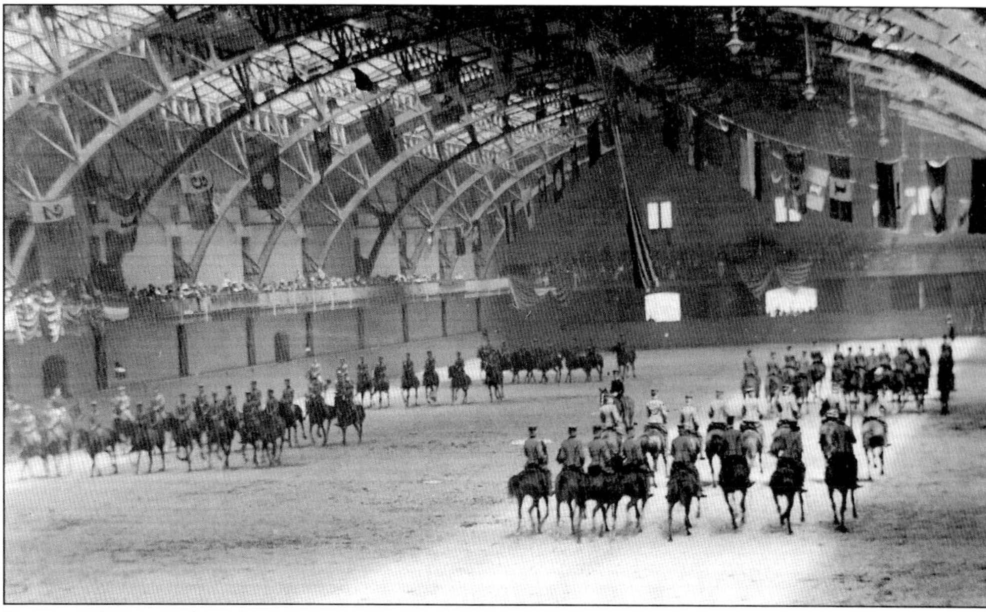

RIDING HALL. Before the mechanization of the army in the late 1940s, great emphasis was placed on horsemanship. The new riding hall, completed in 1909, provided a venue for training, horse shows, and exhibitions. An upper-level gallery for the audience extended around the perimeter. Here, the class of 1917 demonstrates a mounted drill. The riding hall was later renovated for classrooms and renamed Thayer Hall. (USMA Library.)

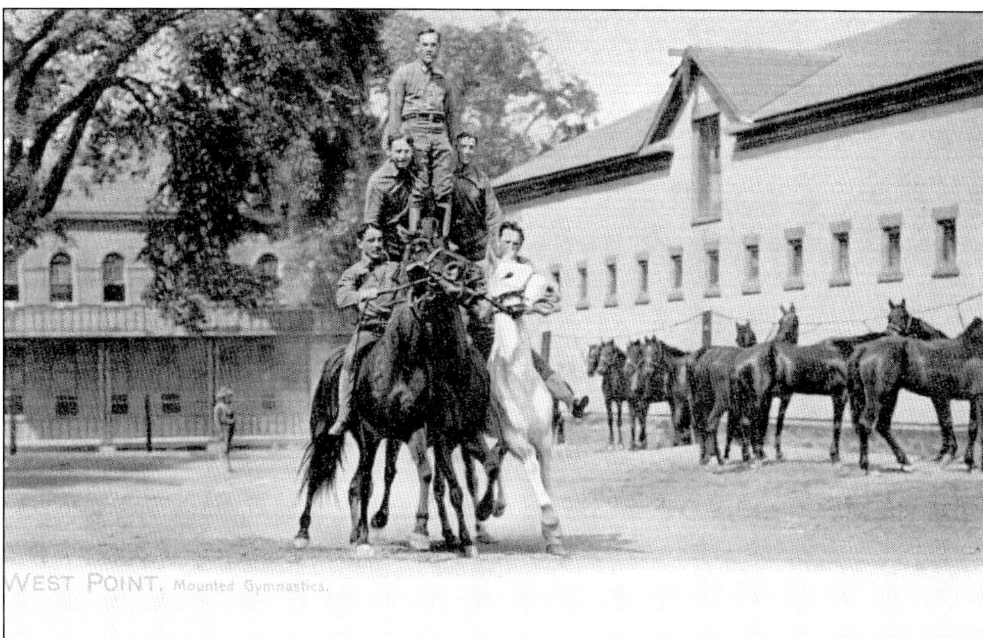

MOUNTED GYMNASTICS. The mastery of equestrian techniques included expert riding, shooting a target while in motion, and mounted gymnastics, the activity shown in this c. 1913 postcard. Visitors thrilled to see bareback riding practice and other daring exercises performed by cadets. (Gunza Collection.)

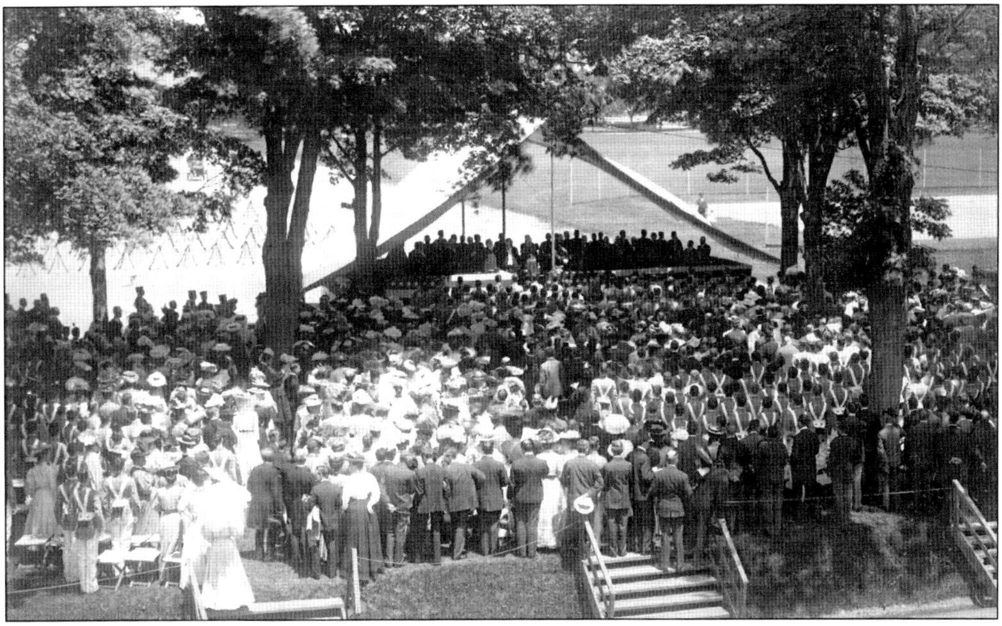

GRADUATION, 1906. Among the many ceremonies guests attend at West Point, one of the happiest is graduation. It is the culmination of days of related festivities known in the past as June Week. Pictured here are the 1906 commencement exercises, held in front of the old library. Secretary of war (and future president) William Howard Taft presented the diplomas to the 78 graduates. (USMA Library.)

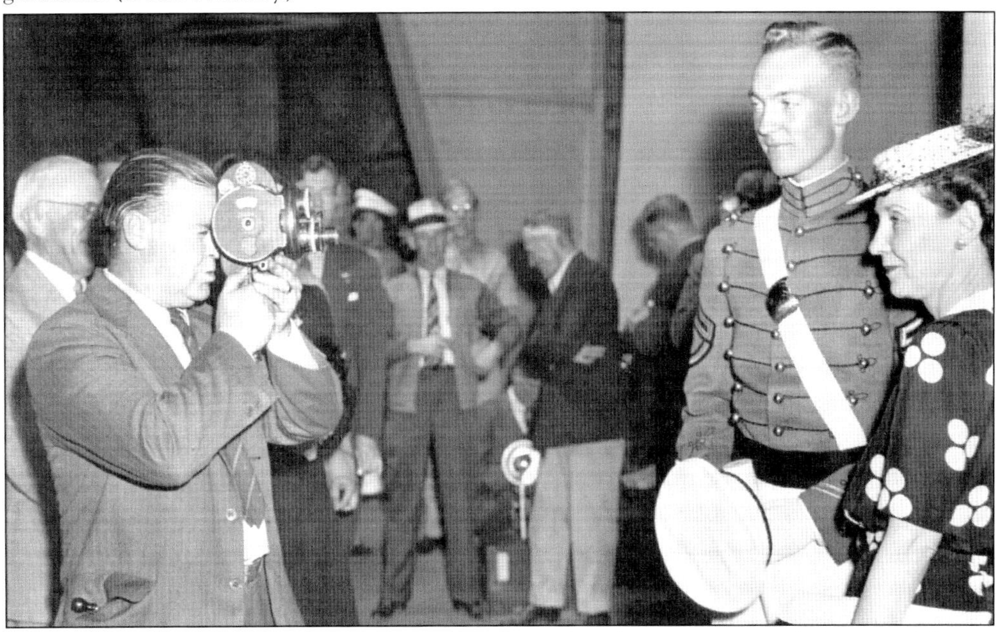

EISENHOWER GRADUATION. Proud parent Mamie Eisenhower poses with her son John at his graduation. His father, Gen. Dwight Eisenhower, was unable to attend because he was commanding forces in Europe during World War II. The date of the graduation was June 6, 1944, also known as D-Day. In 1955, John's wife and children lived in Highland Falls while he served in Korea. (USMA Library.)

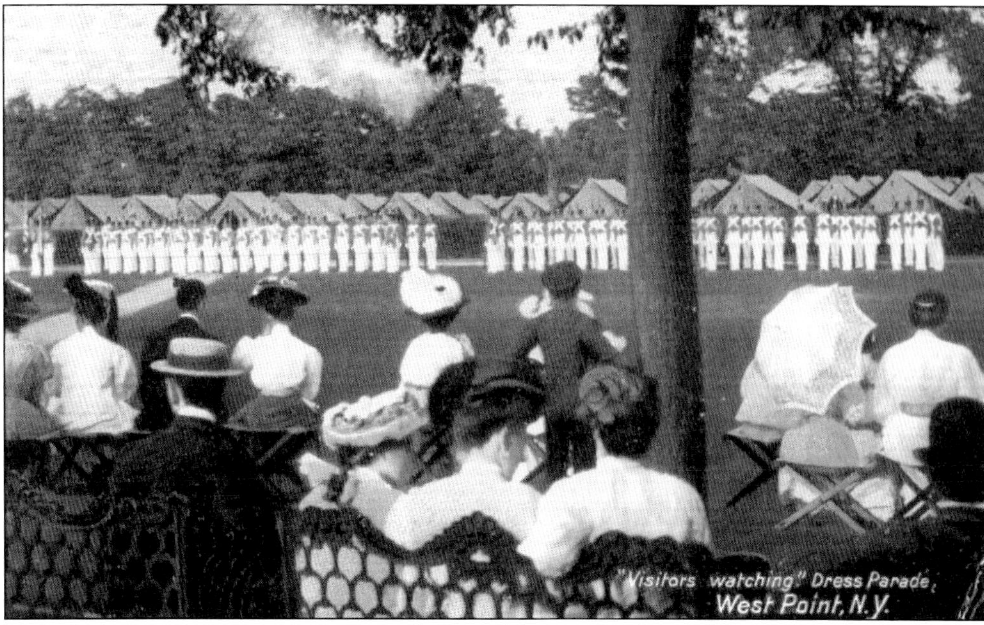

DRESS PARADE. Attending a dress parade is an obligatory tradition for tourists at West Point. In this 1910 postcard view, the tents of the summer encampment form a backdrop for the straight lines of cadets on the plain. Standing at attention in their dress uniforms, they await the order to march. (Gunza Collection.)

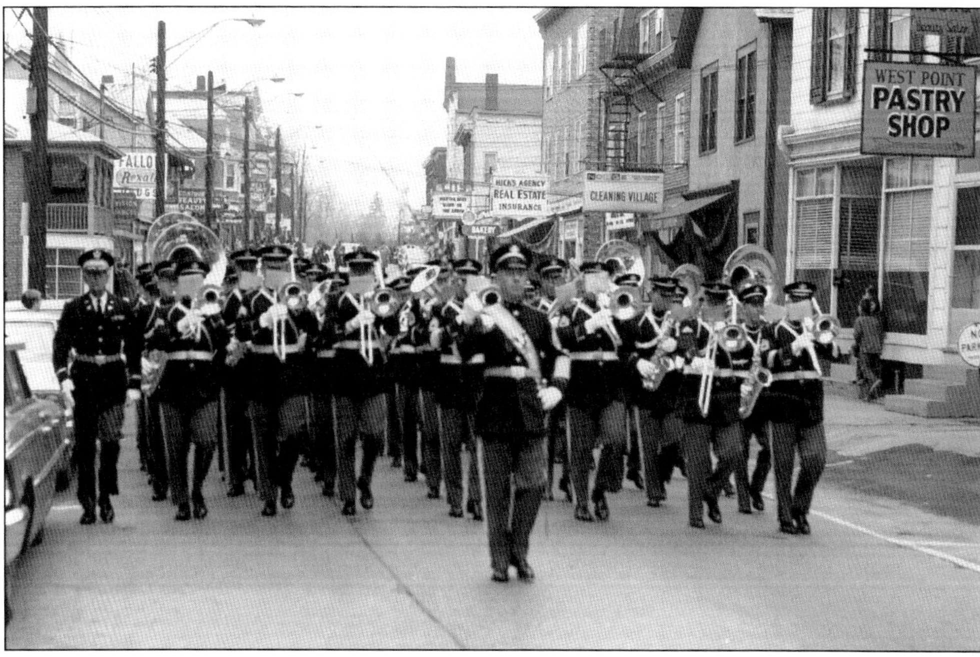

USMA BAND. The United States Military Academy Band has a long and generous tradition of supporting events in the Town of Highlands. Composed of expert musicians, the group marches south on Main Street in the 1964 Veterans Day parade. Thousands of visitors enjoy the band's summer concerts held at West Point every Sunday from June to Labor Day. (Army photograph, Graber Collection.)

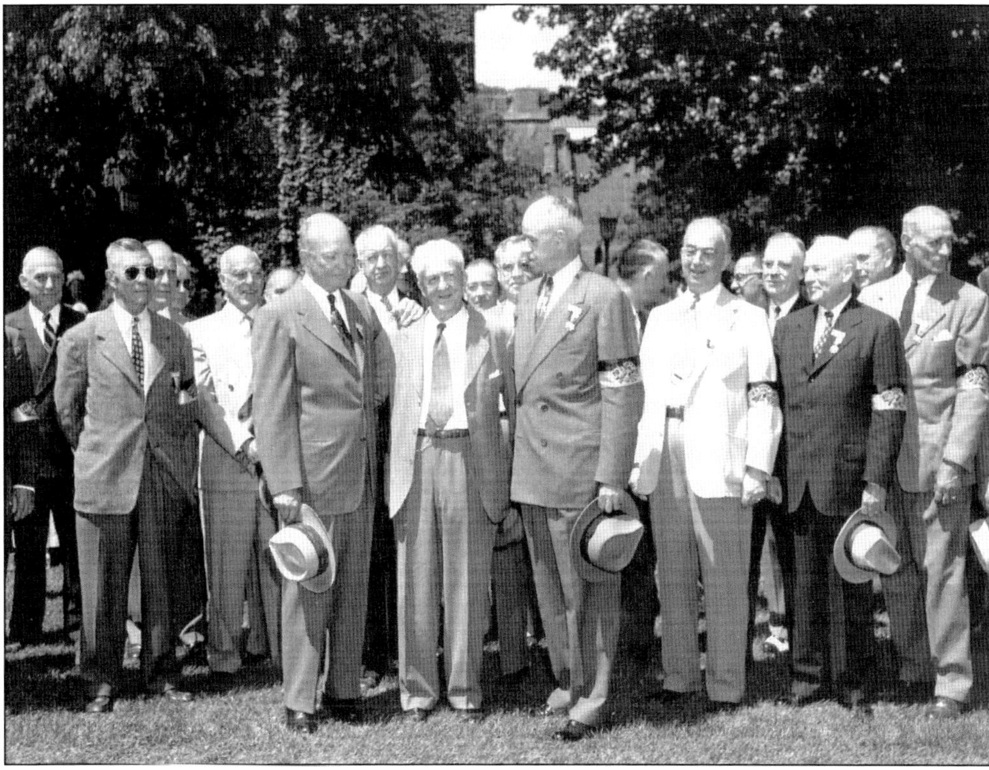

Marty Maher. While a 20-year-old Irish immigrant, Marty Maher (1871–1961) took a job as a waiter in the Cadet Mess at West Point and developed a lifelong devotion to the military academy. He joined the army and began a 55-year career assisting in the training of cadets, among them Dwight "Ike" Eisenhower and Omar Bradley. Above is a 1950 alumni reunion photograph of the class of 1915, showing Maher (center foreground) standing between Ike (left) and Bradley. Maher and his wife, Mary, lived on Lake Street in Highland Falls. In his leisure time, he enjoyed running down to Cohen's Bar (now the Park Restaurant) for a drink and some storytelling. With his Irish wit and charm, Marty was a beloved figure. The 1954 movie *The Long Gray Line* was based on Marty Maher's memoir, *Bringing Up the Brass*, and starred Tyrone Power, pictured below left with a child actor and Marty. (USMA Library.)

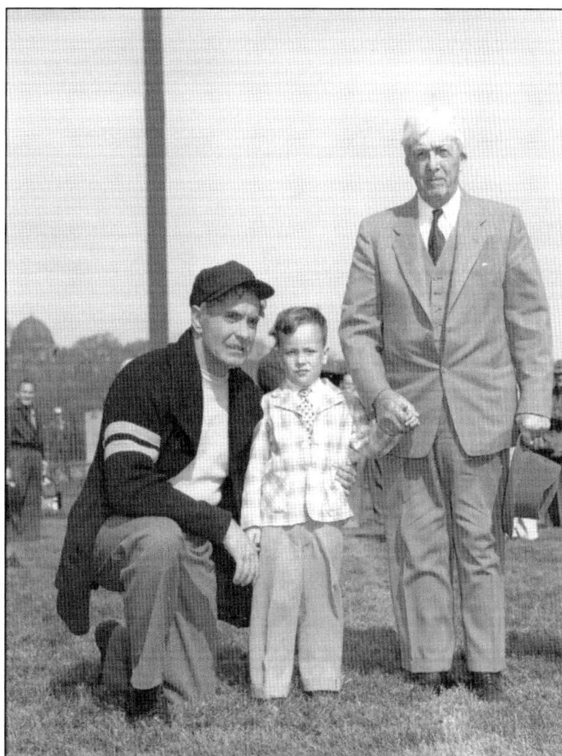

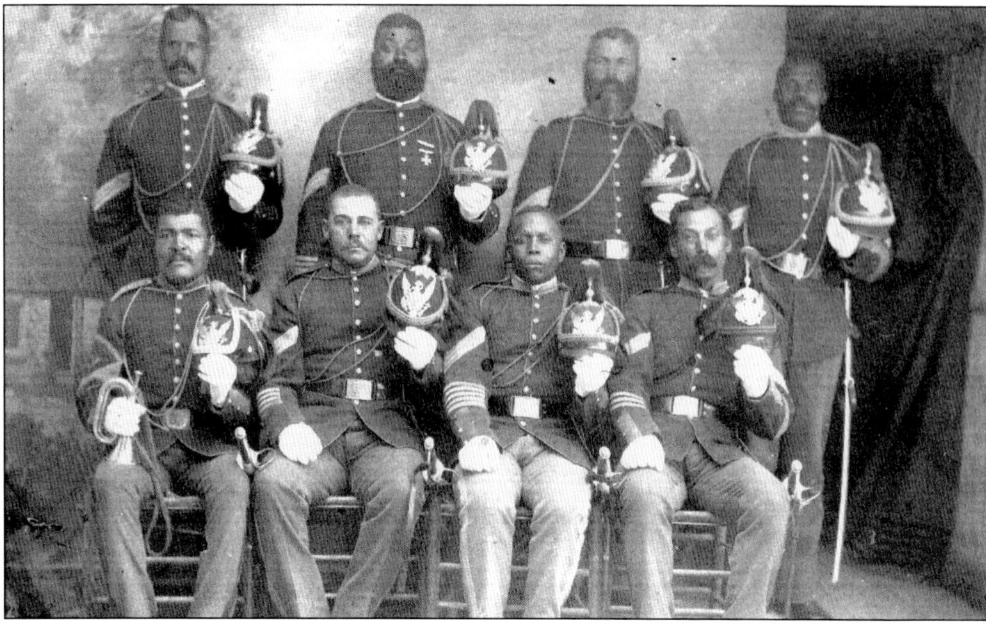

BUFFALO SOLDIERS. Elegantly uniformed members of the 9th Cavalry pose in 1910. After the Civil War, an act of Congress created units consisting entirely of black men, who were sent to the West to repel Native American attacks. American Indian tribes honored them with the nickname "Buffalo Soldiers," a sign of respect for their ability to fight. Stationed at West Point in 1907, their job was to teach cadets riding and cavalry tactics. (USMA Library.)

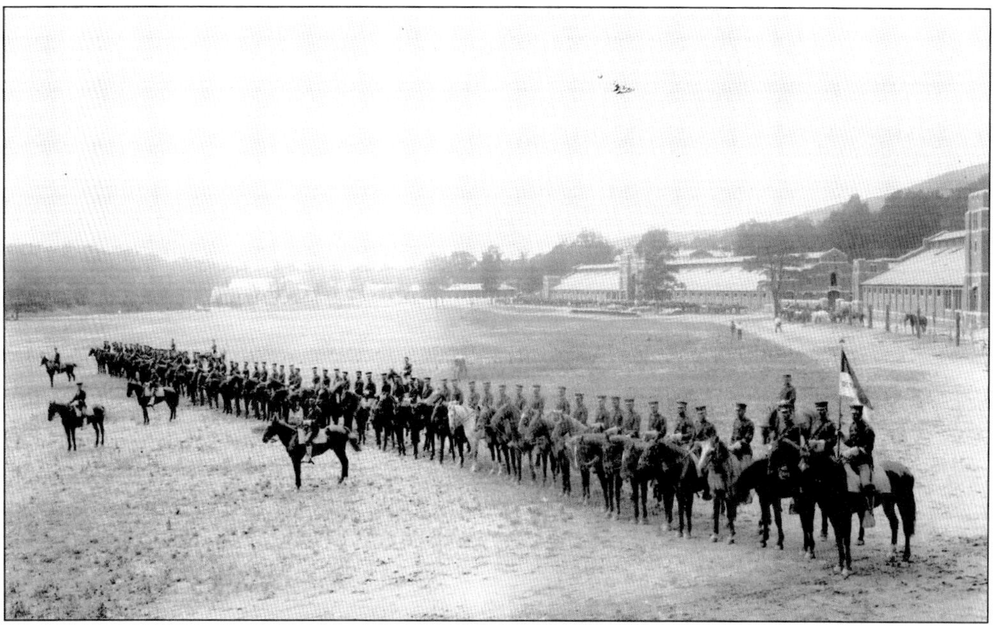

B TROOP, 1910. Buffalo Soldiers drill on the cavalry plain. Famous for their equestrian skills, they often served as escorts and honor guards for high-ranking dignitaries who visited the military academy. Other responsibilities included feeding and grooming the horses, delivering them to the Riding Hall, conducting cadet summer camps, and assisting in the training of cadets in horsemanship and animal care. (USMA Library.)

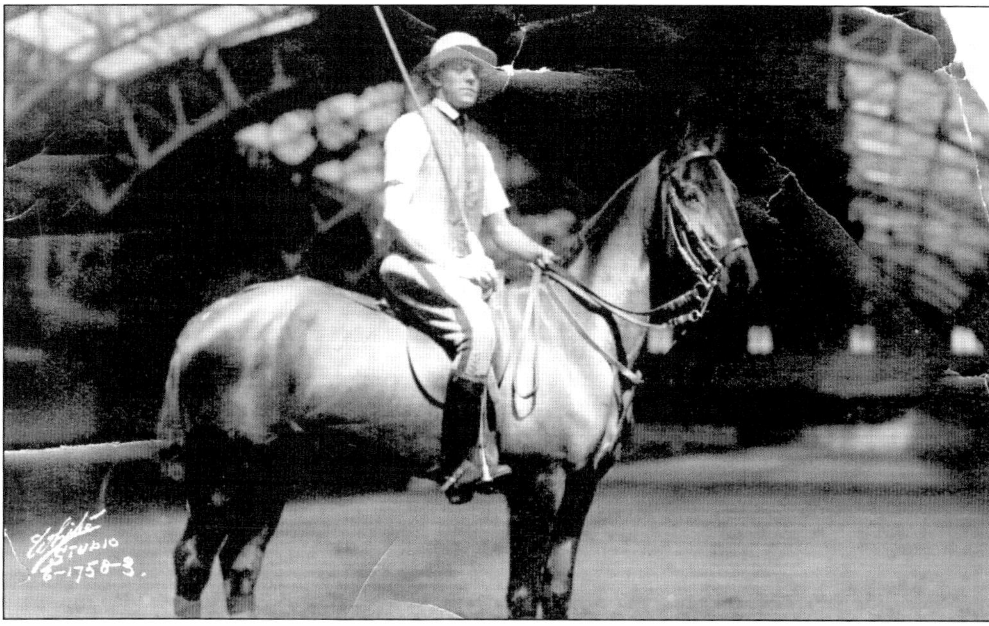

ARTHUR JOHNSON. Ready for play, Arthur Johnson sits astride his horse in the Riding Hall about 1920. Years earlier, Johnson had lied about his age and enlisted in the 10th Cavalry at 14. He was stationed at West Point at a time when the army encouraged their cavalry soldiers to participate in polo in order to improve their riding ability. Johnson later resided with his family in Highland Falls. (Burns Collection.)

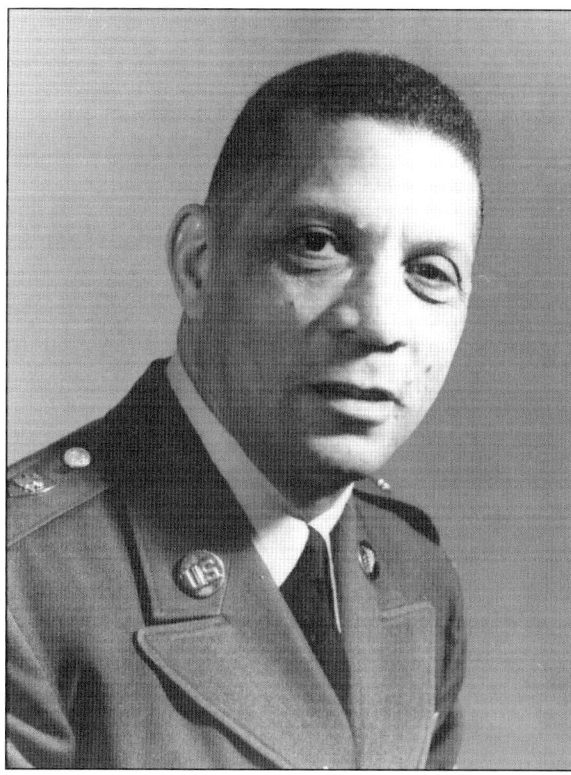

ROBERT JOHNSON. A third-generation Buffalo Soldier, Robert Johnson was raised at West Point and attended Highland Falls High School. He served in the 9th Cavalry until it was disbanded in 1946 and then worked in the Veterinary Detachment. Through his advocacy, the mule became the symbol for the military academy. The animal care facility was the first building on West Point named after an enlisted soldier, Robert Johnson. (Brown Collection.)

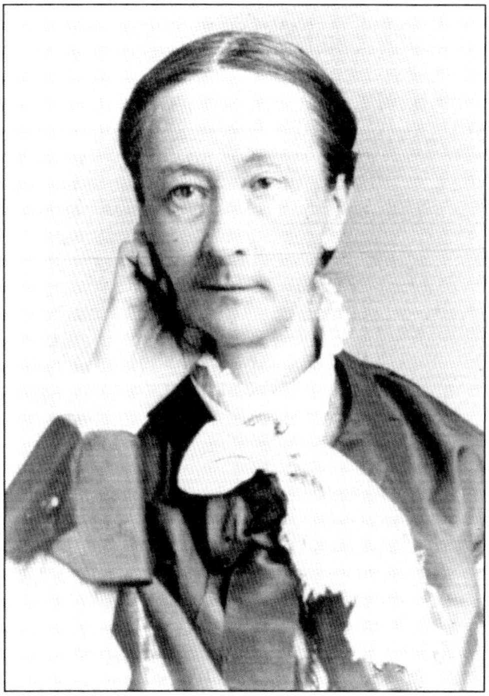

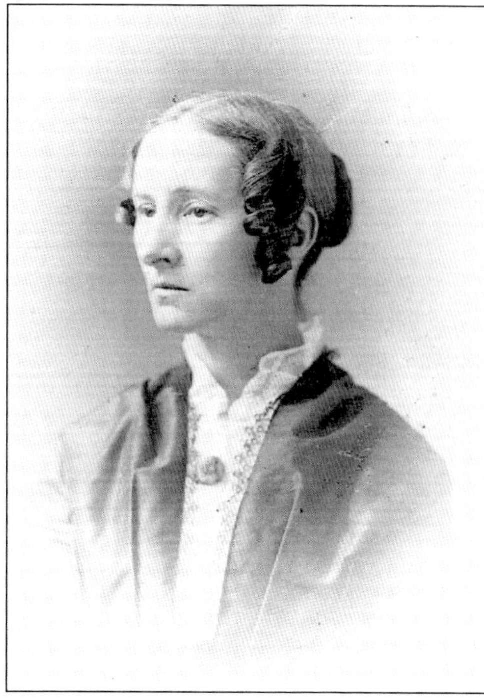

WARNER SISTERS. Opposite West Point, Constitution Island was the site of Revolutionary forts and anchorage for the Great Chain. It later became the home of two 19th-century writers, the Warner sisters. In 1850, Susan Warner, above left, wrote the best-selling novel *The Wide, Wide World*. She followed that with dozens of other novels and also taught Bible classes to West Point cadets. Her younger sister Anna, above right, also a novelist, penned a charming "how-to" book called *Gardening By Myself* but is best known for writing the hymn "Jesus Loves Me." After Susan's death, Anna taught Bible classes for 30 more years. She spent summers at her island home, below, and winters in Highland Falls at John Bigelow's home, called the Squirrels. She died there in 1915. Both women are buried at West Point. (Above left, Constitution Island Archives; above right and below, Sidamon-Eristoff Collection.)

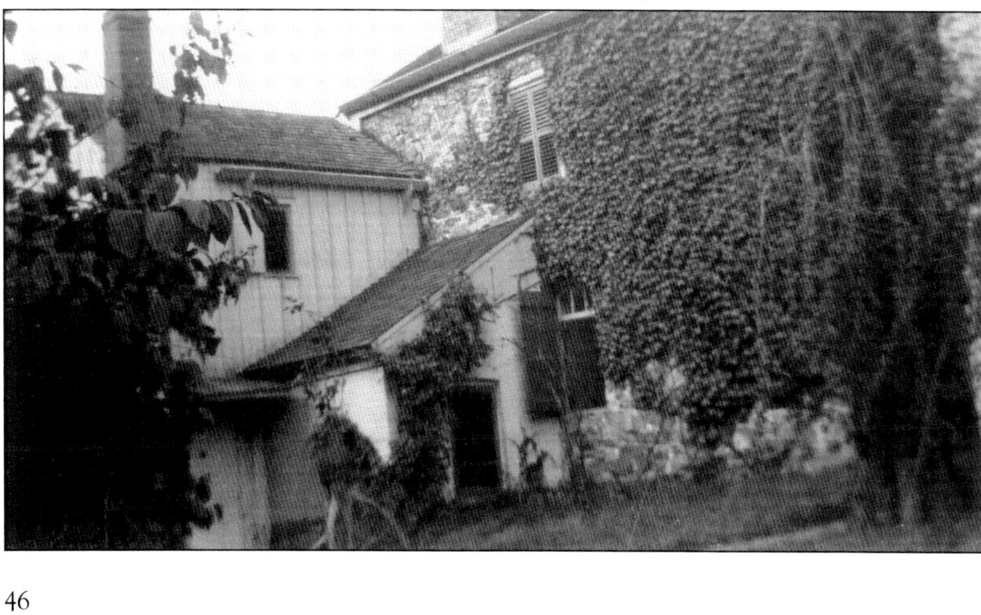

Four

BUSINESS AND INDUSTRY

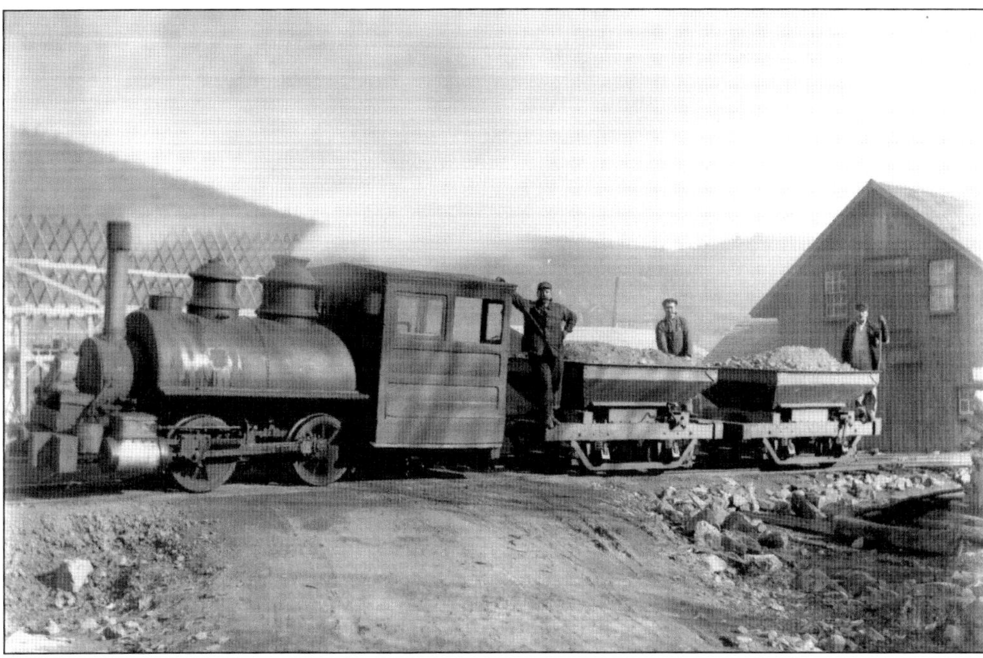

FOREST OF DEAN. Some four miles west of Fort Montgomery, the Forest of Dean Mine was opened in 1754, producing iron ore famous for its high quality. It remained in operation for over 150 years. A community developed around the mine, which included the miners and support personnel like engineer Ralph Conklin, pictured here around 1929. Mining continued until 1931. The federal government acquired the land and created Stillwell Lake, flooding the area. (Woodward Collection.)

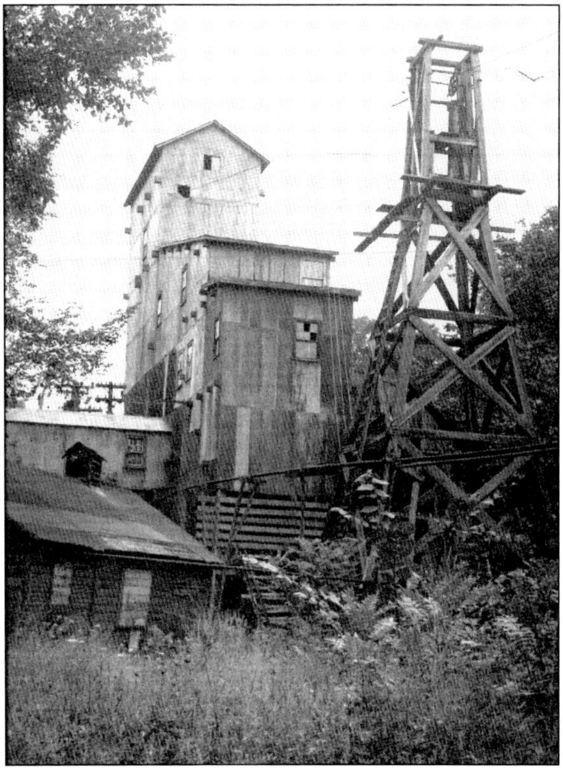

Forest of Dean Crusher. Two shifts of miners wearing headgear with carbide lamps extracted the ore using black powder explosives or dynamite. After removal from the mine, which was 1,700 feet deep and one and one-fourth miles long, the iron ore was pounded by this crusher into small pieces for easy shipment. At a short distance from the mine entrance were residences, farms, two stores, a barracks for single miners, and a school. (PIPC Archives.)

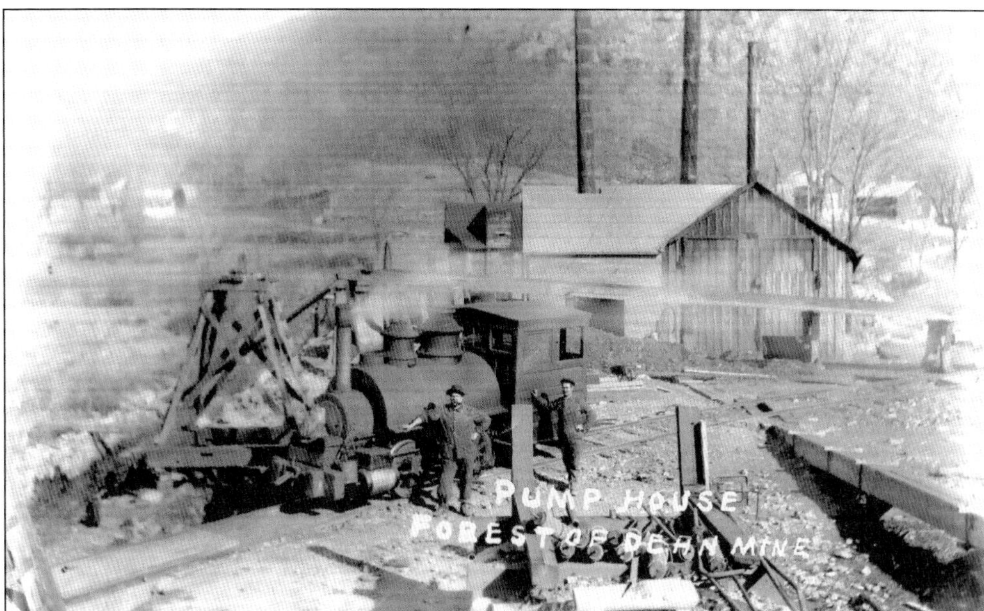

Pump House. After crushing, the iron ore had to be conveyed down to the Hudson River. This was originally accomplished by mule-drawn cars on tracks, but in 1906, a modernized system was put in place. The iron ore was loaded onto cars of the narrow-gauge railroad for a three-mile trip to a loading station. This pump house held the equipment that drained the mine when it filled with water. (Woodward Collection.)

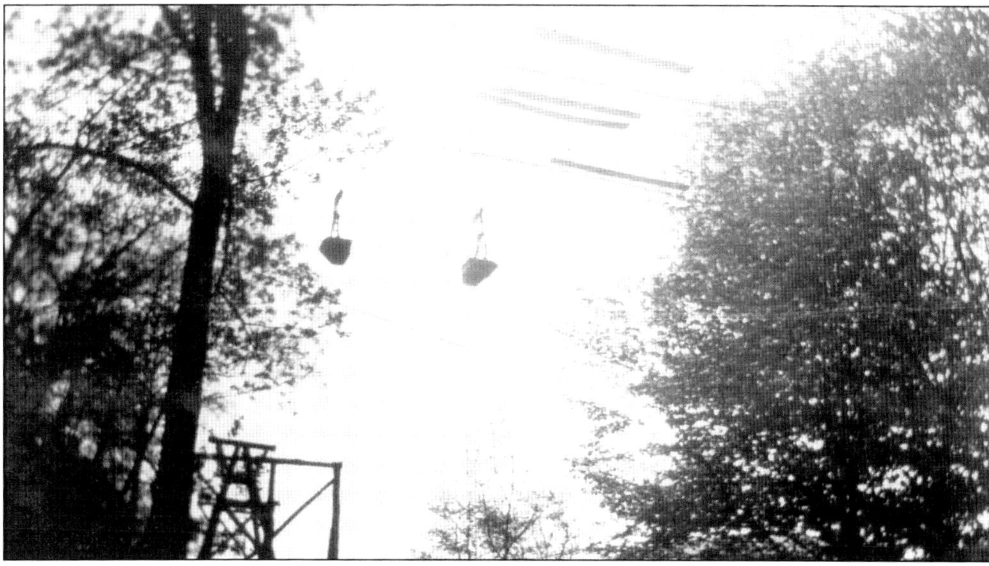

ORE BUCKETS. At the loading station, the iron ore was loaded into buckets of an aerial tramway, which then carried the ore to the river at Fort Montgomery for shipment by boat or train. On the return trip, the buckets carried coal back to the miners. Occasionally, daring children would sneak rides in the ore buckets and jump off as they rode over Brooks Lake! (Bailey Collection.)

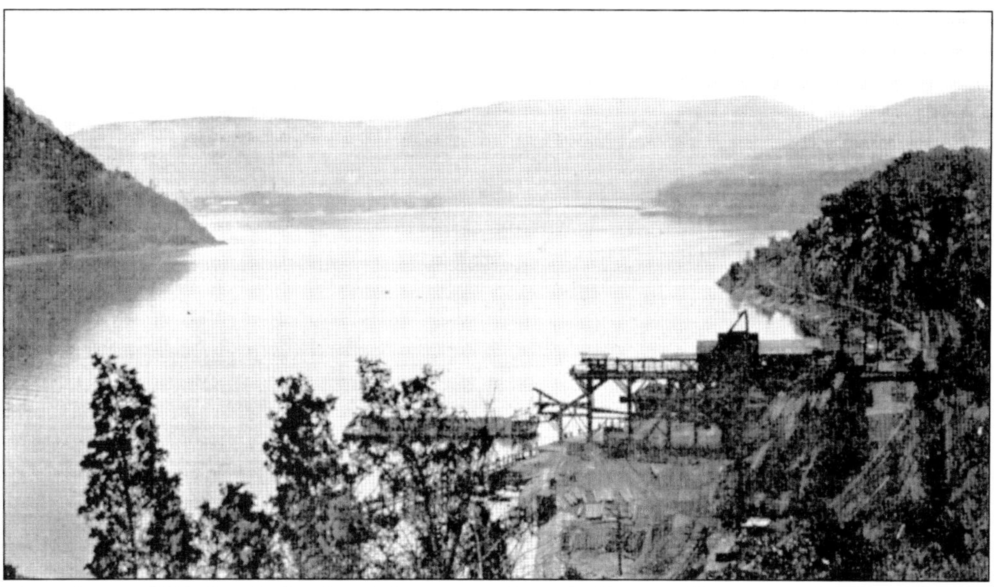

MINE DOCK, 1921. On the last leg of the journey from the Forest of Dean mine, half-ton-capacity buckets filled with iron ore were sent down the aerial tramway to the mine dock at Fort Montgomery, seen here. The ore was then either placed in a 1,000-ton storage bin at the dock or dumped directly into rail cars or boats and sent to an iron furnace in Secaucus, New Jersey. (Gunza Collection.)

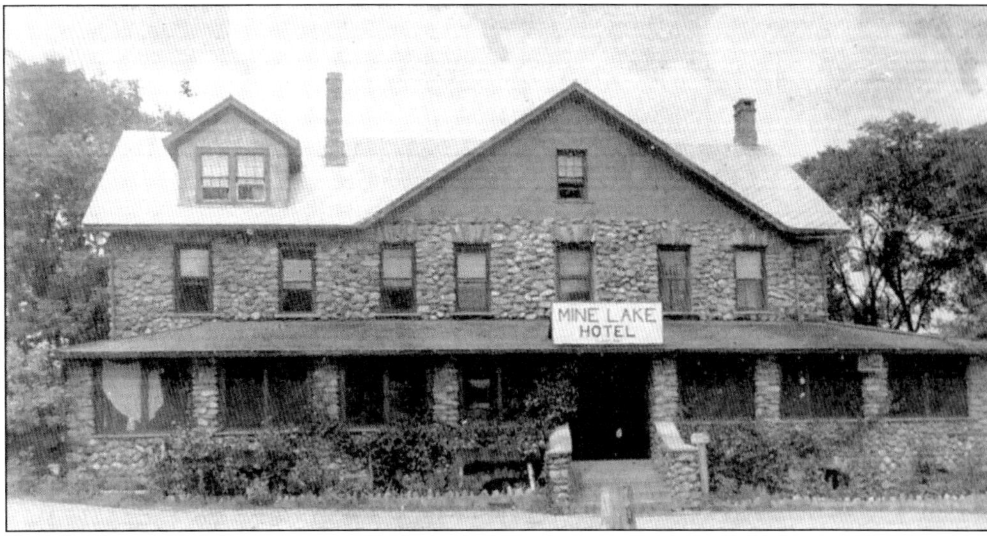

MINE LAKE HOTEL. Operated by the Julian family during the early 1900s, the Mine Lake Hotel also had a well-known restaurant. It overlooked Mine Pond on land now occupied by the army's Camp Buckner. In 1942, the government acquired the hotel site in order to extend the West Point Military Reservation. The stones from the facade of the hotel were used in the construction of the sentry house at Camp Buckner. (Julian Collection.)

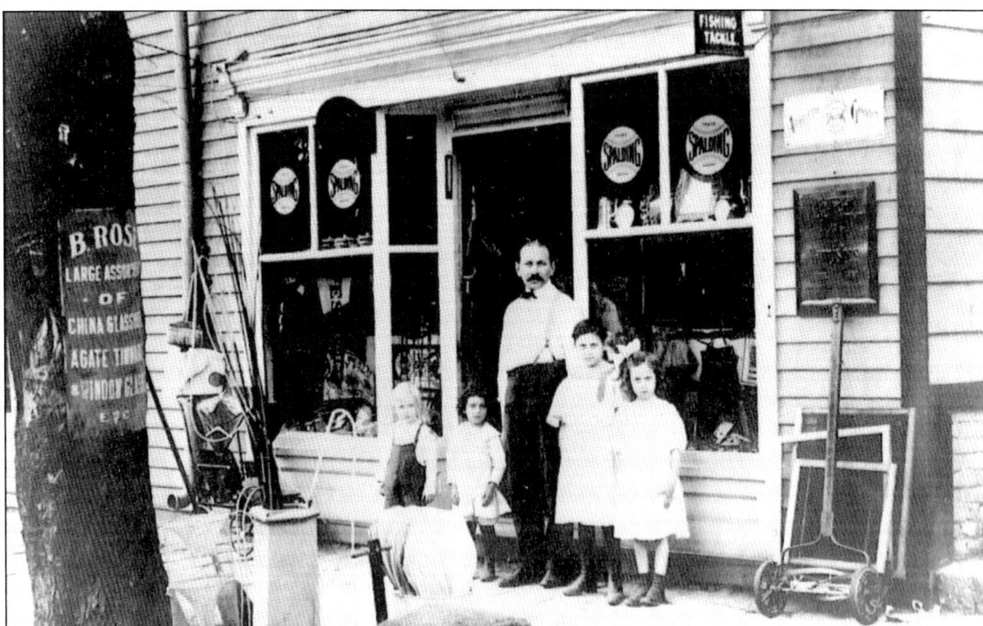

ROSE'S HARDWARE STORE. Proprietor Ben Rose and others pose for a photograph in front of his hardware store on Main Street, Highland Falls, in 1909. With him are, from left to right, neighbor Art Elsen, son Larry, and daughters Hannah and Miriam. The store featured china, tinware, window glass, sporting goods, and equipment for farm and yard. The enterprise later moved to its current location farther north on Main Street. (Rose Collection.)

WEYANT GARAGE SIGN. Lorentz Graber, right, and friends perch daringly on the Studebaker Motor Cars sign along the approach to Highland Falls around 1915. When Chester and James Weyant opened their business on Main Street, it began as a livery service offering carriages, surreys, and road wagons. Since then, the Weyant name has been associated with several successful businesses in the Town of Highlands, including the garage noted on this sign. (Graber Collection.)

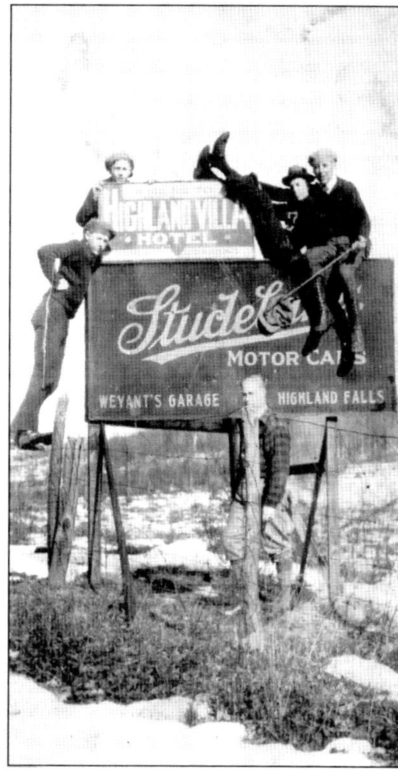

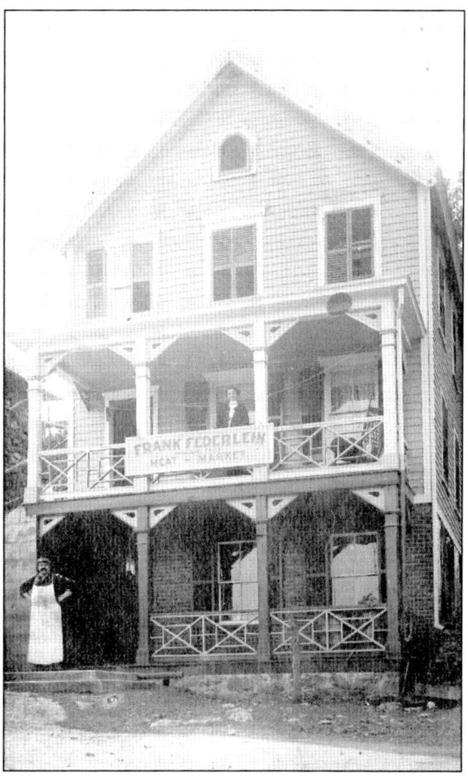

FEDERLEIN MEAT MARKET. Frank Federlein stands in front of his butcher shop on Prospect Street in 1913, while his daughter Marie looks out from the porch of the family living quarters above the store. His wife, Magdelena Federlein, not pictured, helped in the kitchen and made deliveries to local customers, among whom were the many German immigrants who came to the Town of Highlands in the late 1800s. (Feldman Collection.)

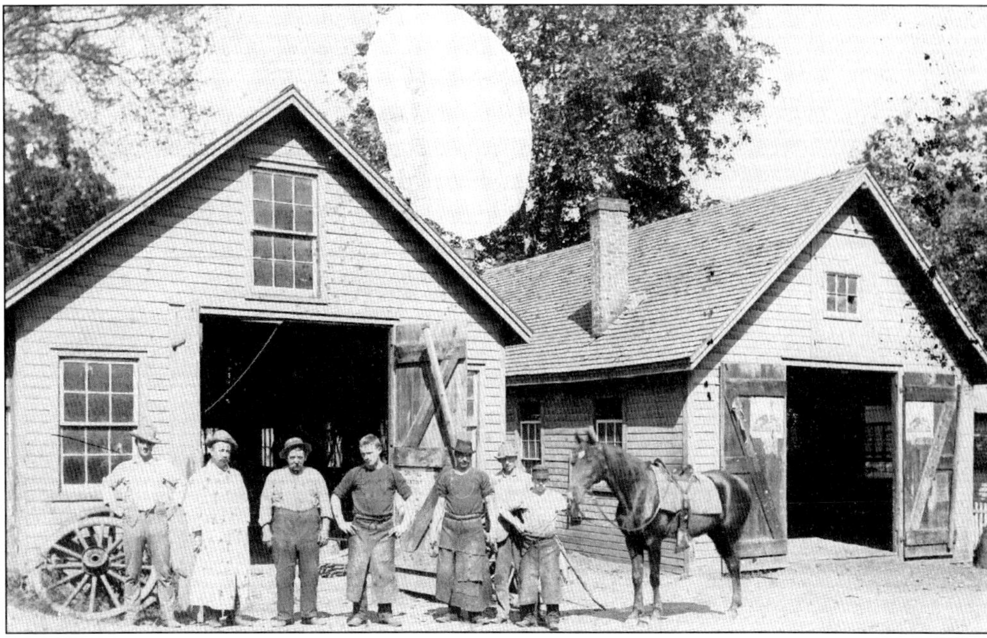

Blacksmith Shop. Alphons Bosch (above and below, fifth from left) owned a blacksmith shop at 14 Cozzens Avenue, Highland Falls. It is best described in a memoir by his daughter Catherine (Sister M. Alphonsus): "It was a busy place from morning until six or seven in the evening. The ring of hammer on anvil could be heard down to the corner of Main Street. The open forge with its red, hot fire heating the horse shoes, tires, and tools to be sharpened, as well as the sparks flying from the anvil as the iron was pounded into shape, were a great attraction to passersby, especially old men and young boys. The hiss of sizzling iron as is was plunged into a barrel of water to cool and the smell of horses hooves as the red, hot shoe was fitted brought many to watch." (Bosch Collection.)

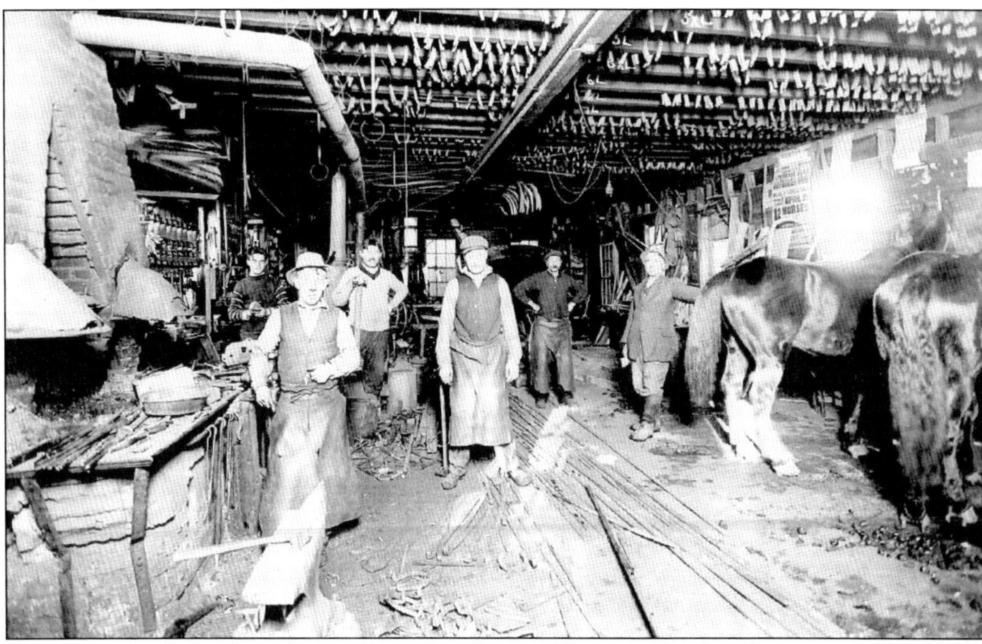

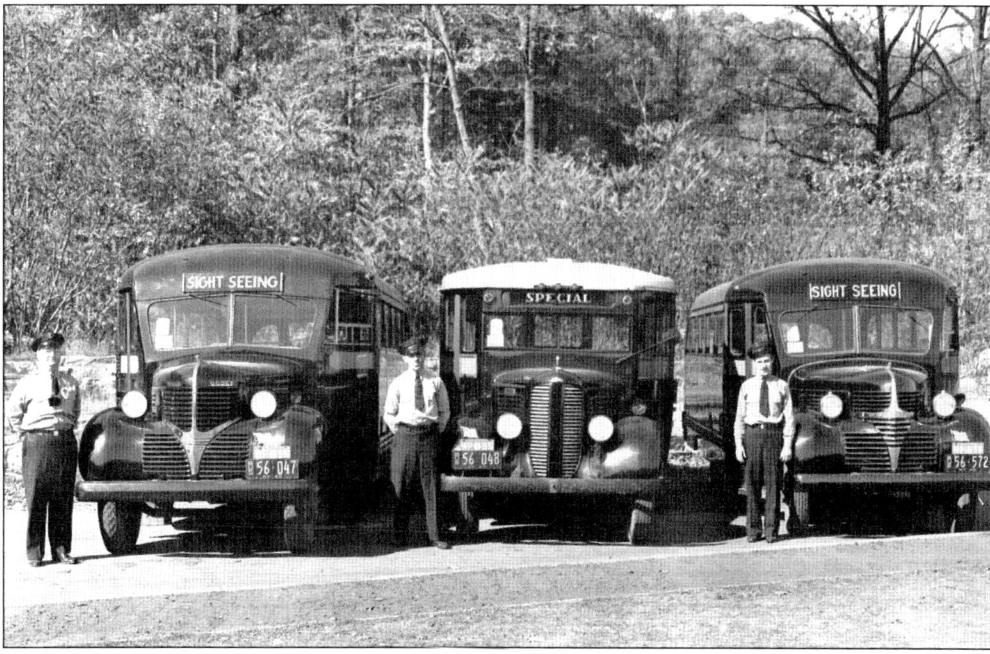

TOUR BUSES. Over the years, the Bosch Blacksmith Shop evolved into an automobile-related business, selling gasoline and cars. This expanded into providing taxi and bus service. Pictured here around 1940 is the fleet of Bosch sightseeing buses, which were used for tours of West Point. The drivers are Calvin Stewart (left), Al Saucier (center), and Clarence Hall. (Bosch Collection.)

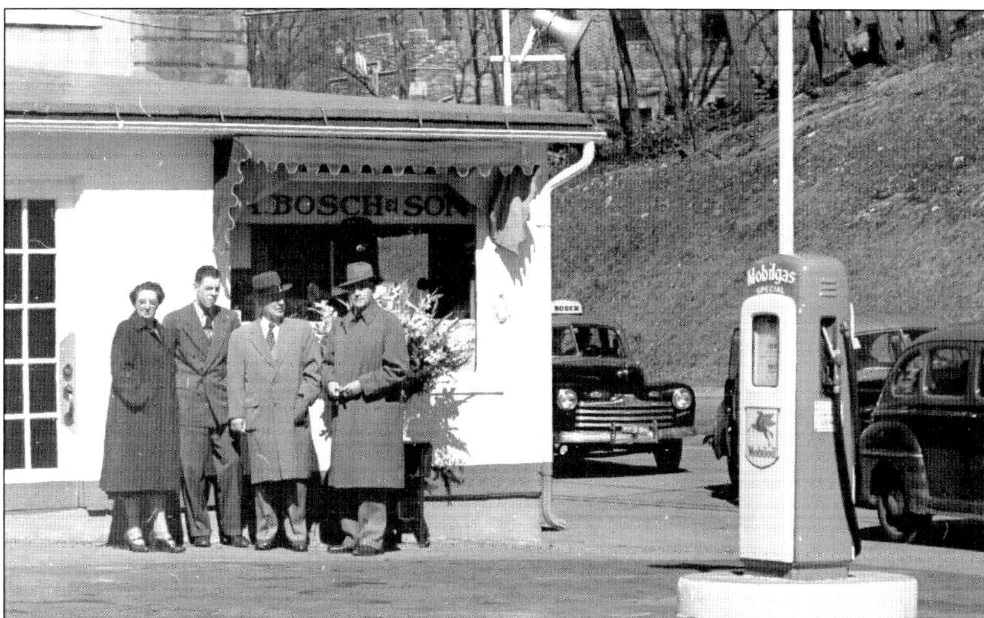

JOSEPHINE BOSCH. For many years, the daughter of founder Alphons Bosch ran the Bosch family business. Standing in front of the taxi headquarters, Josephine and her nephew John speak with two sales representatives. In the 1950s, the company owned 18 taxis, a large body, fender, and motor repair shop, and a Buick sales service. (Bosch Collection.)

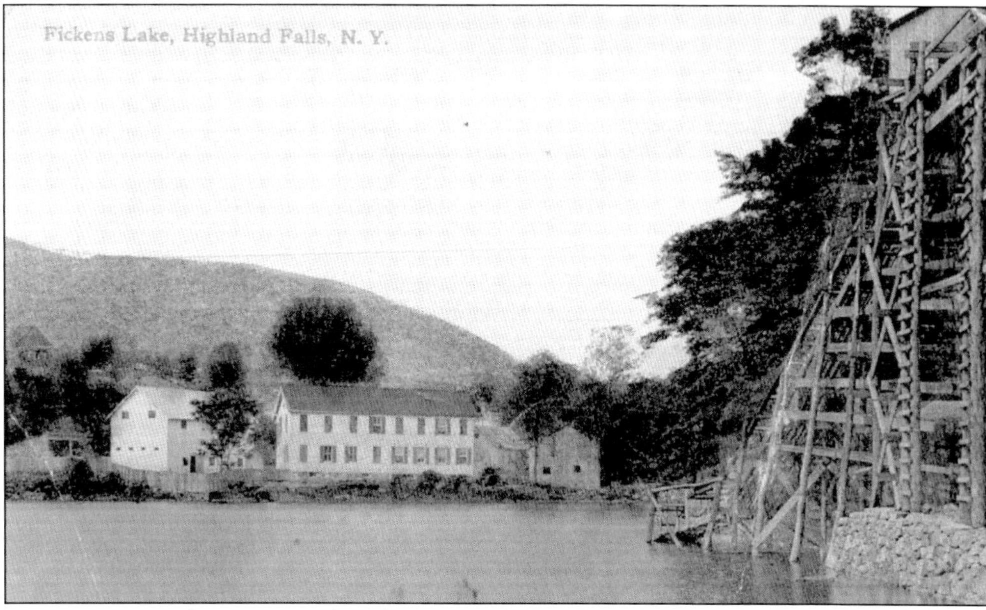

FICKENS LAKE. This 1914 view has three points of interest. The large white building across the lake was the Reppenhagen Razor Strop Company, world renowned for its high-quality products. Visible at right is part of a structure used in winter ice harvests. Blocks of ice were carried mechanically to the top and loaded silo-fashion into an icehouse. The lake itself was filled in during the 1950s and is a well-used ball field today. (Yagel Collection.)

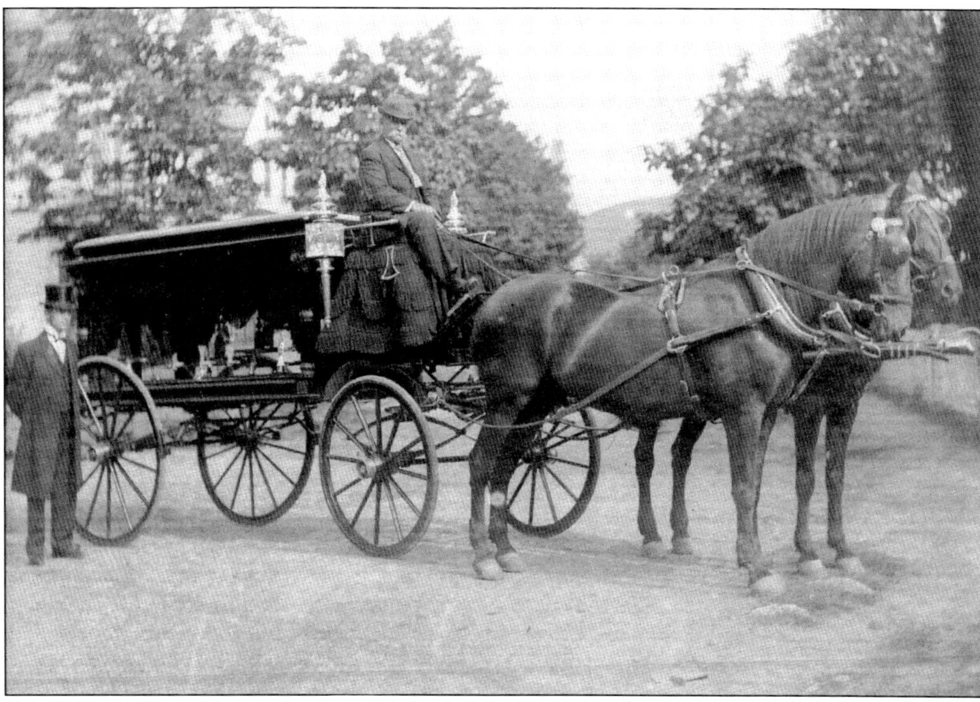

OLD BLACK TEAM. Undertaker Fritz Wolklin, left, stands with his horse-drawn hearse around 1918. Driver Fischer Price holds the reins. This was known as the "Old Black Team." Wolklin's advertising indicates that he also made mattresses and reupholstered furniture. (Yagel Collection.)

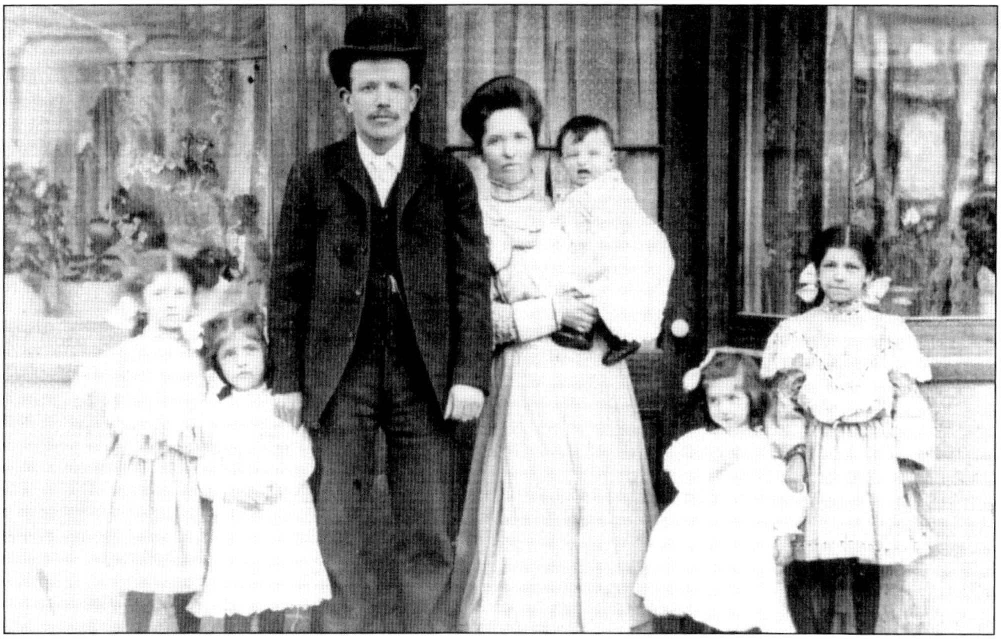

KOPALD FAMILY. Newman and Nettie Kopald and their children—from left to right, Lil, Eva, Abraham, Jennie, and Sadie—stand in front of their Main Street, Highland Falls, home in 1906. The two-story brick structure, now a commercial building, was called the Greenhouse because of the abundant plants in the windows. An Austrian immigrant, Kopald started a dry goods business that flourished in town for over 85 years. (Kopald Collection.)

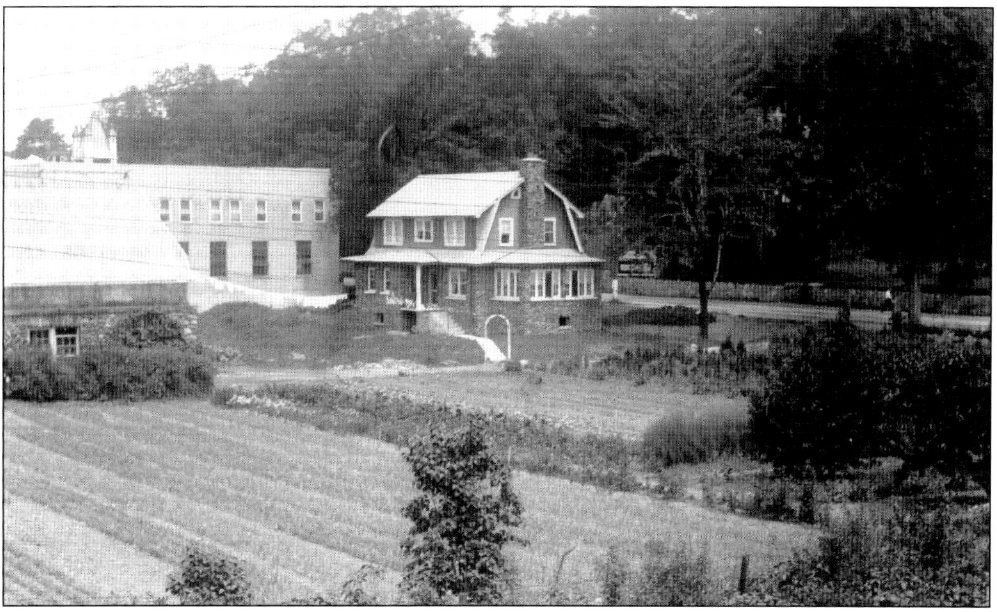

GRABER FLORIST. Highland Falls was the home of a thriving wholesale flower industry from the 1940s to 1960s. The Graber business, pictured here, and nearby Michel's greenhouses were major suppliers throughout the tri-state area. Poinsettias, lilies, and bedding plants were produced but Graber's specialty was carnations. Townspeople looked forward to the florist's showy summer display in fields of neat, colorful rows. (Graber Collection.)

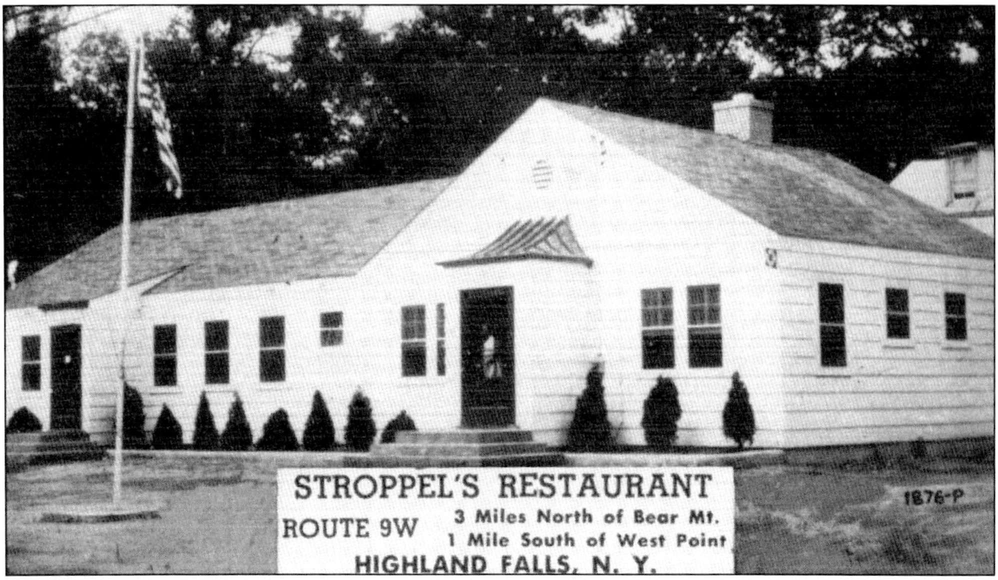

STROPPEL'S RESTAURANT. Conveniently located on Route 9W between Bear Mountain and West Point, Stroppel's Restaurant was a favorite of locals and travelers for many years. The menu offered delicious sandwiches and dinners. On Friday and Saturday evenings there was dancing. It later became Joseph's and now operates as the Hacienda Restaurant. (Gunza Collection.)

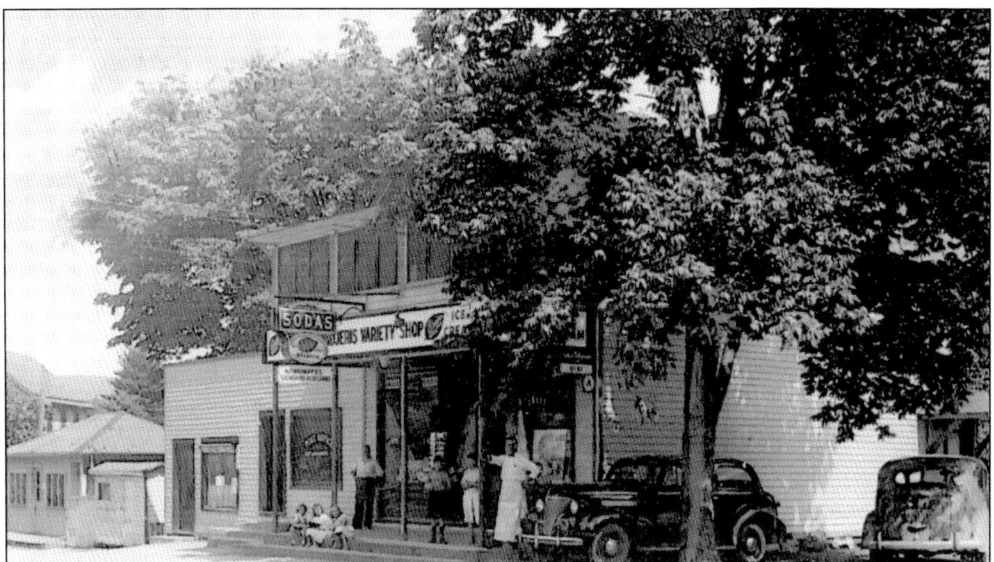

COUNJERIS'S STORE. Wearing a bow tie and long white apron, Nick Coundjeris stands in front of his variety store in Fort Montgomery around 1940. Several young customers join him. A Bell sign on the shop indicated that a public telephone booth was available for use inside. The building to the left is the post office. The Fort Montgomery Post Office occupies this site today. (Gunza Collection.)

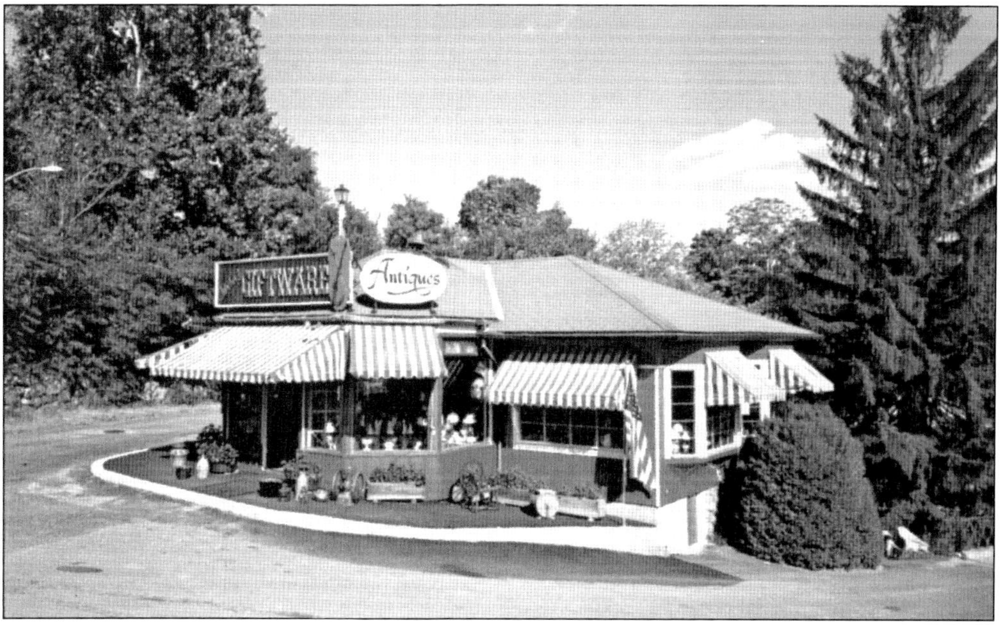

MICHEL'S. Now the community room of Weyant Green Apartments, this building was Michel's Antique and Gift Shop, known for its large assortment of gift ware. The Michel family also ran a successful flower-growing operation. Decorated in this 1955 view with cheerful, striped awnings, the shop sold dinnerware, lamps, glass, old prints, bric-a-brac, and candles. (Gunza Collection.)

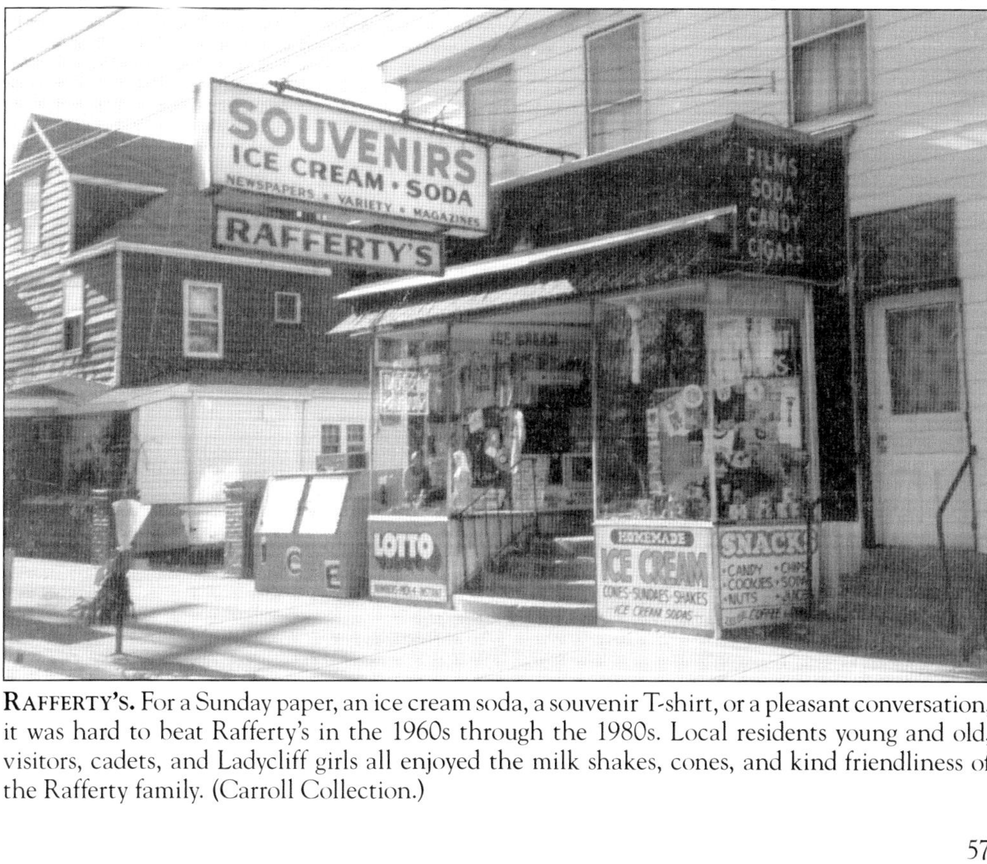

RAFFERTY'S. For a Sunday paper, an ice cream soda, a souvenir T-shirt, or a pleasant conversation, it was hard to beat Rafferty's in the 1960s through the 1980s. Local residents young and old, visitors, cadets, and Ladycliff girls all enjoyed the milk shakes, cones, and kind friendliness of the Rafferty family. (Carroll Collection.)

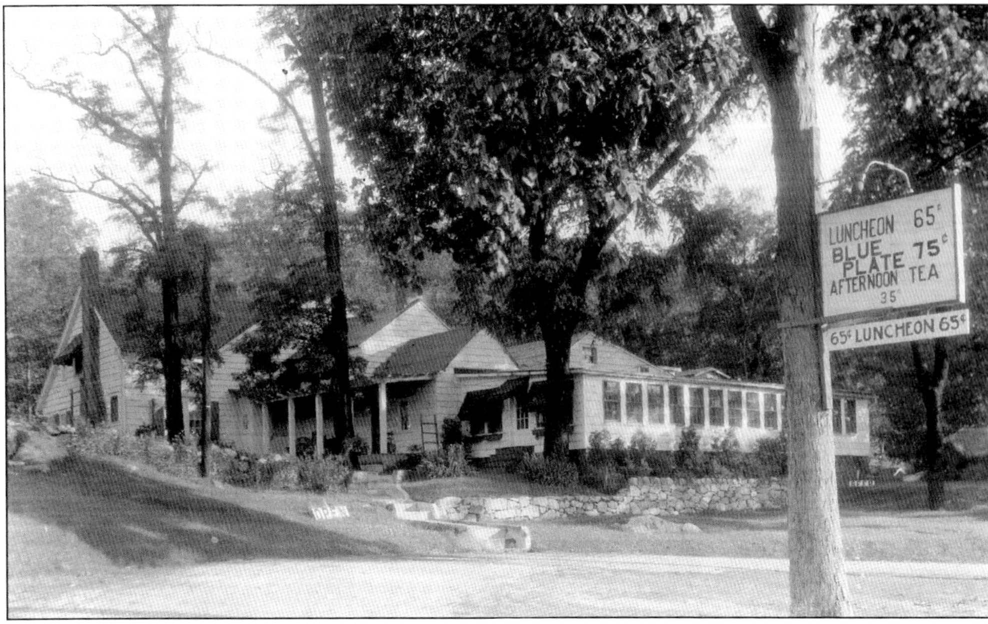

CHIMNEY CORNER, C. 1931. By the early 1930s, the Garrison house, which had previously been the home of patriot Isaac Garrison and the residence of Molly Corbin, had become a fashionable teahouse called the Chimney Corner. With its Colonial furnishings, wide plank boards, and expansive porch, it was a delightful spot for tea. Still overlooking Garrison Pond in Fort Montgomery, it survives as a private residence. (Scott Collection.)

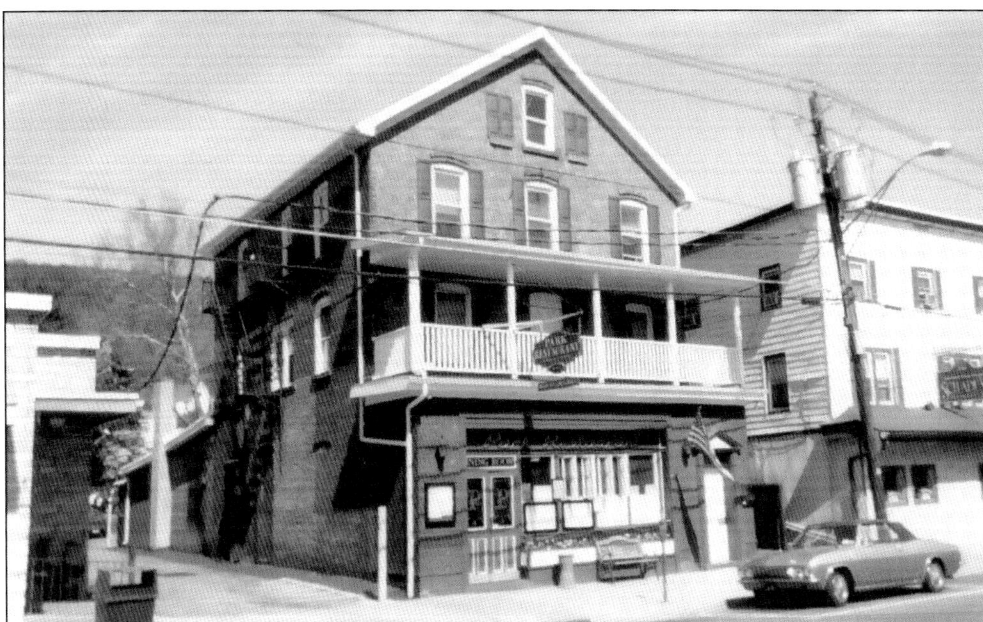

PARK RESTAURANT. For more than 50 years, the Park Restaurant has been a favorite dining place in Highland Falls. Previously a pub known as Cohen's, it was purchased by John and Anna Pozo in 1956. It is now in its third generation as a family business. (Photograph by Kevin Coffey.)

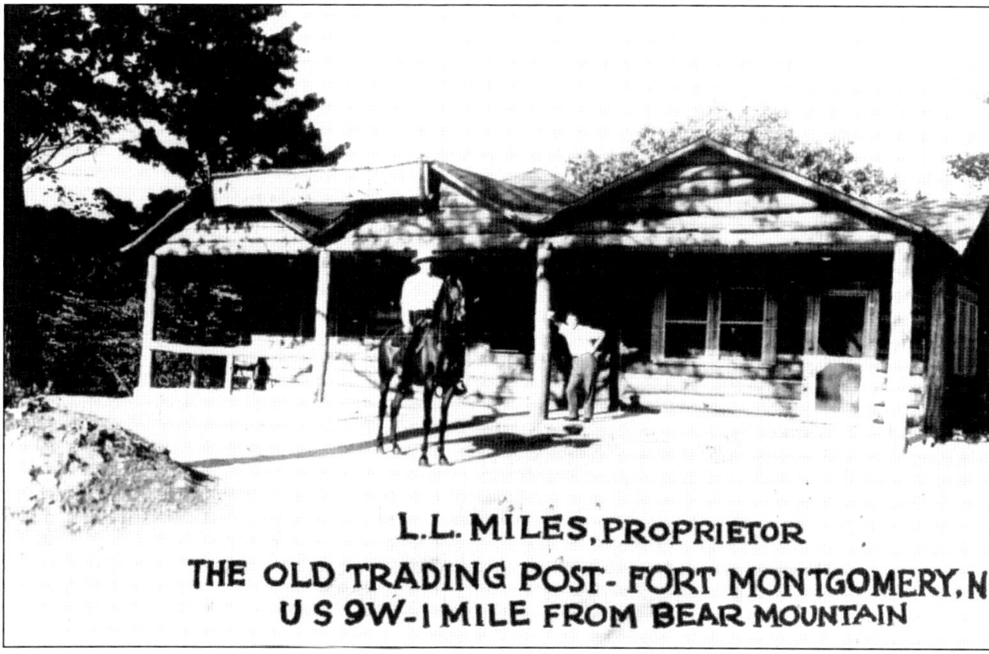

TRADING POST, C. 1920. Pictured here is the Trading Post, or simply TP, a longtime favorite gathering place on the east side of Route 9W in Fort Montgomery. This original log building was later replaced by an updated structure. A popular restaurant and catering venue for more than 50 years, it closed in 2003. (Gunza Collection.)

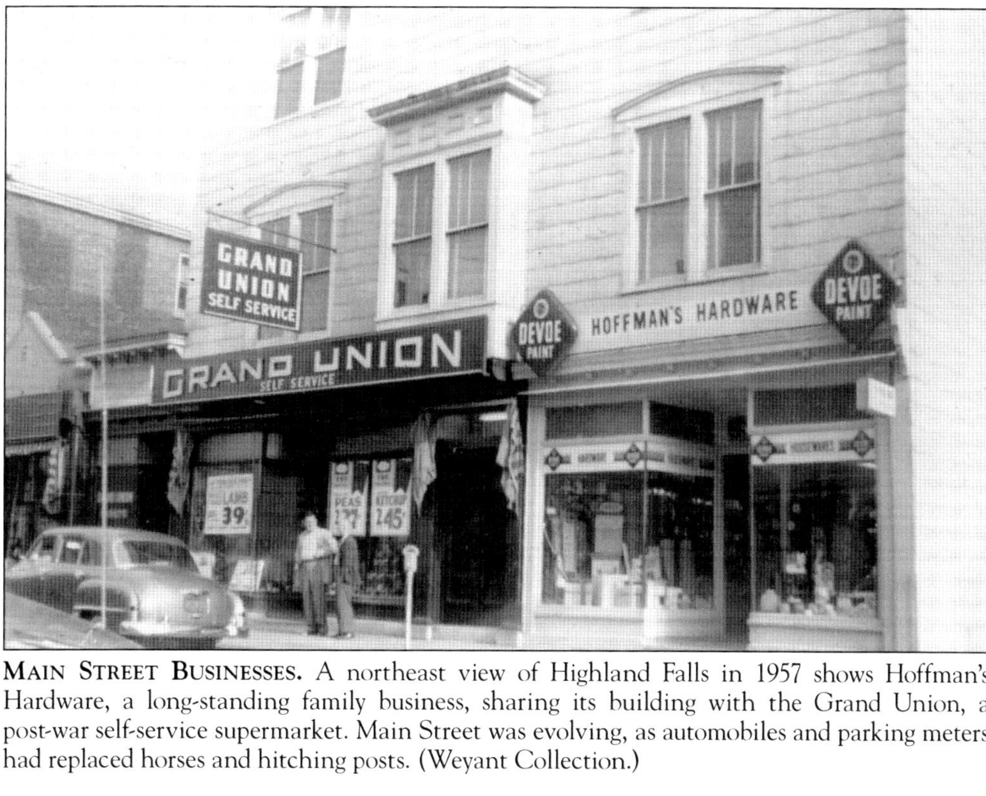

MAIN STREET BUSINESSES. A northeast view of Highland Falls in 1957 shows Hoffman's Hardware, a long-standing family business, sharing its building with the Grand Union, a post-war self-service supermarket. Main Street was evolving, as automobiles and parking meters had replaced horses and hitching posts. (Weyant Collection.)

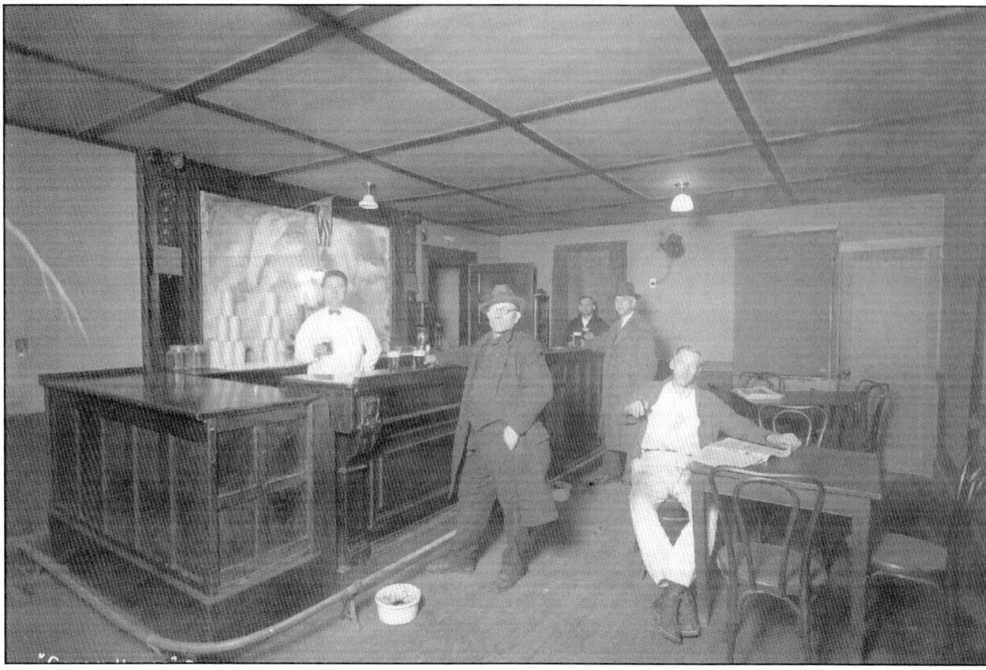

THE GREENHOUSE. In a rustic setting north of Old Fort Montgomery, on what is now Oakwood Road, stood a small pub called the Greenhouse. Among the several patrons pictured here is William Cobey, fourth from left. During Prohibition, the establishment was reportedly a lively speakeasy. No doubt this photograph was taken before the law went into effect! (Hansen Collection.)

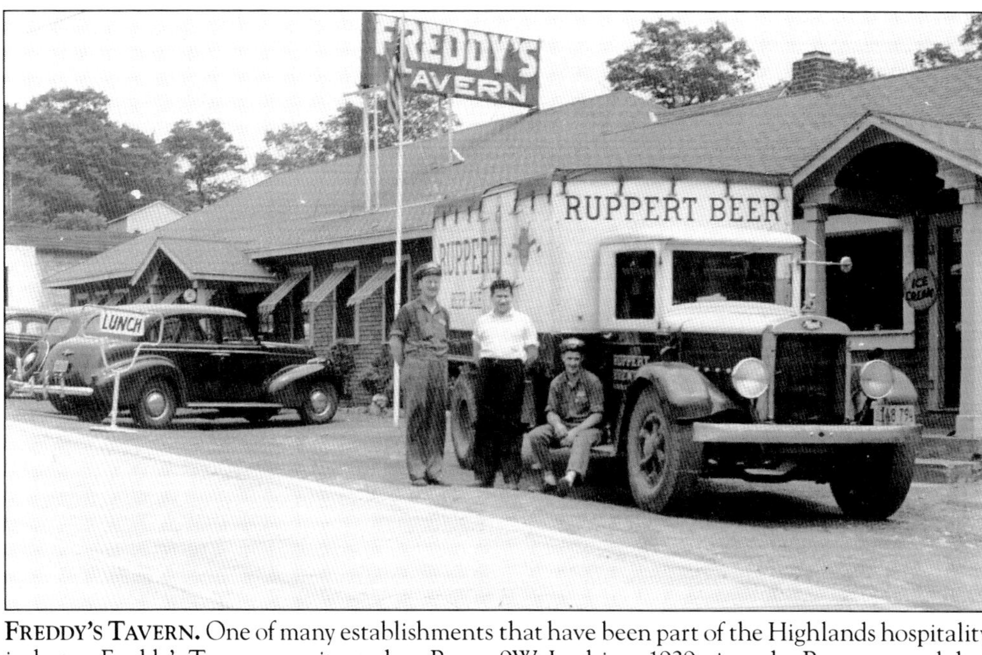

FREDDY'S TAVERN. One of many establishments that have been part of the Highlands hospitality industry, Freddy's Tavern was situated on Route 9W. In this c. 1939 view, the Ruppert truck has stopped for a delivery. Freddy's later became the Drummer Boy Restaurant and is today the site of the parking lot for Marchese Chevrolet. (Gunza Collection.)

Five

The Great Estates

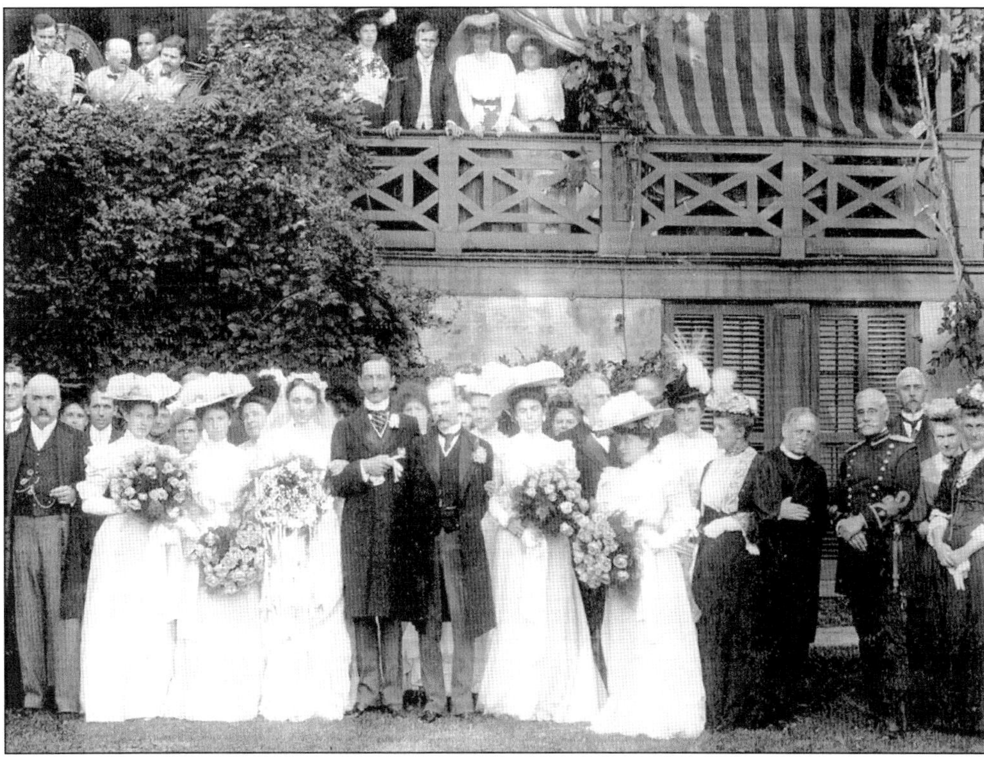

Pell Wedding. The 1905 marriage of Frances Pell and Martin Archer-Shee took place at Pellwood, the bride's Highland Falls home. It was an elegant gathering of notable Hudson River families. Standing from left to right are Franklin D. Roosevelt, J. P. Morgan, Anne Tracy (seventh), and Jenny Bigelow (ninth). Standing tenth from right is John Bigelow and fourth from right, Gen. Charles Roe. Eleanor Roosevelt and Sara Delano Roosevelt attended but are not pictured. The Bigelows, Morgans, Pells, Roes, and Tracys owned estates in Highland Falls. (Sidamon-Eristoff Collection.)

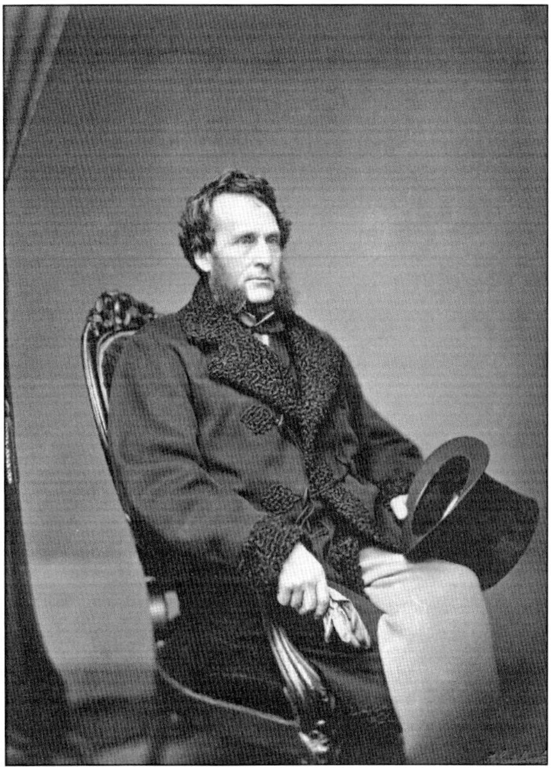

John Bigelow. One of the distinguished residents of Highland Falls was John Bigelow (1817–1911), a lawyer, writer, and statesman. Under Abraham Lincoln he served as minister to France and is credited with preventing the French recognition of the Confederacy. He and William Cullen Bryant were co-owners of the *New York Post*. Active in New York and international politics, he was a founder of the New York Public Library and an ardent supporter of building the Panama Canal. A list of his correspondents reads like a Who's Who of the 19th century and includes Edgar Allan Poe, Charles Dickens, Mark Twain, John Fremont, Andrew Carnegie, William Seward, Winfield Scott, Ulysses Grant, J. P. Morgan, and Theodore Roosevelt. At his Highland Falls estate, the Squirrels (below), he hosted Samuel Tilden, Oscar Wilde, and Edward, Prince of Wales. (Left, Sidamon-Eristoff Collection; below, photograph by Kevin Coffey.)

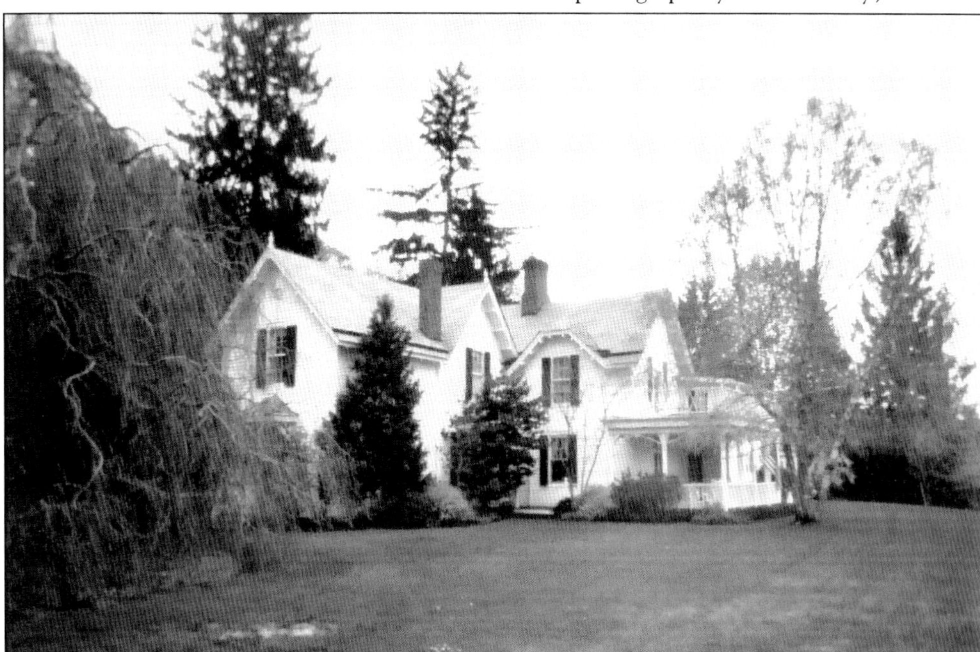

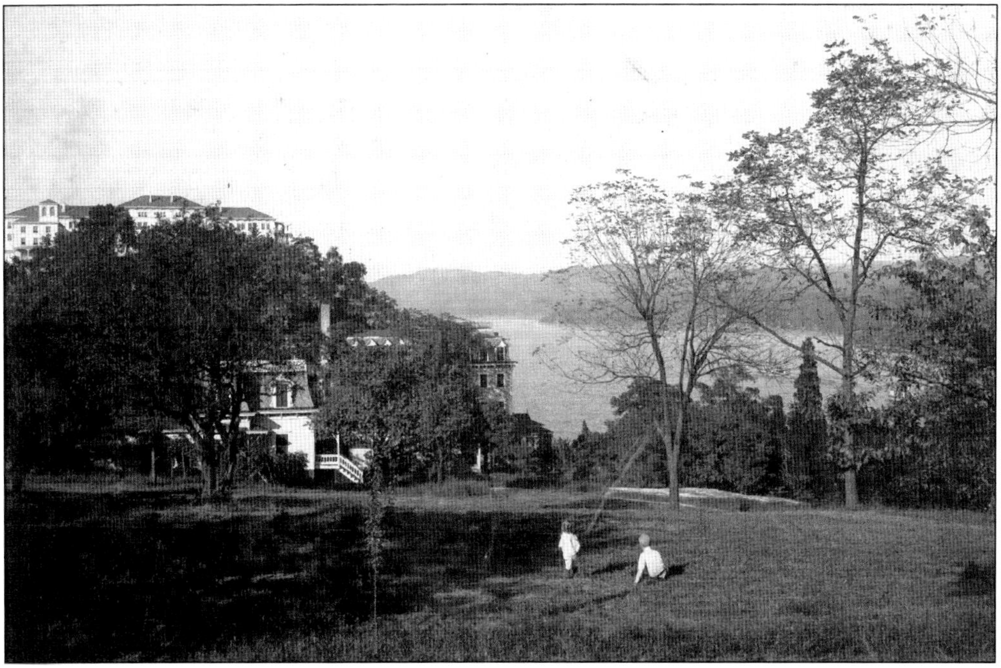

GOODSELL ESTATE. In this view looking north from the estate of Louis Goodsell, the highest point is occupied by Cozzens' Hotel. The center building overlooking the river is the Rocks, also a hotel. Goodsell, a Highland Falls native and Civil War veteran, was a state senator from 1898 to 1906 as well as a major property owner in town. (THHS Archives.)

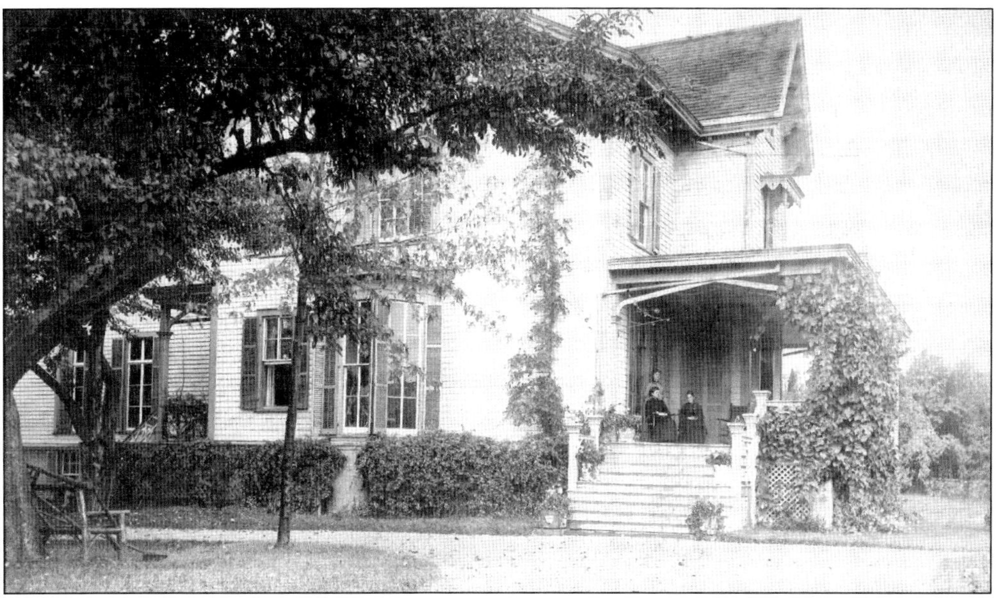

STONIHURST. Purchased by lawyer Charles Tracy in 1874, Stonihurst commands a breathtaking view of the Hudson. Charles and his wife lived here until 1885. Their son Charles Edward Tracy occupied the home with his wife, Jenny Bigelow. It later became the residence of their daughter Anne Tracy and her husband, Simon Sidamon-Eristoff. (Sidamon-Eristoff Collection.)

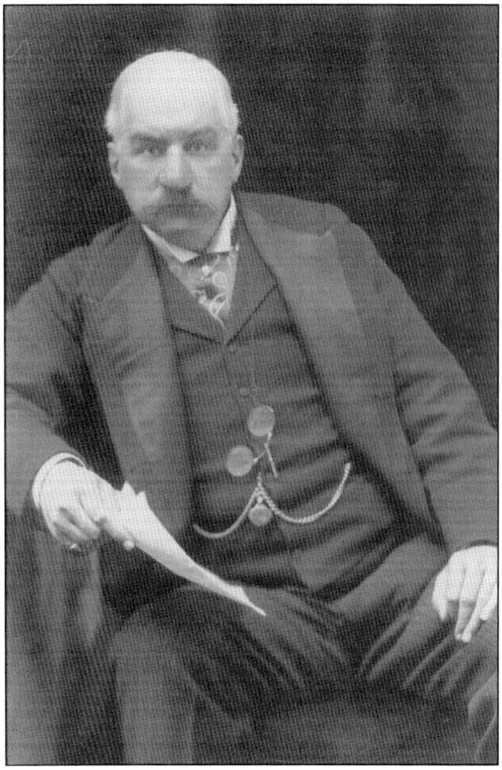

J. P. MORGAN. Another distinguished property owner in Highland Falls was John Pierpont Morgan (1837–1913), often called the greatest banker of all time. An excellent mathematician and astute businessman, he amassed wealth through investments in railroads, public utilities, steamships, communications, and steel. He was known for his skill, integrity, and self-assurance. At the conclusion of the Civil War, he helped refinance the United States war debt. Again in 1893 his financial intervention rescued the country from bankruptcy. (Sidamon-Eristoff Collection.)

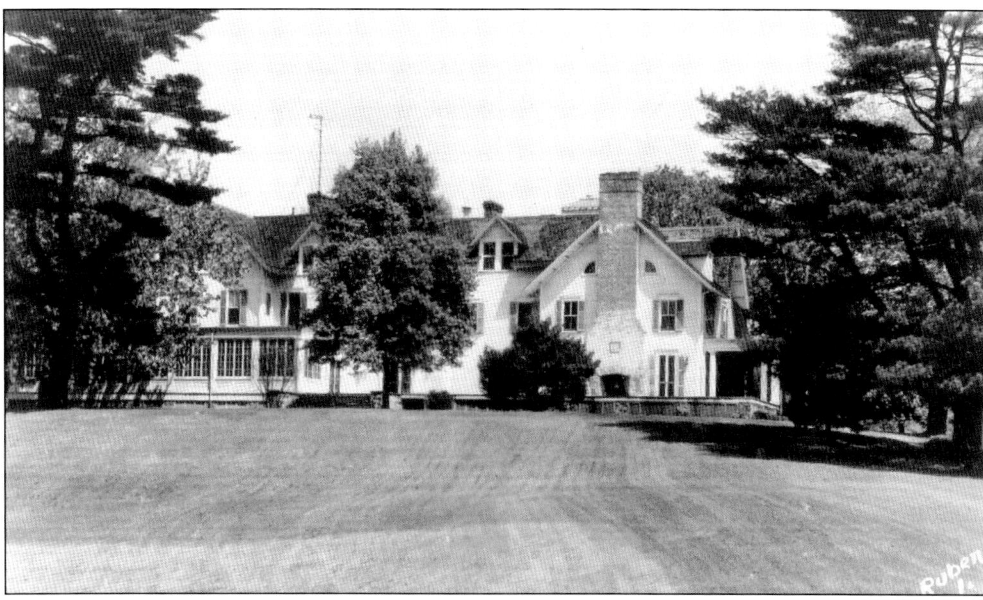

CRAGSTON. In 1872, J. P. Morgan and his wife, Frances, bought the estate Cragston along the river in Highland Falls. The estate included a farmhouse, agricultural outbuildings, a lake, stables, kennels, a dock, and a carriage house. After remodeling the house, J. P. planted thousands of daffodils down the hill; they still bloom every spring. He dearly loved the country life of Cragston. After his death, the property was sold and became a country club. (Gunza Collection.)

FRANCES TRACY MORGAN. The wife of J. P. Morgan, Frances Tracy Morgan (1842–1924) enjoyed summers and weekends with her husband and four children at their Highland Falls estate. She became a generous benefactress of the town. Through her philanthropy, the Morgan Circulating Library was established on Main Street. She also endowed a trade school and sponsored sewing classes. (Sidamon-Eristoff Collection.)

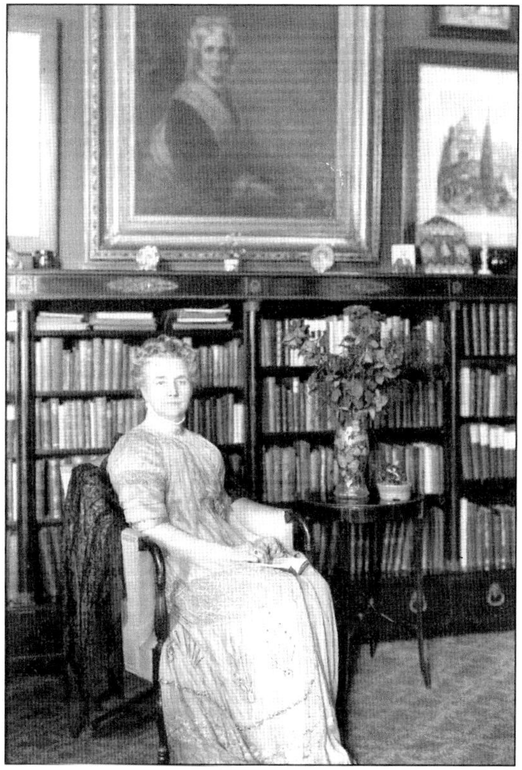

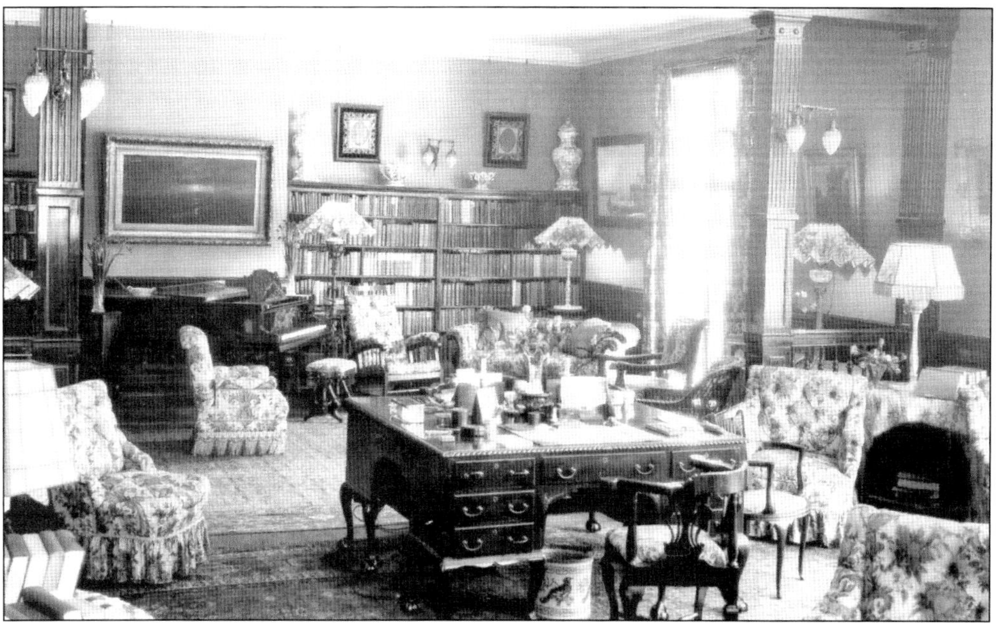

CRAGSTON INTERIOR. With its floral fabrics, oriental carpets, and elaborate lamp shades, the interior of J. Pierpont Morgan's house at Cragston was a classic example of Victorian design. Dark furniture, paintings, porcelains, and books abound. Five lamps and other light fixtures are visible. J. P. was fascinated by electricity and was an early and faithful supporter of Thomas Edison. (Highland Falls Library.)

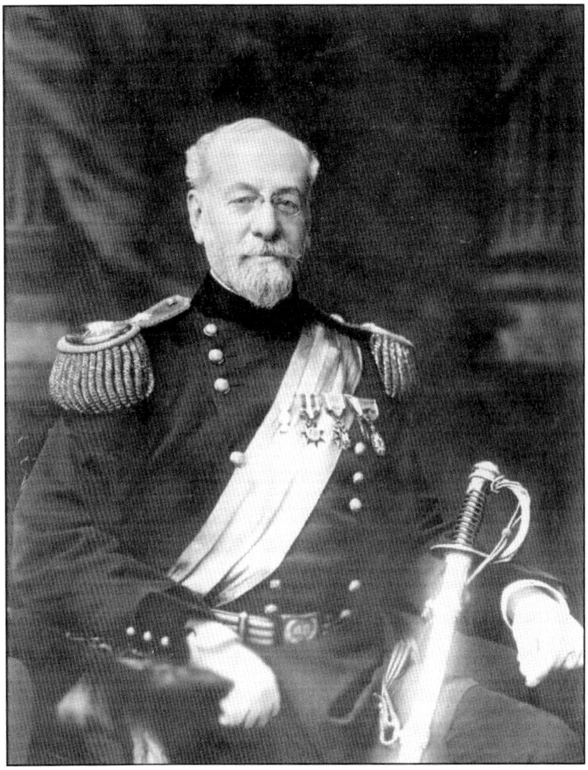

GENERAL ROE. Charles Roe was a leading citizen of the town in the early 1900s. During his childhood, Roe's mother operated the West Point Hotel. He attended the military academy, graduating in 1868. As a cavalry officer, he served in the American Indian wars and later led the New York National Guard. The general owned a substantial estate in Highland Falls and was a senior warden of the Church of the Holy Innocents. (USMA Library.)

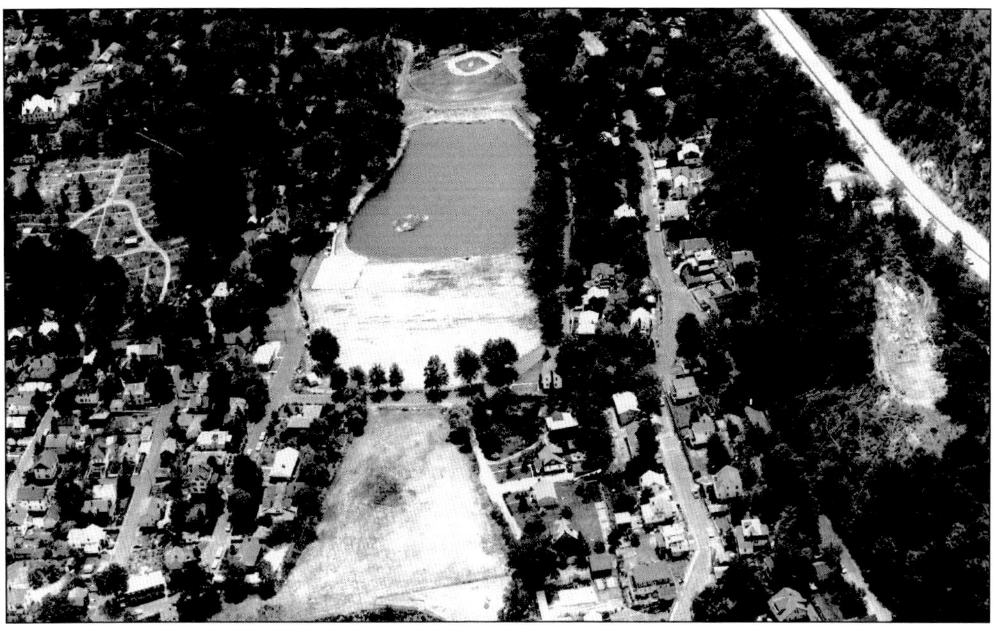

ROE PARK. In 1906, the *News of the Highlands* reported that General Roe had donated land "to fit up a park and provide a suitable place where innocent games can be indulged in." The plan included tennis courts and a baseball diamond. This southward view shows Fickens Field, once a pond, in the foreground. Roe Park begins at the line of trees and extends across Roe Pond to the ball field. (USMA Library.)

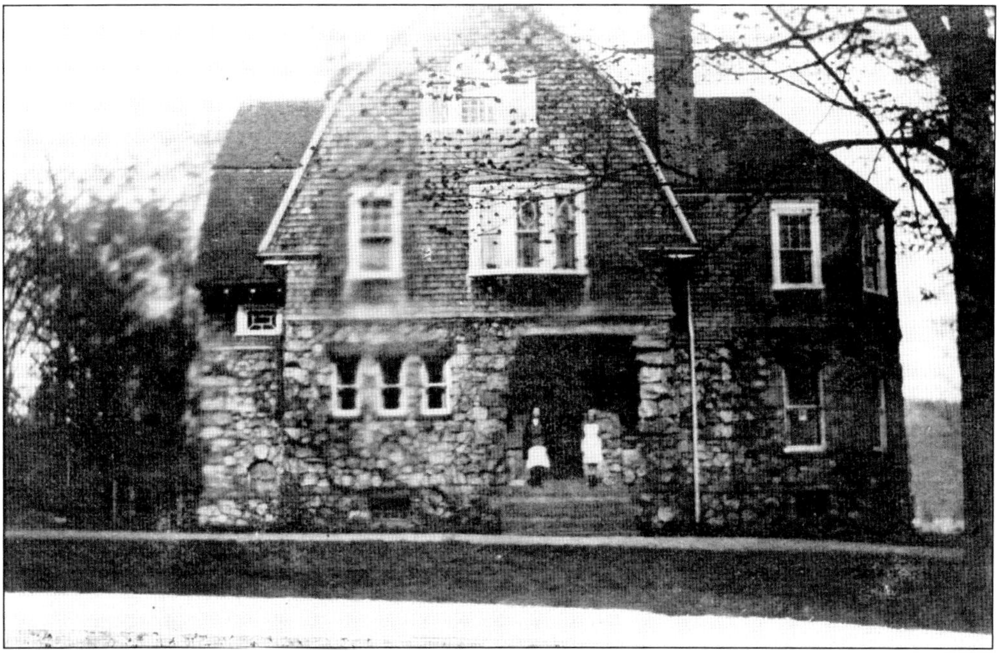

HOME STATION. Two uniformed servants stand on the steps of the stone mansion about 1910. A fine example of Highlands stonework, Home Station was the residence of Gen. Charles Roe's mother. The home, redesigned and now owned by the Weyant family, remains on the lot immediately behind their Lustron house on Main Street. (Graber Collection.)

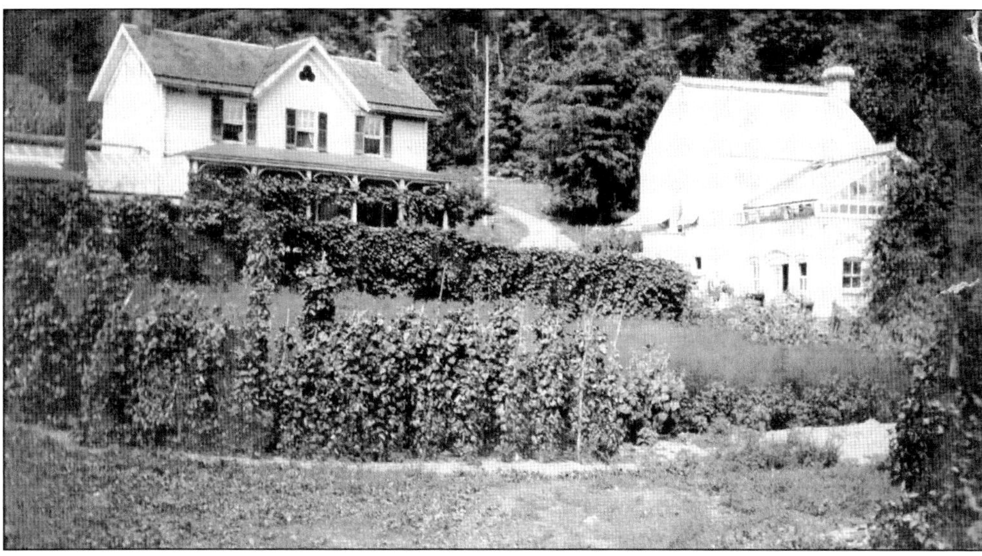

ROE ESTATE. In 1924, the Roe estate, shown in a partial view here, was divided. The main house was sold to Herman Schildkraut. A letter to Joseph Graber, the manager of the Roe estate, mentions that included in the sale are "two bob sleighs, one very old farm wagon, and two old carriages." Schildkraut operated his new holding as a resort hotel catering to vegetarians. Today, it is an apartment building called Peregrine Hall. (Graber Collection.)

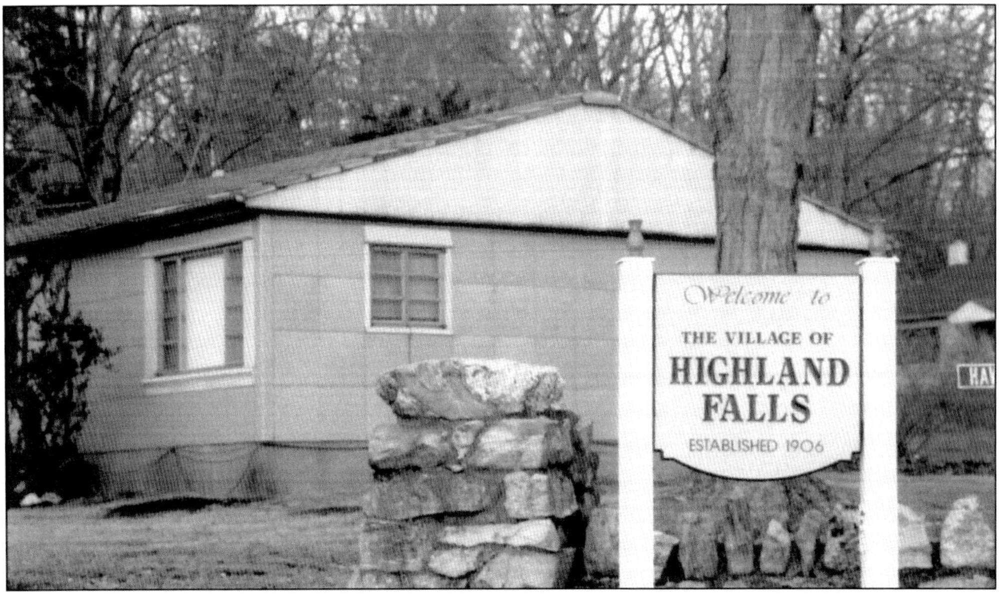

LUSTRON HOME. Constructed entirely of steel, prefabricated homes like this one, on the old Roe estate, were intended to be the answer to the post–World War II housing shortage. Coated with porcelain, the houses were termite-proof, decay-proof, and maintenance-free. Assured by the fact that Lustron homes were also fireproof, the Weyant family purchased this residence after their previous one burned down. Only 2,680 Lustrons were sold before the company went bankrupt in 1950. (Photograph by Veronica Coffey.)

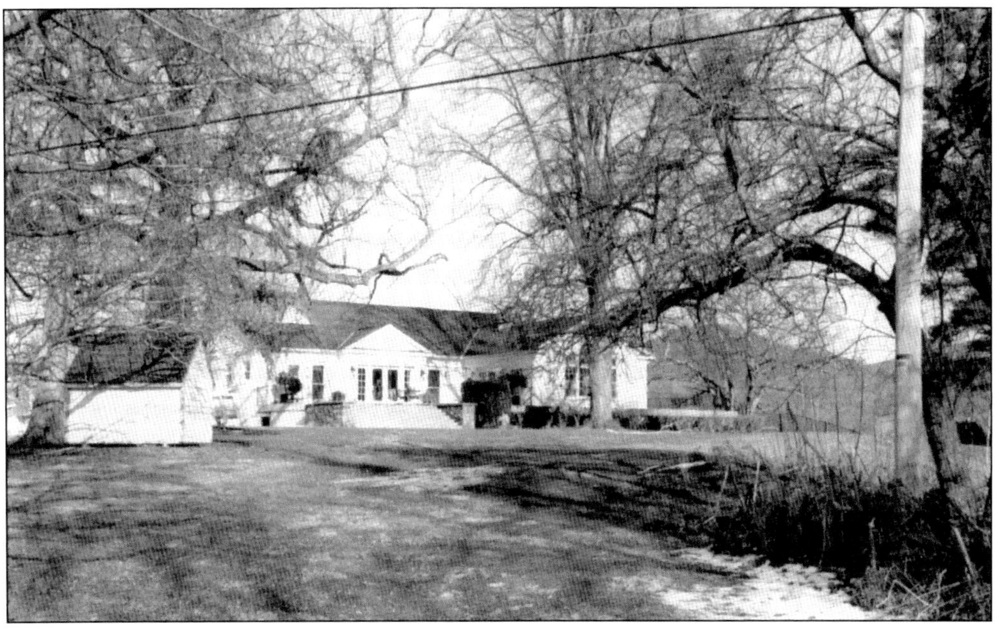

SUMMER, HIGHLAND FALLS. From 1974 to 1975, singer-songwriter Billy Joel and wife, Elizabeth, rented this home, built on the original site of the J. P. Morgan farmhouse. A stairway to the second floor was enlarged to accommodate the delivery of a grand piano to an upstairs room. Joel's contemplative masterpiece "Summer, Highland Falls" was recorded shortly after his stay here. (Photograph by Veronica Coffey.)

Six

BEAR MOUNTAIN

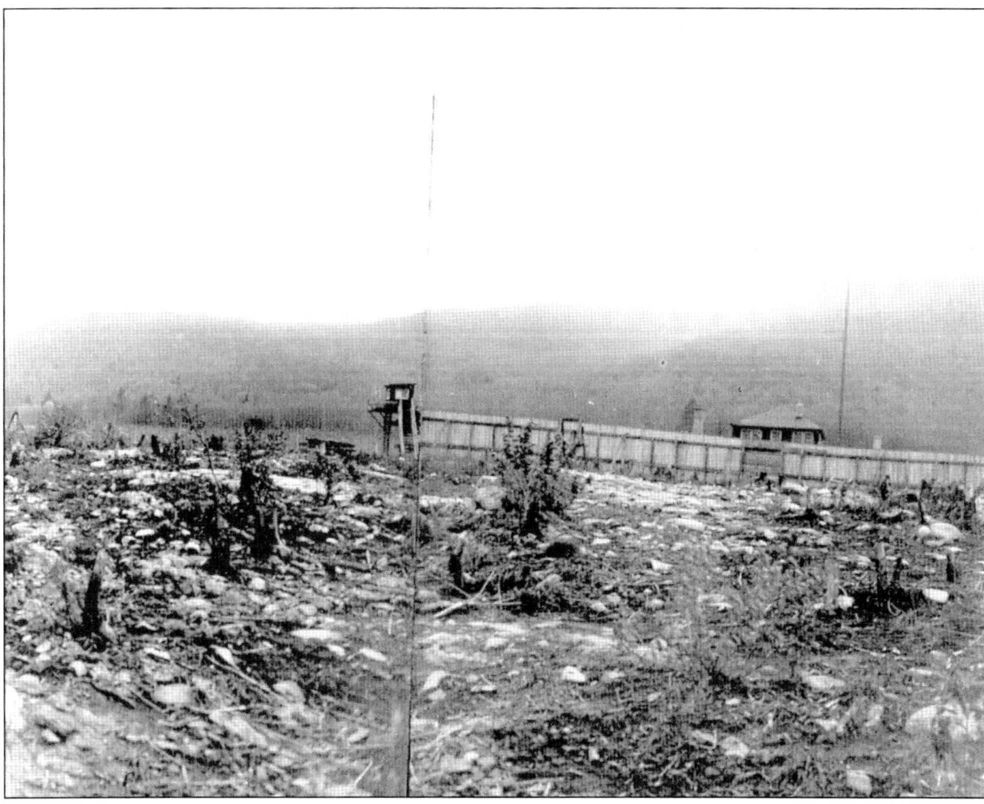

SING SING. In 1908, the state began relocation of Sing Sing Prison from Ossining to Bear Mountain. This enclosure housed prisoners who cleared the land. Concern for the environment soon caused a public outcry. The donation of the land to the Palisades Interstate Park Commission led to the abandonment of the planned prison and the construction of Bear Mountain State Park in 1910. The playing field occupies this area today. (PIPC Archives.)

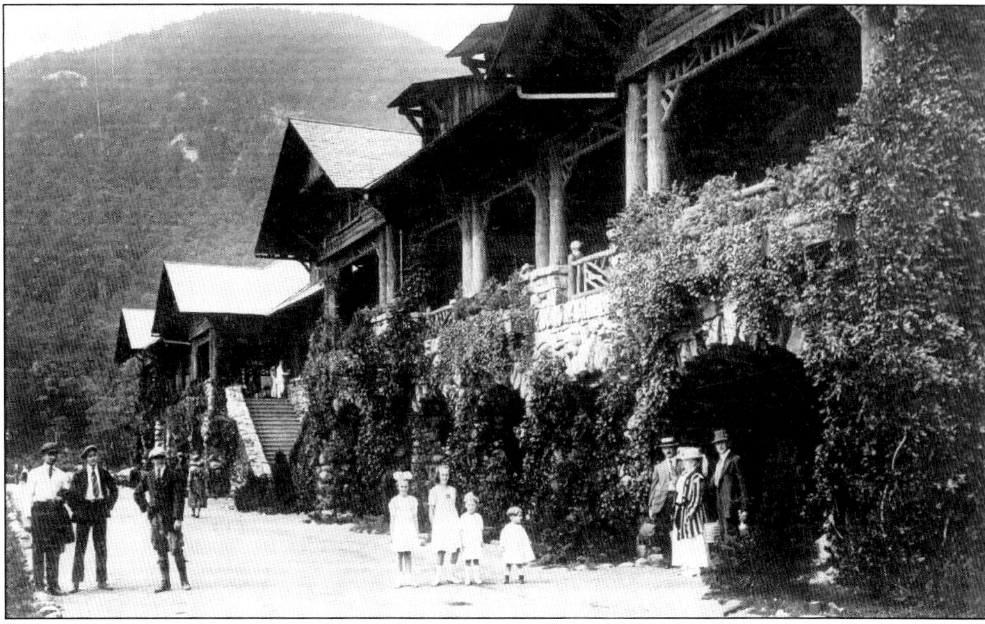

Bear Mountain Inn. One of the first park structures, the Bear Mountain Inn was completed in 1915. It was constructed of boulders and chestnut logs to be compatible with its environment. Inside, it was a marvel of modernity equipped with electric refrigeration and on site laundry facilities. Immediately popular with visitors, it also offered a bakery, cafeteria, restaurant, and staff dormitories. (Carroll Collection.)

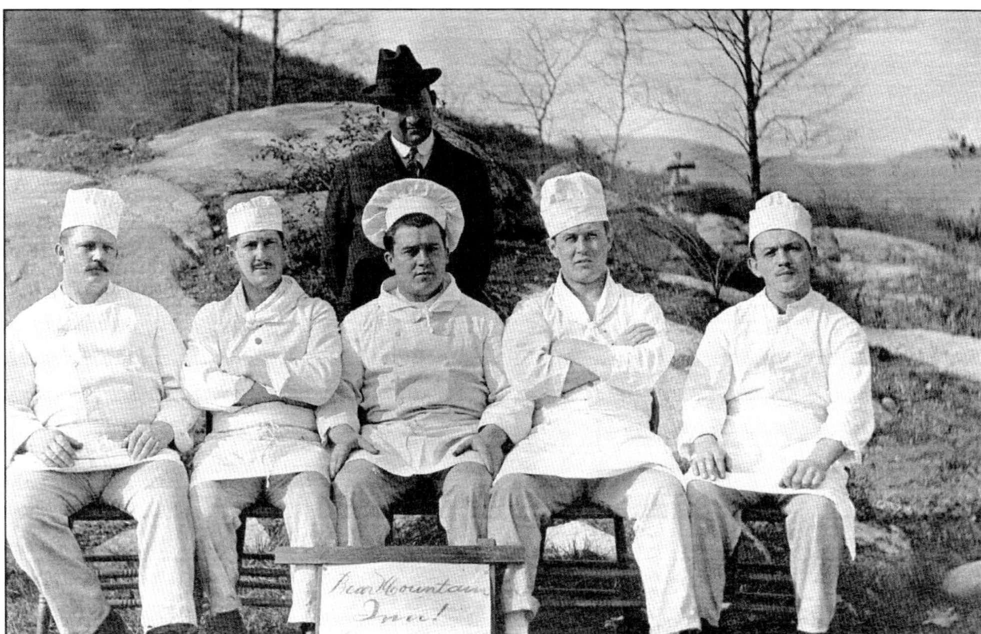

Bear Mountain Chefs. Cooking was serious business at the Bear Mountain Inn in 1916, when these chefs posed for a photograph. The Palisades Interstate Park Commission was committed to offering good food at affordable prices. Food service was monitored for quality, sufficient portion size, and value. (Scott Collection.)

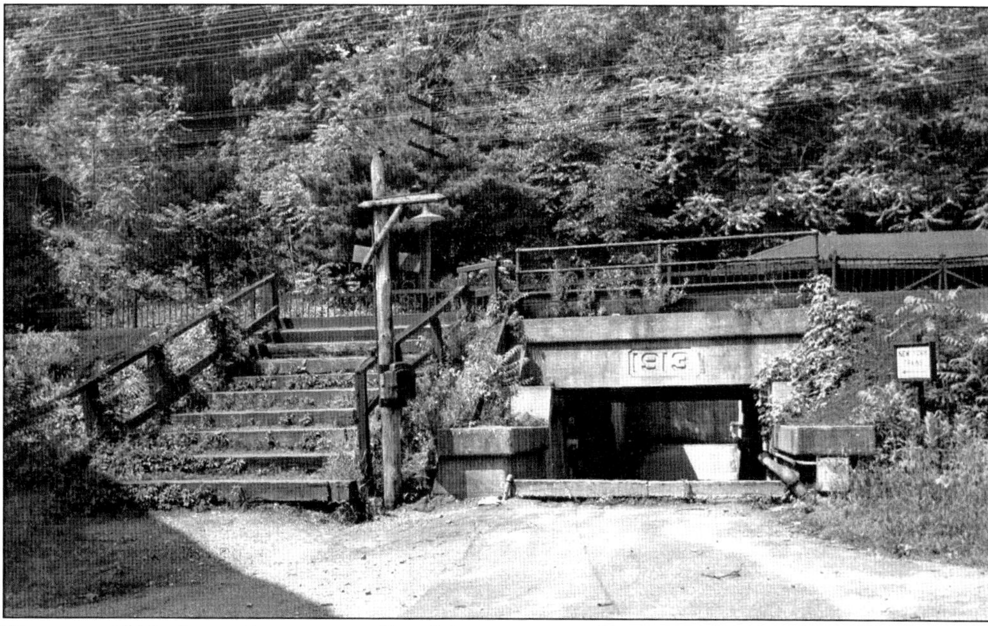

TUNNEL, 1913. An early project at Bear Mountain was the construction of a tunnel under the West Shore Railroad tracks for the safety of patrons arriving at the riverside dock. Above the tunnel to the right was the newly completed Bear Mountain station. Laborers were paid $2 per day to build these and other amenities, including lawn tennis courts, trails, and a running track. (PIPC Archives.)

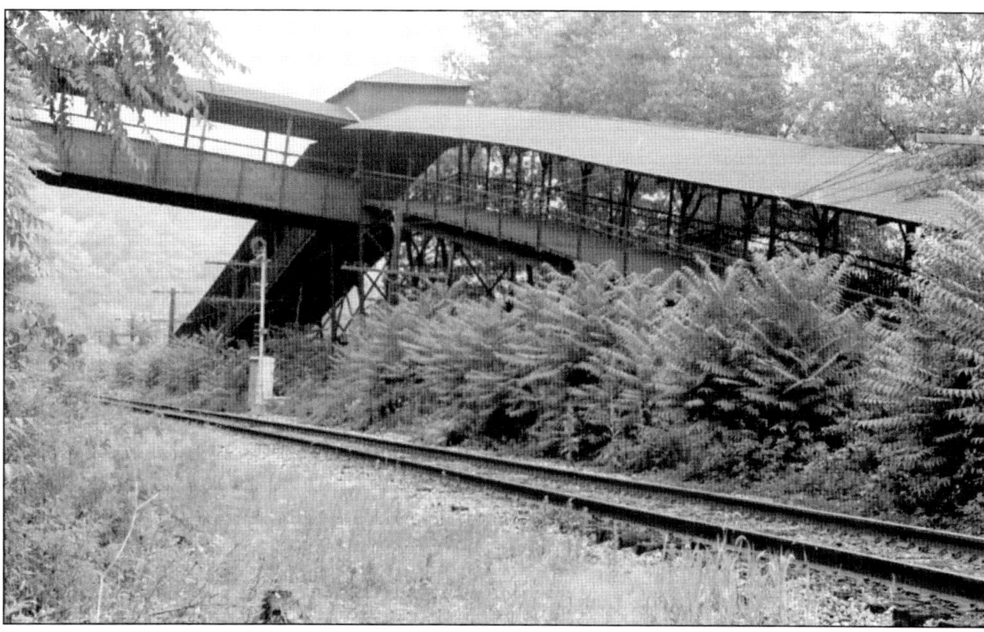

PEDESTRIAN WALKWAY. This overpass was an important safety feature at Bear Mountain. Depending on their mode of transportation, visitors possibly had to cross railroad tracks and a highway as they walked up the hill to the inn and playing field. To provide shaded comfort and prevent accidents, the Palisades Interstate Park Commission installed this walkway. (PIPC Archives.)

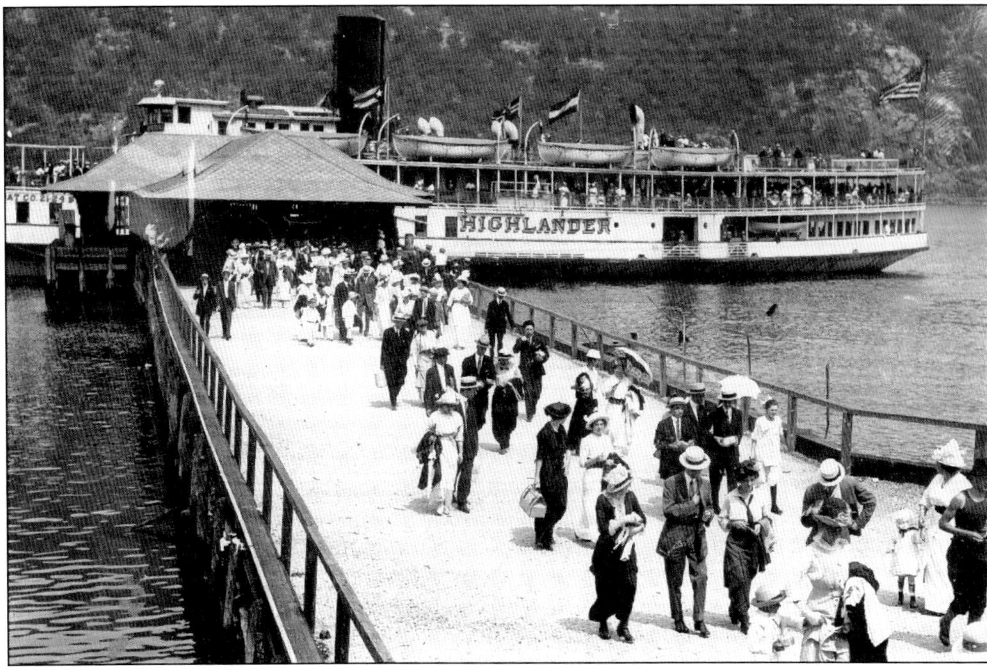

THE *HIGHLANDER*. Owned by the McAllister Steamboat Company, the *Highlander* sailed every day from the Battery in Manhattan to Bear Mountain State Park during the summer of 1915, bringing passengers to enjoy the newly constructed Bear Mountain Inn. The rate was 50¢ per person. The park, still in its infancy, provided an escape from urban over-crowding in the form of refreshing wilderness. If only for an afternoon, a city dweller could be a "Highlander." (PIPC Archives.)

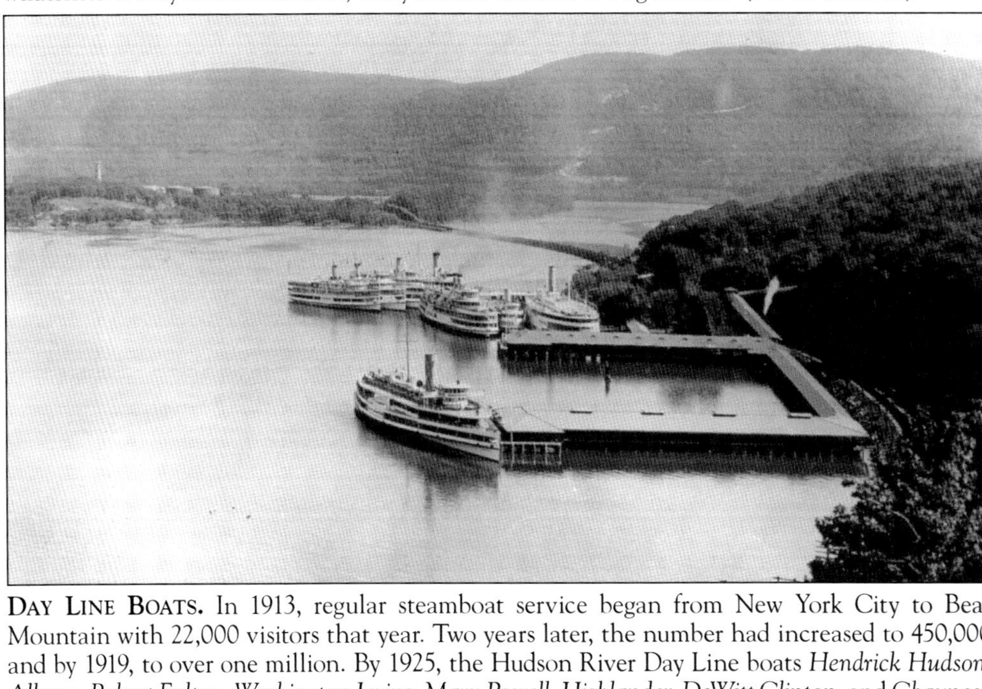

DAY LINE BOATS. In 1913, regular steamboat service began from New York City to Bear Mountain with 22,000 visitors that year. Two years later, the number had increased to 450,000 and by 1919, to over one million. By 1925, the Hudson River Day Line boats *Hendrick Hudson*, *Albany*, *Robert Fulton*, *Washington Irving*, *Mary Powell*, *Highlander*, *DeWitt Clinton*, and *Chauncey M. DePew* all stopped at Bear Mountain along their routes. (PIPC Archives.)

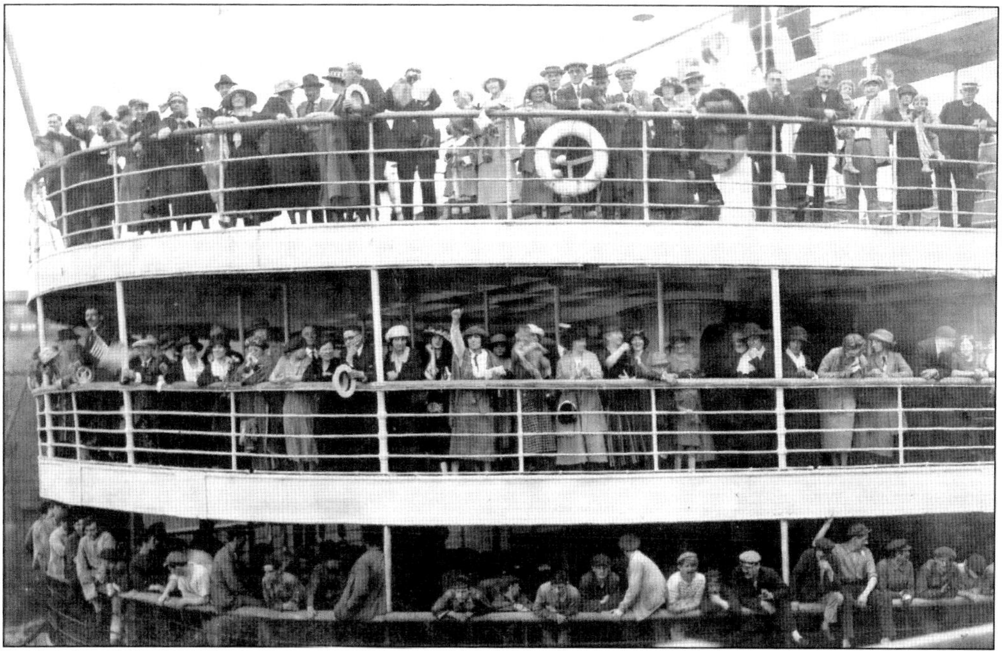

STEAMBOAT DEPARTURE. People crowd the deck of a steamboat preparing to depart Bear Mountain Dock around 1919. Passengers sometimes threw coins into the water; local children would then dive into the river to find them. At the height of their popularity, Day Line vessels serviced every landing from New York City to Troy, a distance of 150 miles. A separate Night Line with sleeping cabins operated between Manhattan and Albany until 1938. (Scott Collection.)

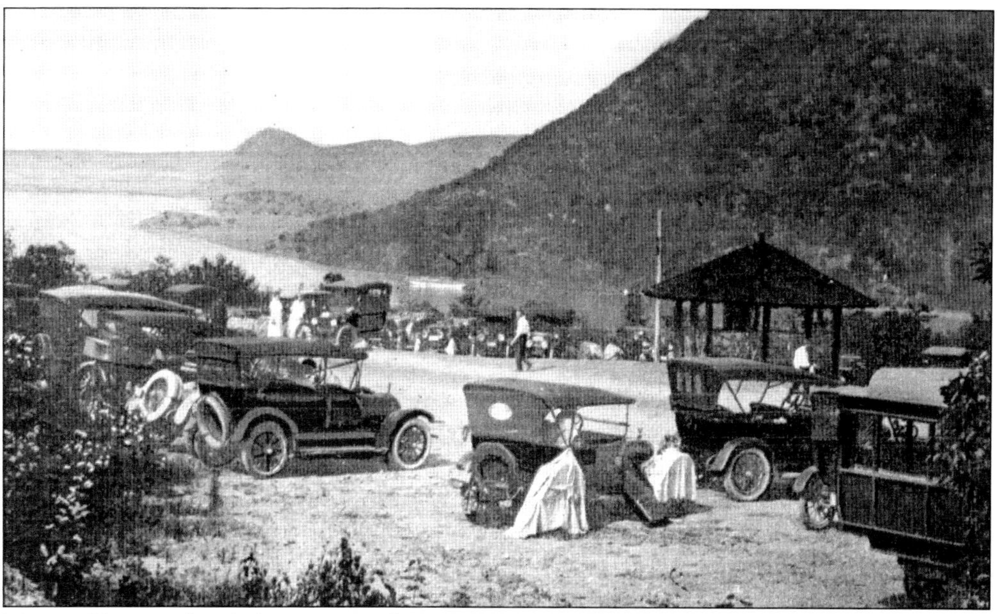

MOTOR TRAVEL. By 1916, motor travel was increasing in popularity. That year, 2,150 automobiles arrived at the Bear Mountain Inn. Records show that five years later more than one million visitors came by car. This picturesque unpaved "parking space" overlooks the Hudson and the opposite mountain, called Anthony's Nose. (Carroll Collection.)

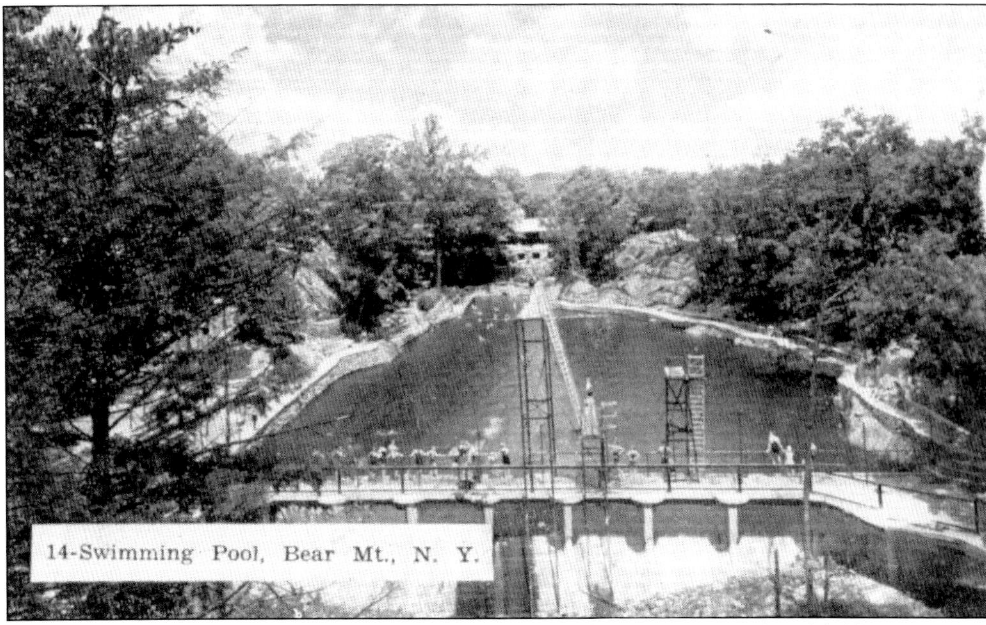

BEAR MOUNTAIN POOL. In 1924, a rustic swimming pool was constructed and fed by water from Hessian Lake. The pool was a major summer attraction and underwent several modifications over the years. Land nearby would become the site of the Trailside Museums and Zoo, an adjunct to the American Museum of Natural History in New York. A serious scientific research station, the museums and zoo also became a beloved attraction of the park. (Gunza Collection.)

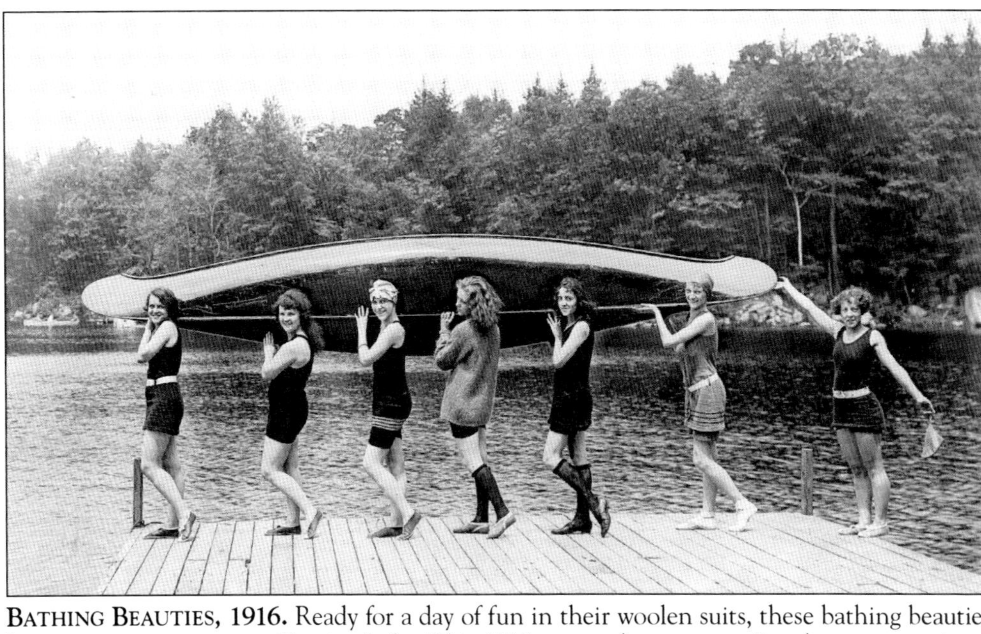

BATHING BEAUTIES, 1916. Ready for a day of fun in their woolen suits, these bathing beauties line up to go canoeing on Hessian Lake. This 1916 postcard announces "outdoor sports, winter and summer, at Bear Mountain Inn." In the early years of the park, many new lakes were created by damming streams. Forests, which had been depleted by woodcutters, were reclaimed through the planting of thousands of seedlings. (PIPC Archives.)

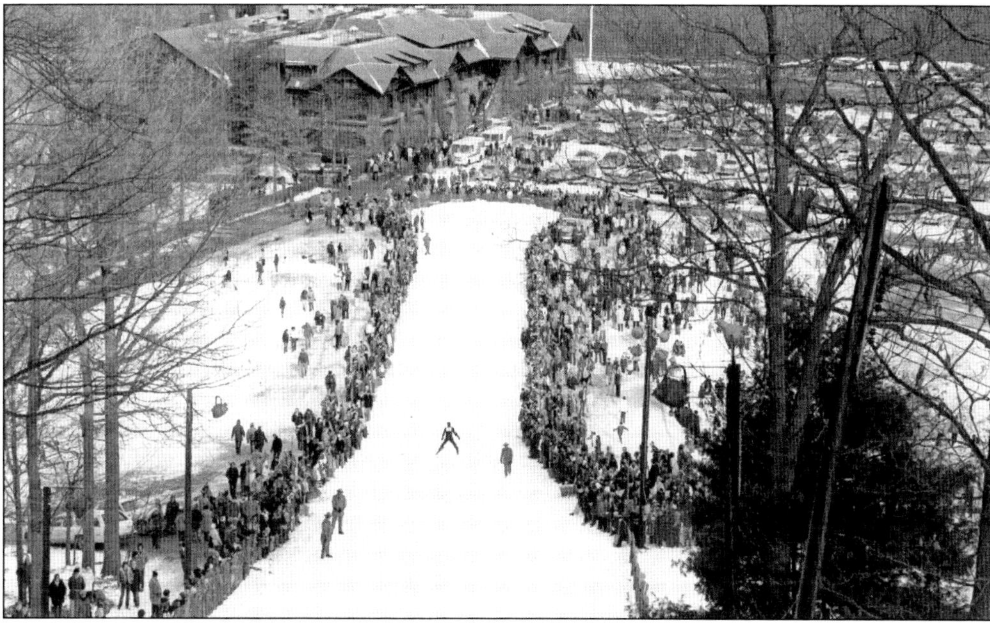

WINTER SPORTS. Lovers of outdoor life enjoyed the development of winter sports at Bear Mountain. Between 1922 and 1923, the inn was heated for winter accommodations and facilities were provided for snowshoeing, ice-skating, tobogganing, and skiing at nearby Silver Mine. Competitive ski jumping and skating were added shortly after. In 1942, an indoor roller rink was constructed. (PIPC Archives.)

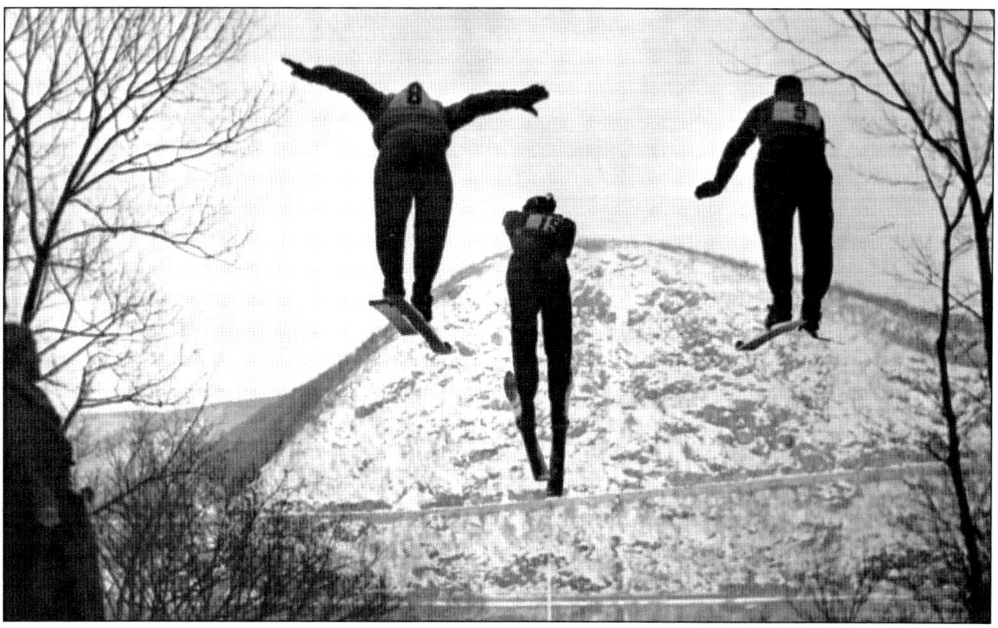

SKI JUMP. The Palisades Interstate Park Commission continually made a concerted effort to upgrade winter sports opportunities. Ski jumping championships began in 1927 and remained one of the park's most popular attractions for over 50 years. The slope had been designed by Scandinavian engineers to rival the one at Dartmouth College. This view looks east across the Hudson River. (PIPC Archives.)

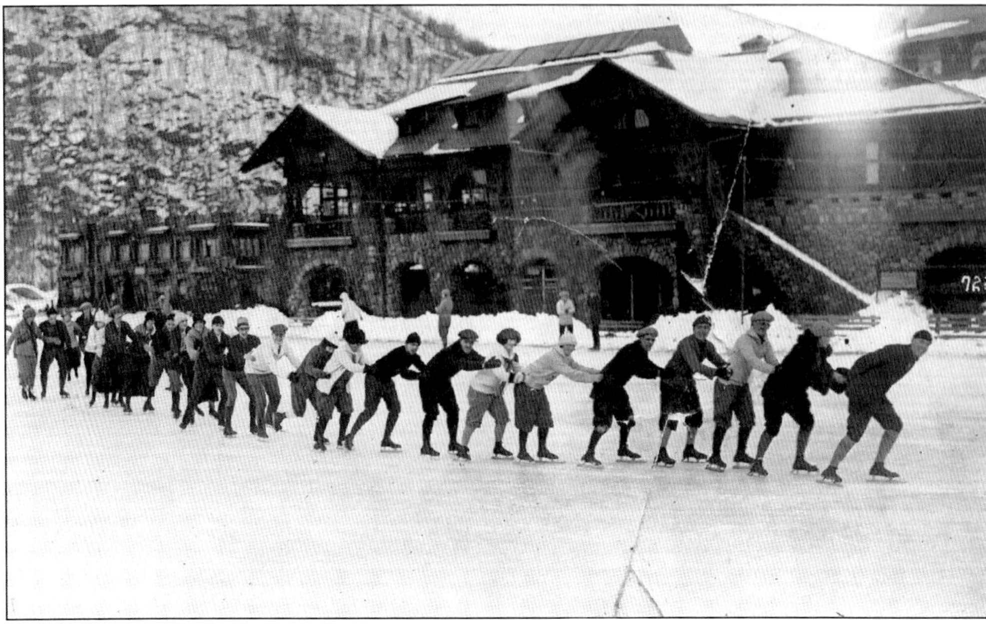

ICE SKATERS. In-line skating had a different meaning in 1920. A parade of exuberant skaters crosses the ice beside the impressive stone facade of the Bear Mountain Inn. An ice rink was created by laying a huge canvas tarpaulin with upturned edges on the playing field and flooding it with water from Hessian Lake. Speed-skating races were also held throughout the winter. (PIPC Archives.)

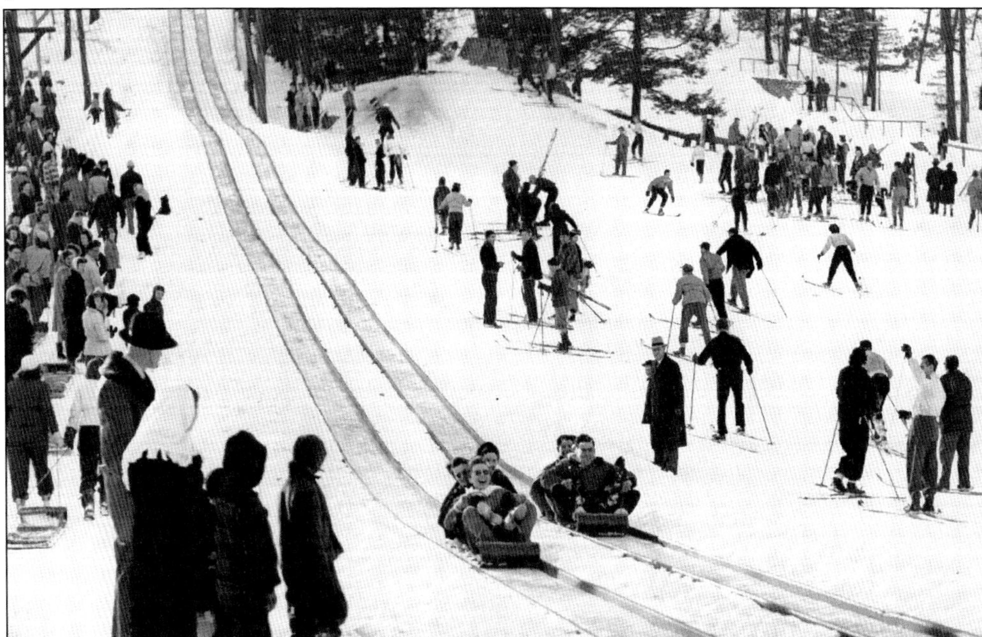

TOBOGGAN SLIDE. Hurtling down the steep toboggan slide was one of Bear Mountain's most thrilling offerings, a fact to which these 1945 adventurers can attest. The exciting toboggan run was over 1,000 feet long with a rocket-like finish. To the right was the landing area for ski jumpers. (PIPC Archives.)

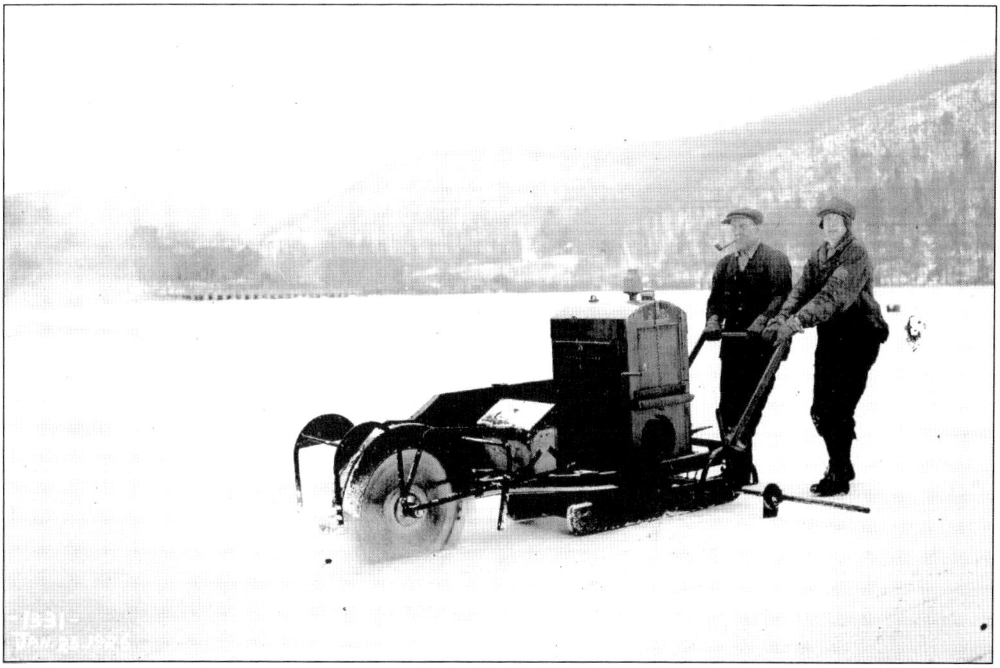

ICE HARVESTING. Ice harvesting was a common sight in the Highlands before the widespread use of refrigerators in the 1940s. Large blocks were carved from frozen lakes and ponds with an ice saw, which retraced its cuts, back and forth, until the blocks of ice could be freed. A power-driven ice saw, like this one on Hessian Lake in 1926, was a great improvement over the manual saws used previously. After cutting, men with long-handled ice picks and ice tongs maneuvered the blocks to the shore of the lake, where they were removed by horse teams. Then the blocks of ice could be stored or readied for delivery to consumers. Ice was packed in sawdust for shipment or kept in a special icehouse. Properly stored, it would last for several months. (PIPC Archives.)

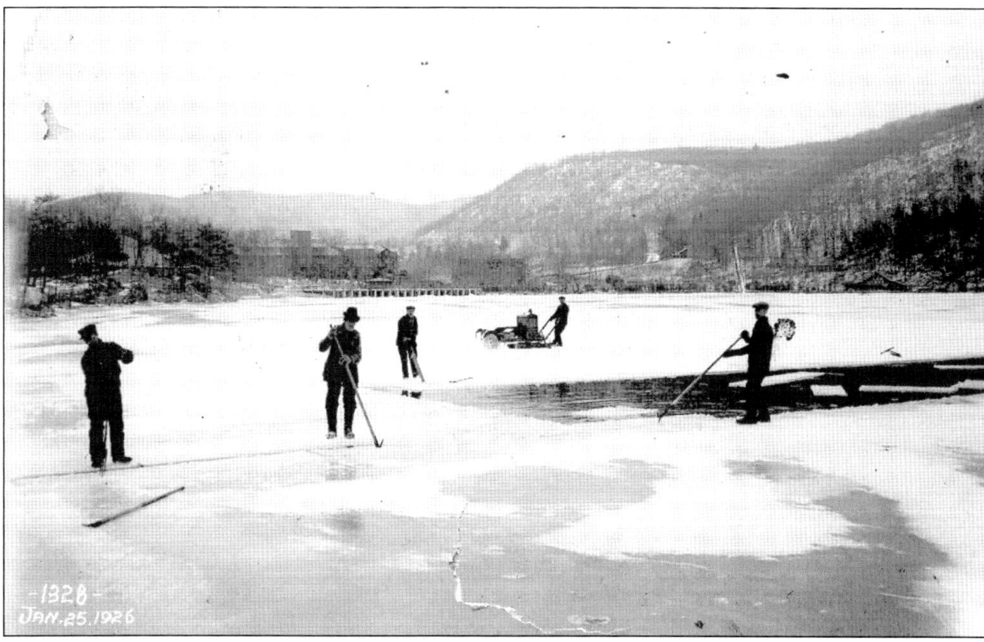

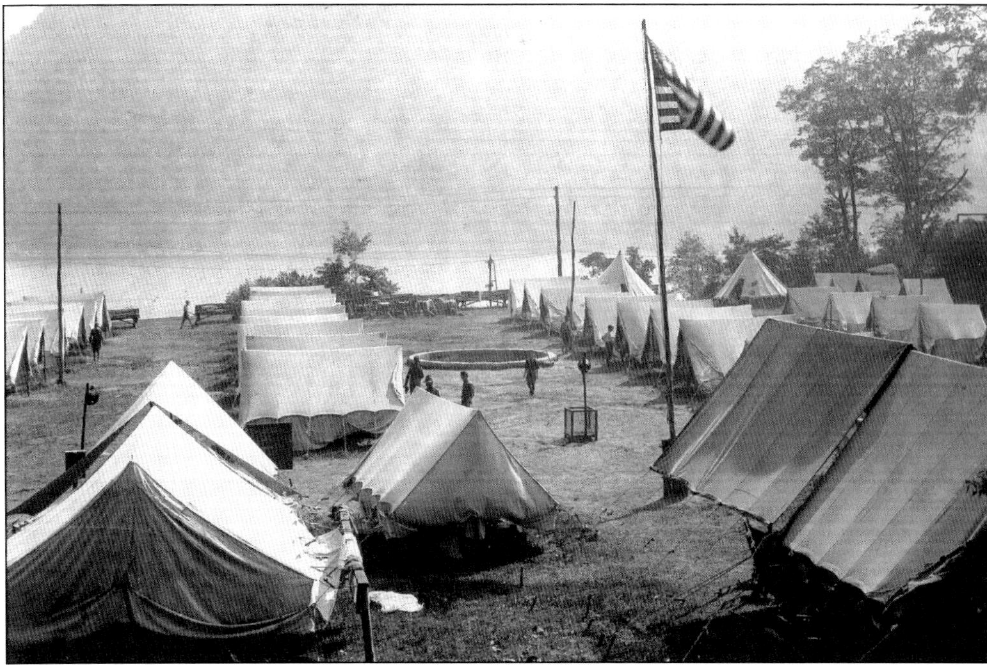

WORLD WAR I BIVOUAC. During World War I, the army used Bear Mountain as a bivouac area. Soldiers camped there awaiting deployment. Rows of tents can be seen in this *c.* 1917 view looking east toward Anthony's Nose. (PIPC Archives.)

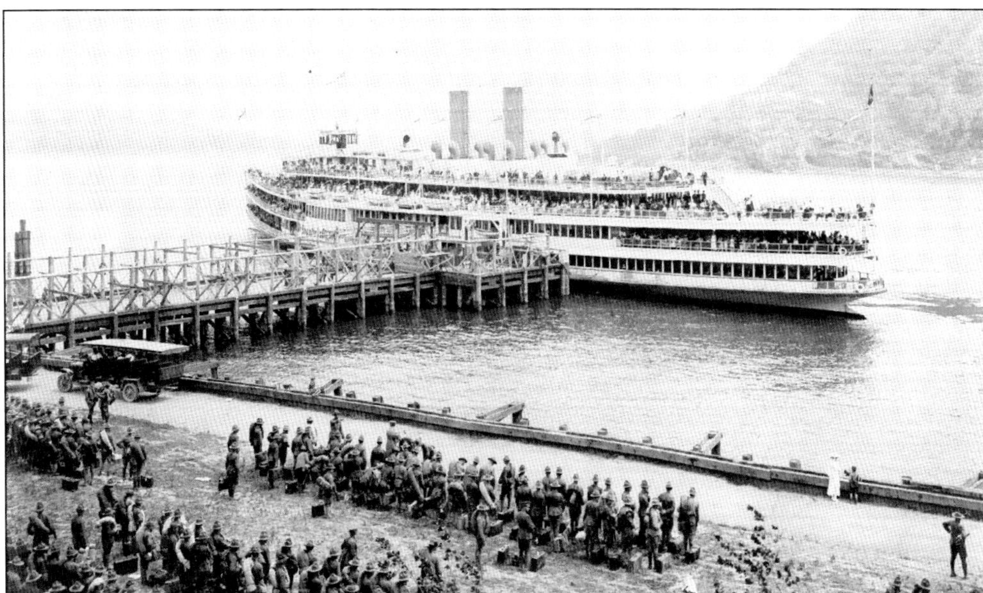

WORLD WAR I TROOPS. Soldiers carrying bedrolls and suitcases watch the Hudson River Day Line boat *Hendrick Hudson* dock at Bear Mountain. They wait in readiness for transportation to New York and then to Europe. Another Day Line boat, the *Manhattan*, was renamed *Nopatin* and converted by the government for service as a troop transport vessel. By May 1919, she had carried over 150,000 soldiers across the English Channel. (PIPC Archives.)

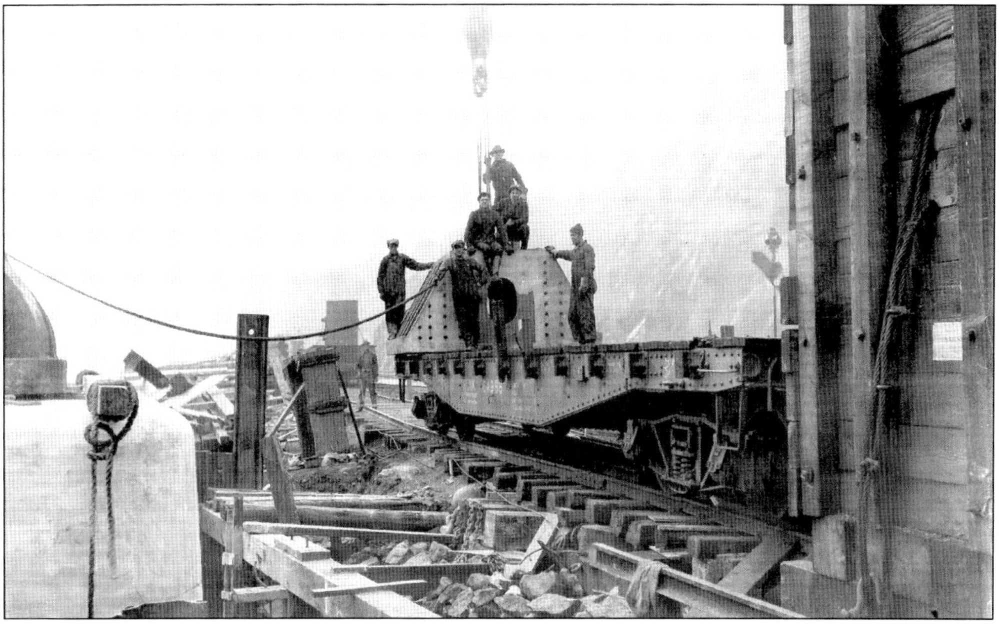

Bear Mountain Bridge. Under consideration for two decades, the contract for construction of the Bear Mountain–Hudson River Bridge was signed on March 24, 1923. Work began immediately. The intent was to enable people to cross the Hudson day or night, regardless of weather, and to provide a short route between the middle states and New England. It would be the first highway across the river south of Albany. (THHS Archives.)

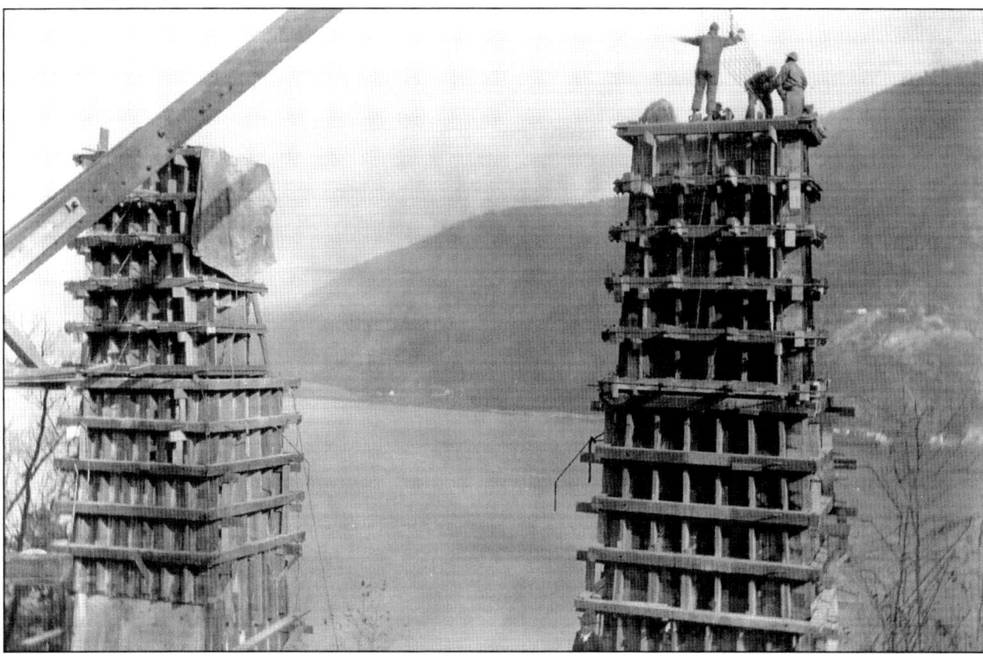

Western Piers. Four concrete piers built on solid rock formed the bases of the span. The western piers in this 1923 photograph are nearing completion. The workmen's bunkhouse and foremen's quarters were located nearby. The total length of the bridge would be 2,257 feet. (THHS Archives.)

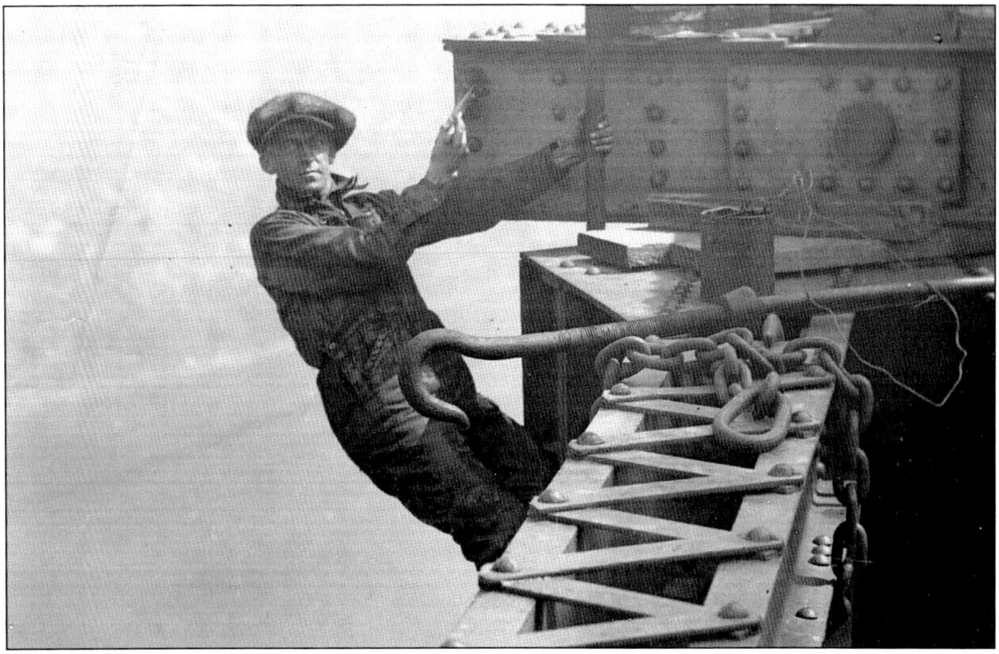

Daring Bridge Man, 1924. High above the Hudson without a safety harness, a young man paints the rivets of the Bear Mountain Bridge superstructure. Great skill and daring were required of the bridge men as they worked on the towers and the footbridges connecting them. Despite the lack of modern-day safety precautions, the bridge was completed without the loss of any lives. (Scott Collection.)

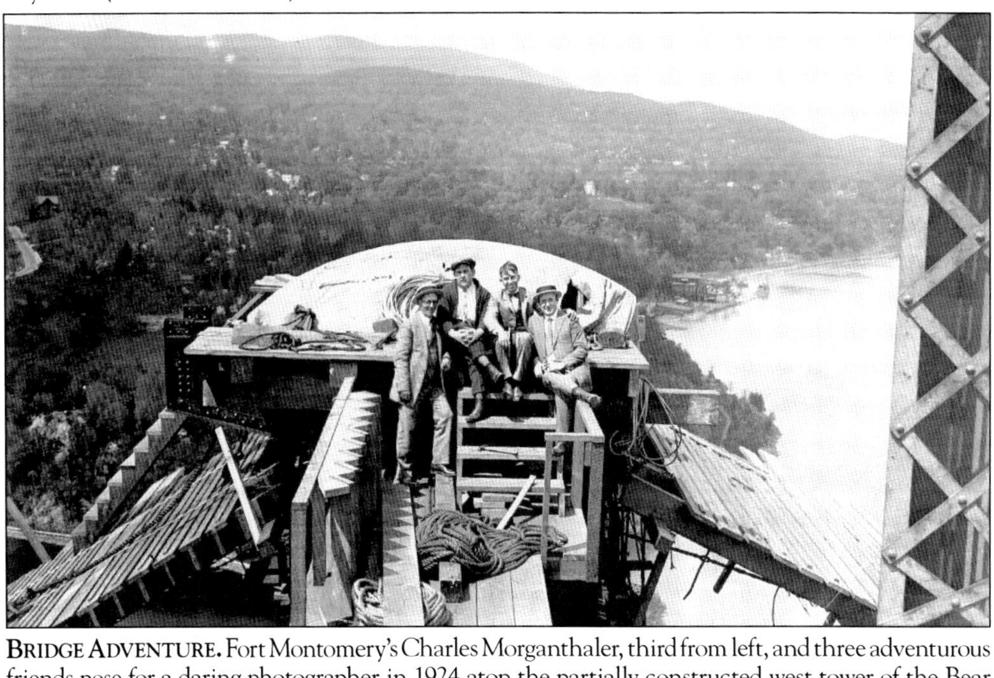

Bridge Adventure. Fort Montomery's Charles Morganthaler, third from left, and three adventurous friends pose for a daring photographer in 1924 atop the partially constructed west tower of the Bear Mountain Bridge. Beyond them are the mountains and homes of the Town of Highlands and the shoreline of the Hudson River. (Photograph by Leroy Davies, Scott Collection.)

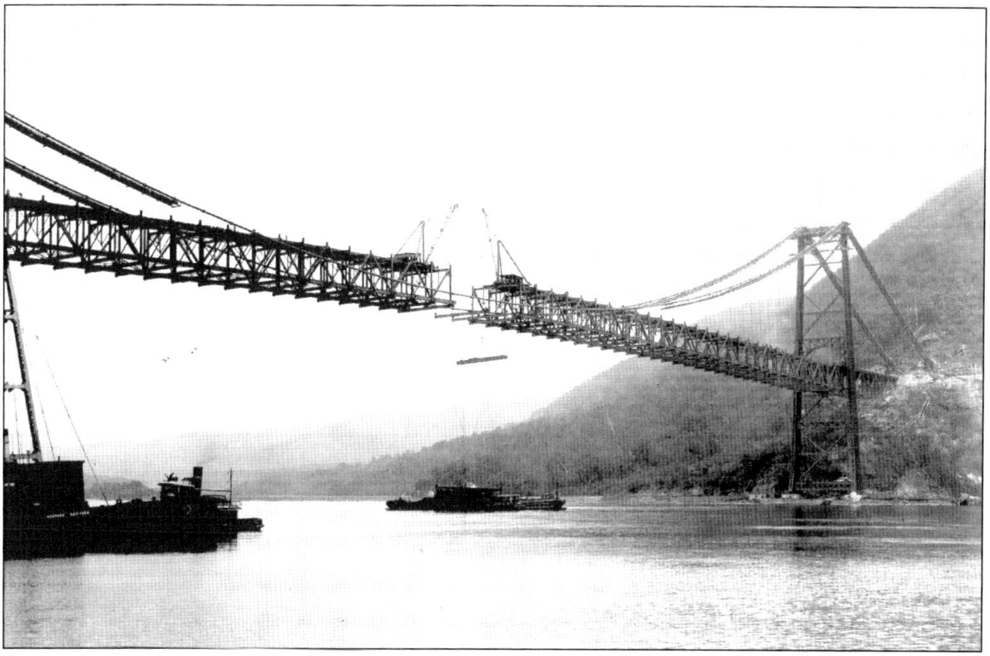

Bear Mountain Bridge Deck. Made of twisted strands of wire, two 18-inch-thick cables were manufactured by the Roebling Company, builders of the Brooklyn Bridge. The floor system was suspended from these main cables by wire rope suspenders. Starting at the towers, working toward the center, crews hoisted steel for the decking from barges in the river below. (THHS Archives.)

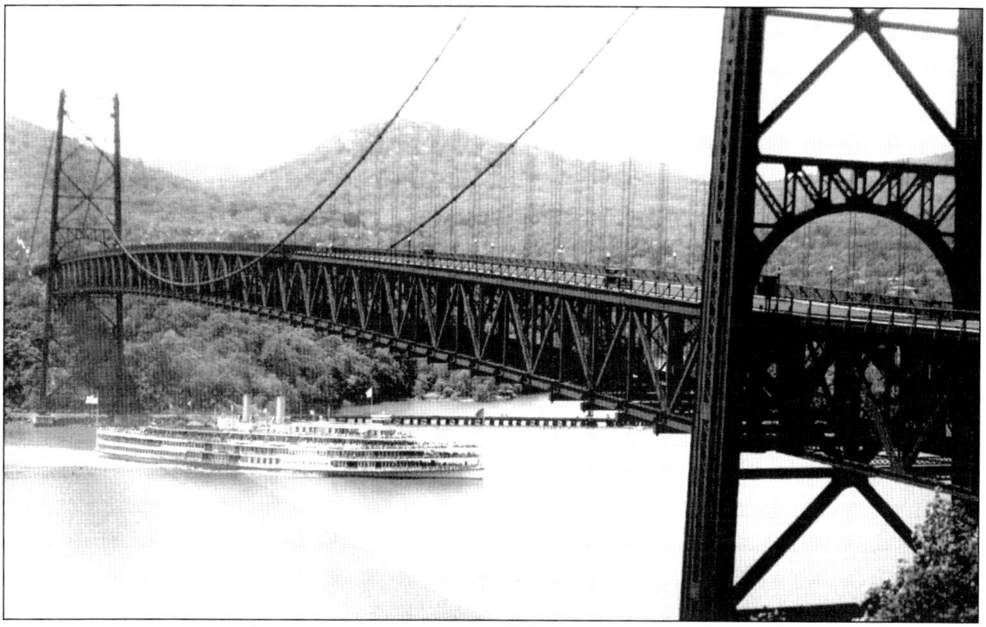

Completed Bridge. The Bear Mountain Bridge was completed in only 20 months, opening on November 26, 1924. The West Point Band led a motorcade across the bridge to a reviewing stand on the west side, where a plaque honoring all the workers was unveiled. A private company headed by the Harriman family had financed the span. It became the property of the state of New York in 1940. (PIPC Archives.)

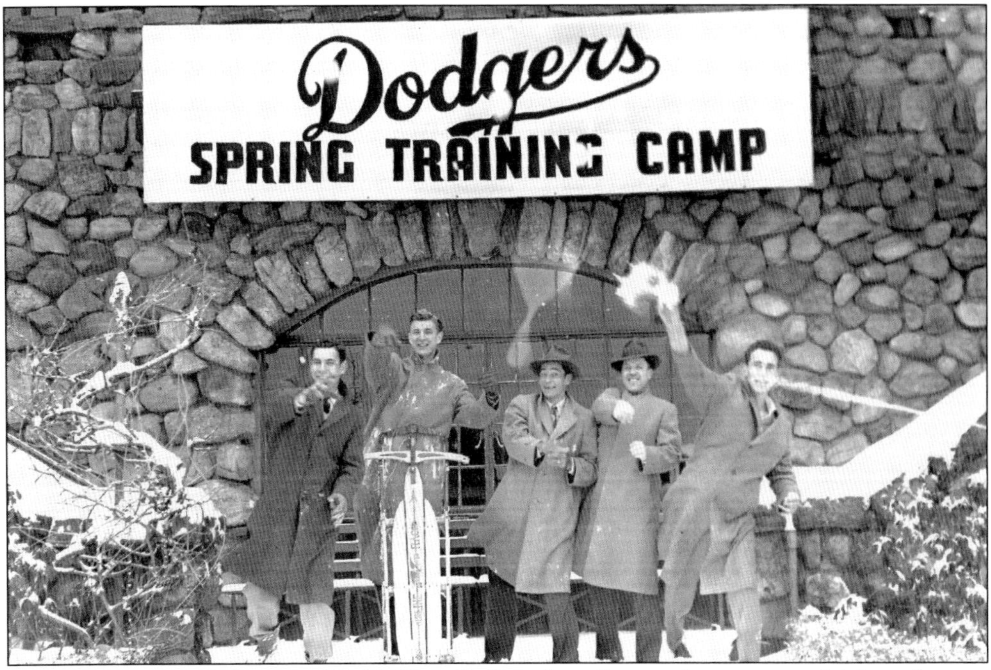

Spring Training? During World War II, President Roosevelt encouraged Major League Baseball to continue as a morale booster for the American people. Wartime travel was restricted, so teams who trained in Florida had to find a venue closer to home. From 1943 to 1945, the Brooklyn Dodgers used Bear Mountain for spring training. With palm trees a distant memory, players enjoy a snowball fight in front of the inn. (Los Angeles Dodgers' Archives.)

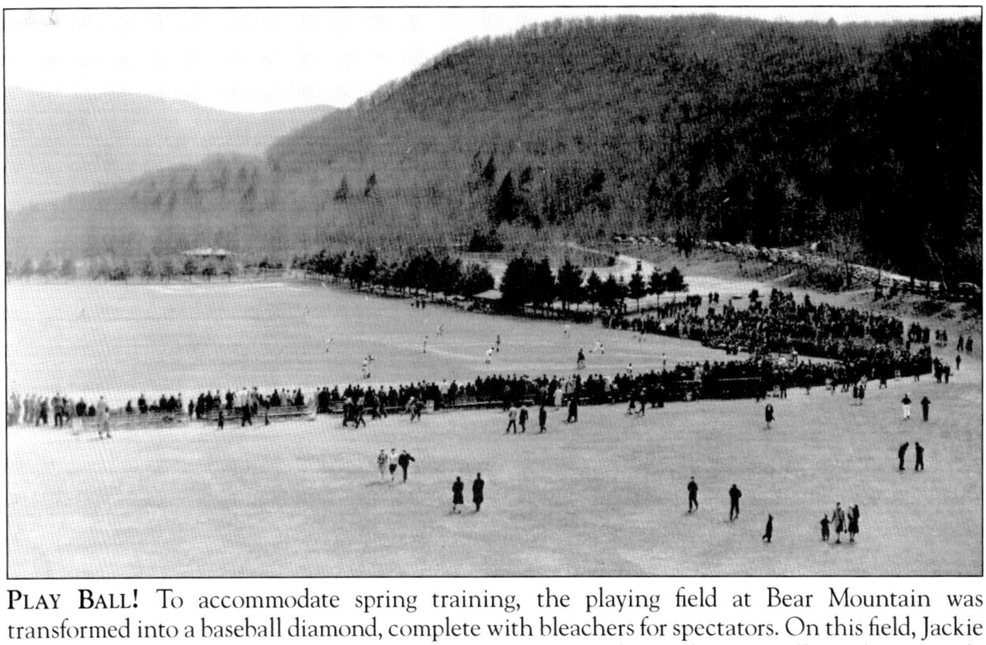

Play Ball! To accommodate spring training, the playing field at Bear Mountain was transformed into a baseball diamond, complete with bleachers for spectators. On this field, Jackie Robinson took some of his first batting practices for the Dodgers. Players recall watching people ice skate while they worked out. In severe weather, batting practice was held at the West Point Field House. (PIPC Archives.)

DODGERS AT WEST POINT. For an extra workout, the Dodgers occasionally traveled five miles to West Point to play exhibition games against the cadets. Taking time out from a practice in 1944, Dodger shortstop Pee Wee Reese, right, talks with a wounded World War II soldier and multi-talented cadet athlete Glenn Davis. (USMA Library.)

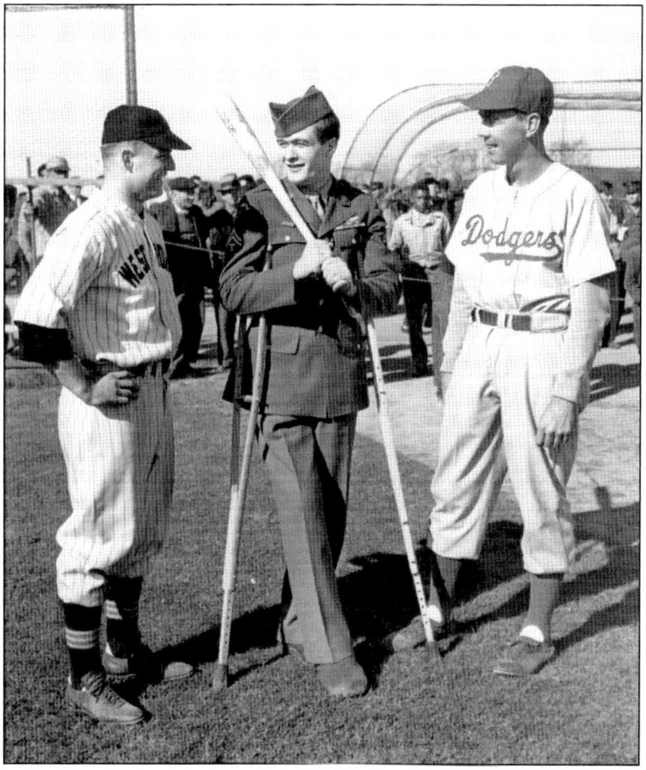

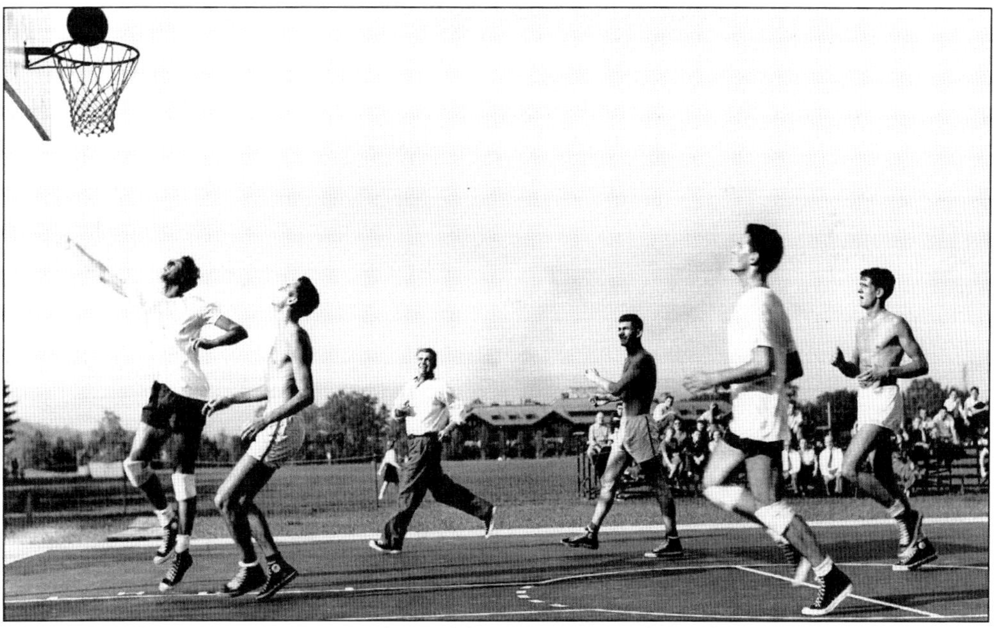

NEW YORK KNICKERBOCKERS. Members of the 1949 New York Knickerbockers basketball team practice on the courts at Bear Mountain. During the 1940s, the inn was managed by Jack Martin, a charismatic entrepreneur and sports fan who also hosted the New York Giants, the Green Bay Packers, the Cleveland Rams, a Golden Gloves team, and various college teams. The presence of athletes brought sports writers and generated publicity for the inn. (PIPC Archives.)

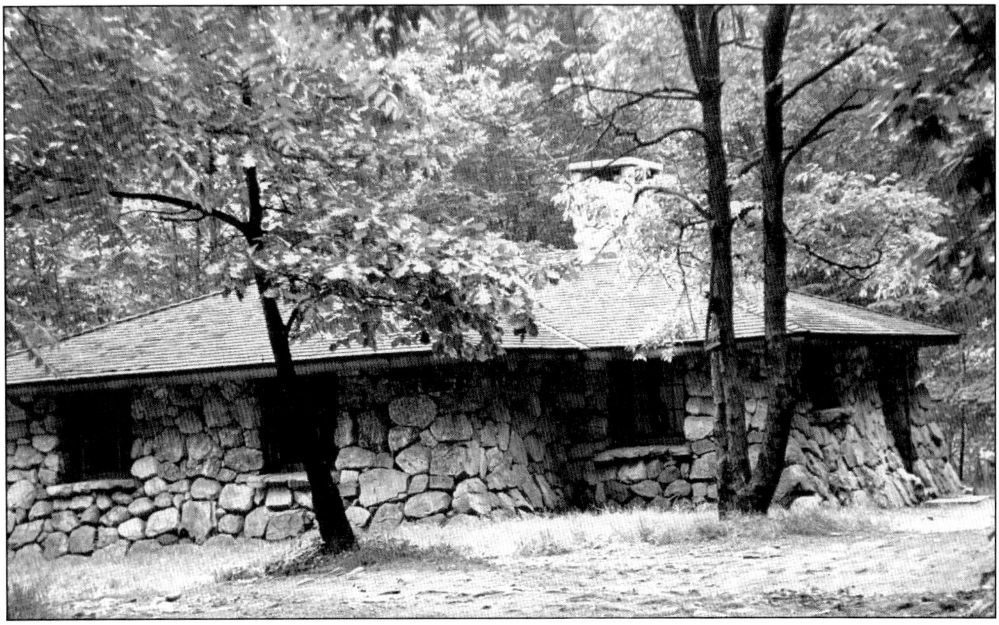

GAZAWAY HOUSE. Enhanced by its woodland setting, this home is one of several constructed in the 1930s for employees of the Palisades Interstate Park Commission. Built by the Works Progress Administration, the dwellings were crafted of native stone and timber. This residence was occupied by park police captain James Gazaway and his family between 1945 and 1950. Several of the park homes remain in use today. (Wallace Collection.)

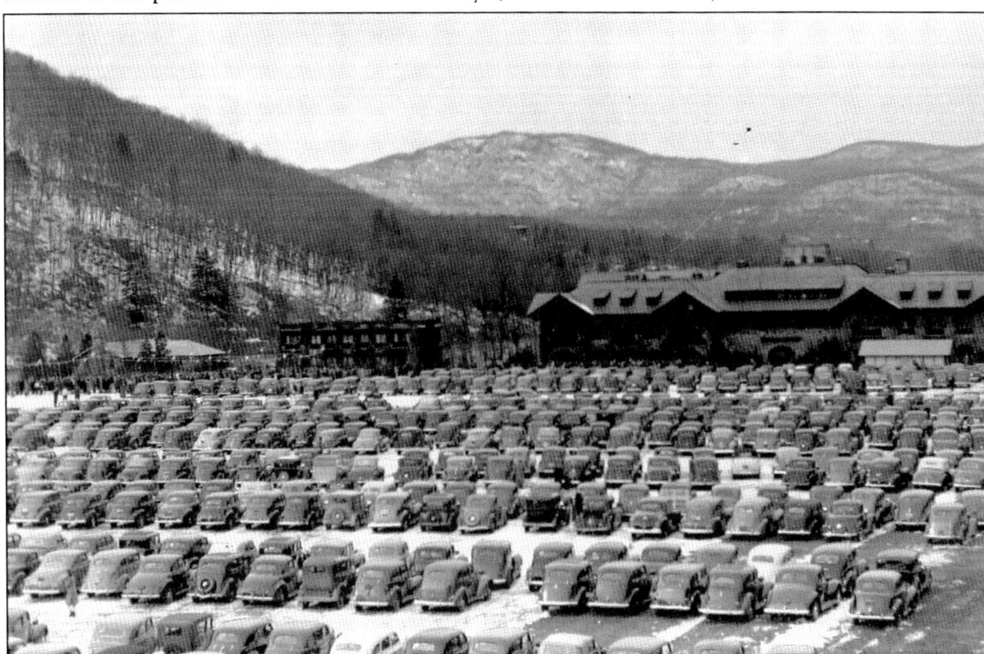

PARKING LOT, C. 1935. In the decades following its opening, Bear Mountain State Park grew in popularity. Visitors enjoyed a full array of year-round activities, and motorists found it just as hard to find a parking place in winter as in summer. (PIPC Archives.)

Seven

SCHOOLS AND CHURCHES

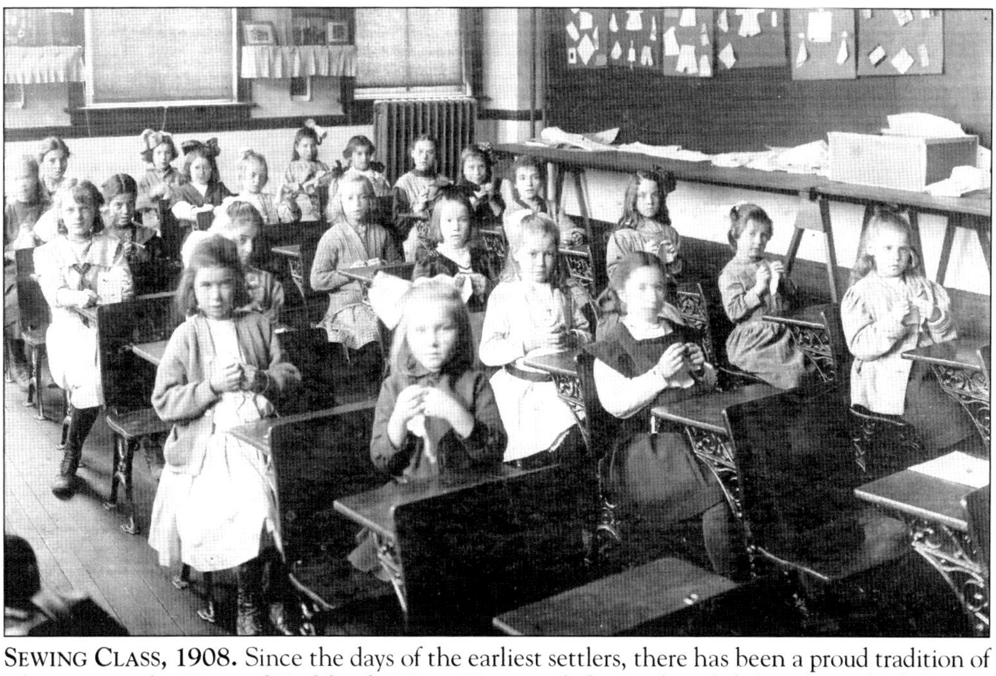

SEWING CLASS, 1908. Since the days of the earliest settlers, there has been a proud tradition of education in the Town of Highlands. Here, 22 young ladies with stylish hair bows, high button shoes, and charming dresses pause from their handwork to pose for a photograph. The Union Free School in Highland Falls followed the common practice of providing sewing lessons for girls during the 19th and early 20th centuries. (Graber Collection.)

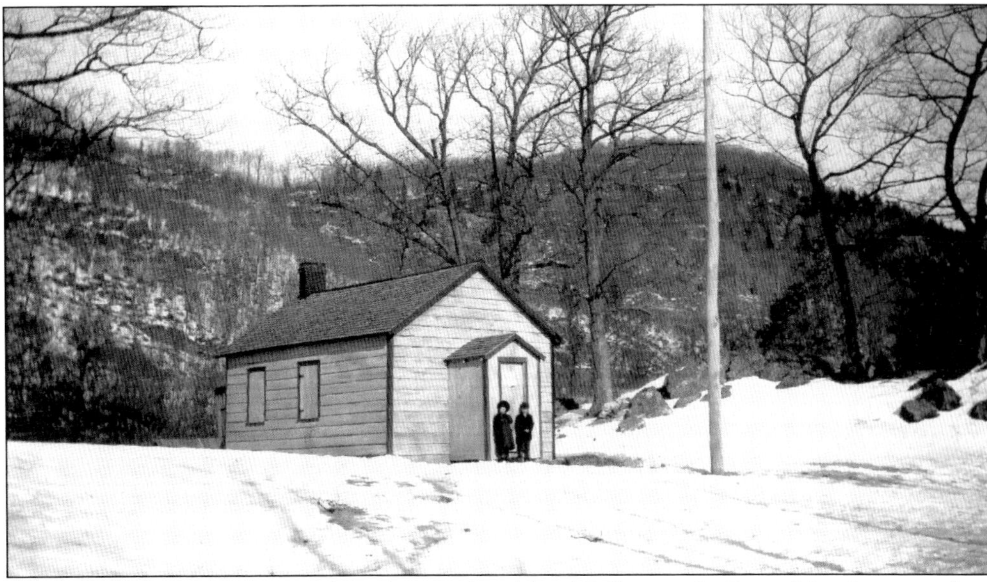

WEST GROVE SCHOOL. Located northwest of Highland Falls near the Round Pond crossroads in the valley of Bog Meadow Creek, the West Grove School was the first public education institution in the area. The school was built in 1814, and many of its first students were children of parents who had fought in the American Revolution. Other pupils came from mining and farming families who lived nearby. The historic school remained in use for over 100 years. (PIPC Archives.)

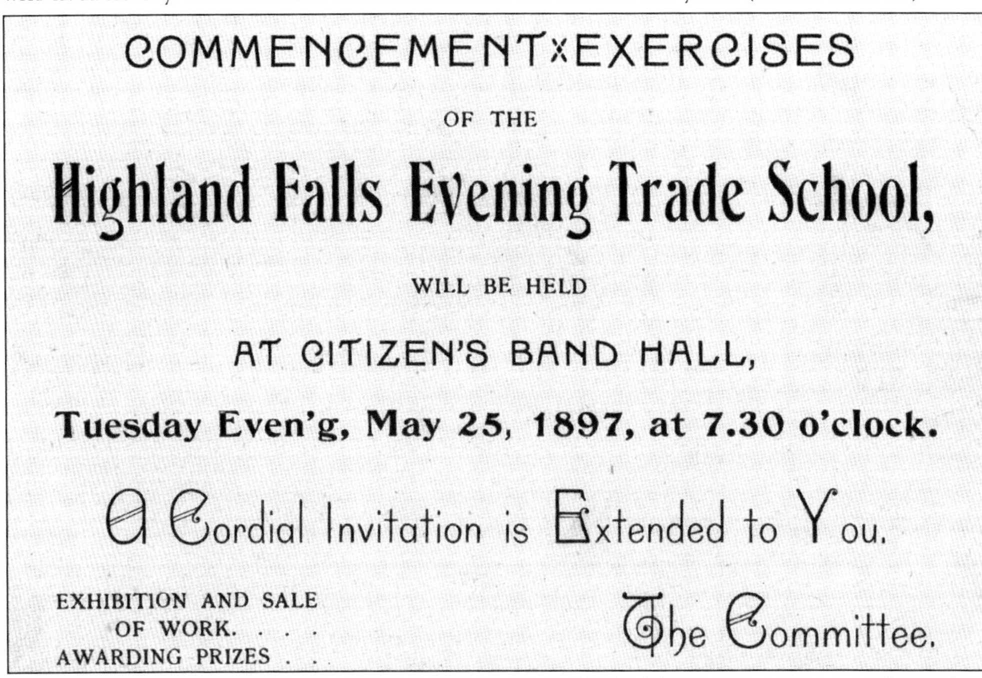

COMMENCEMENT EXERCISES

OF THE

Highland Falls Evening Trade School,

WILL BE HELD

AT CITIZEN'S BAND HALL,

Tuesday Even'g, May 25, 1897, at 7.30 o'clock.

A Cordial Invitation is Extended to You.

EXHIBITION AND SALE
OF WORK. . . .
AWARDING PRIZES . .

The Committee.

HIGHLAND FALLS TRADE SCHOOL INVITATION. Established by Frances Morgan, the wife of J. P. Morgan, the Highland Falls Trade School opened in 1896. It was modeled after successful vocational schools in New York City. Part of the library, also endowed by Frances, was outfitted with workbenches and carpentry tools. The *News of the Highlands* hailed it as a "grand opportunity for the youth of our village." Free tuition and uniforms were provided. (Yagel Collection.)

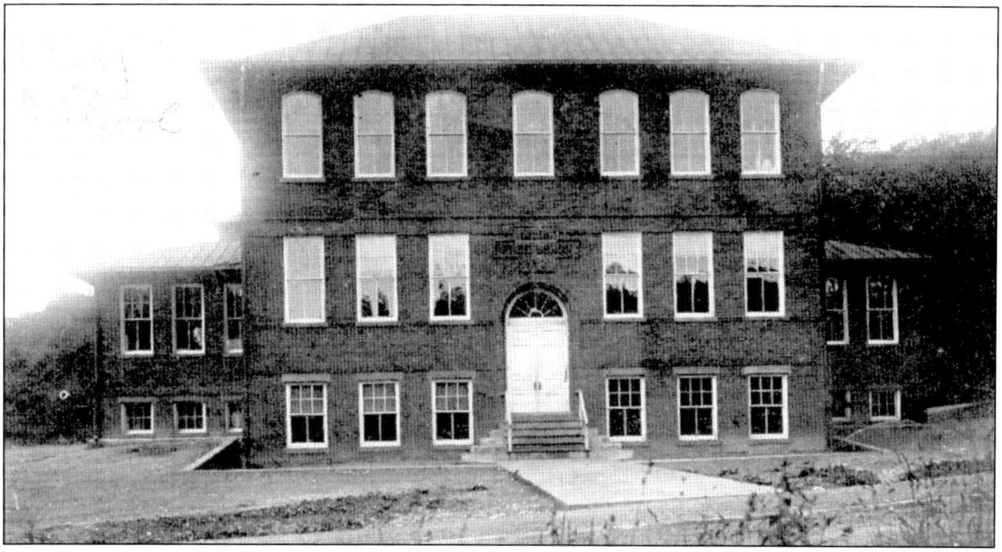

UNION FREE SCHOOL. The first brick school in the Town of Highlands was the Union Free School, located on Mountain Avenue on the site of the present elementary school. In September 1893, the *News of the Highlands* reported that preparations were under way for the first day of school. "Workers are scrubbing the wood, varnishing the furniture, and oiling the floors. The people have reason to be proud of our new temple of learning." (Storms Collection.)

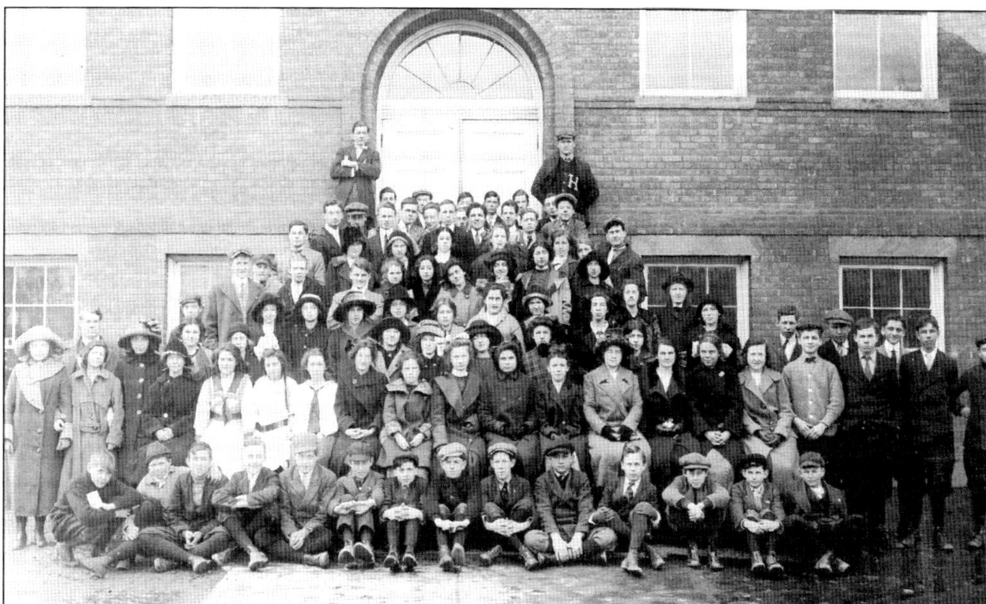

UPPER GRADES. Members of the upper grades of the Union Free School assemble for a group photograph at the Main Entrance about 1915. An elected school board managed education. Unlike national elections, which prohibited women from voting, school board elections were advertised as open to all, "regardless of race, color, sex or previous condition of servitude." (Bosch Collection.)

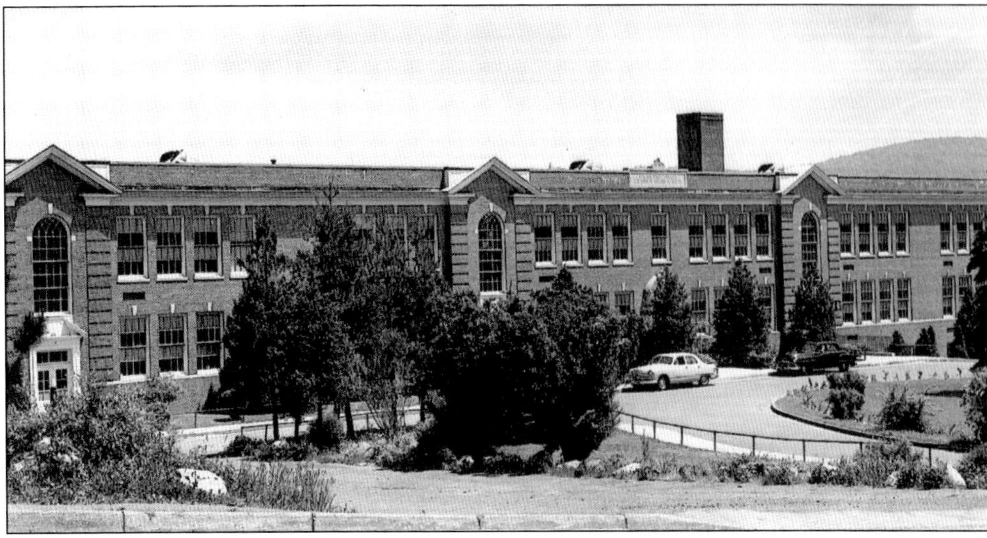

HIGHLAND FALLS HIGH SCHOOL. Built to accommodate kindergarten through 12th grade, a modern facility was constructed on Mountain Avenue in 1930 opposite the Union Free School, which had become obsolete. With an eye to the future, the school was engineered so additions could be made without destruction of the building. As the town grew, this became strictly a high school. It still serves the community, now as a middle school. (Gunza Collection.)

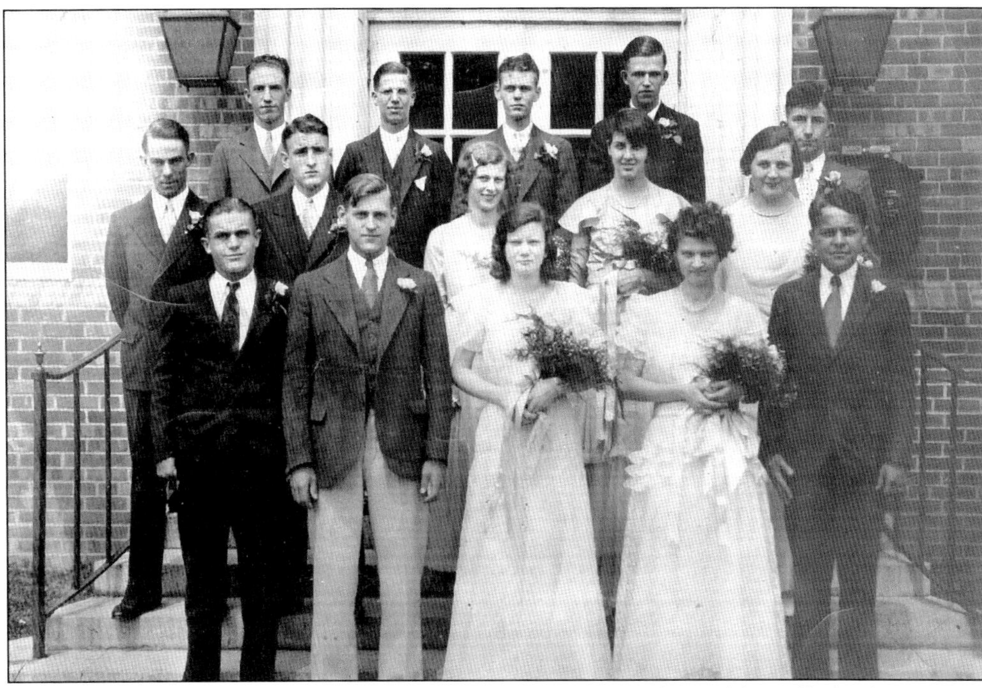

CLASS OF 1932. The Highland Falls High School class of 1932 dressed formally for the occasion of their graduation. Pictured in front of their new school, from left to right, are the following: (first row) Clayton Hager, Franz Van Buskirk, Clare Hansen, Helen Slavicek, and Claudio Haines; (second row) Joe Volkringer, Nick Tangney, Gertrude Adams, Marjorie Flickenchild, and Berenice Coffey; (third row) Jasper Baker, Thomas Parks, Rodney Boyce, Valentine Seria, and unidentified. (Baker Collection.)

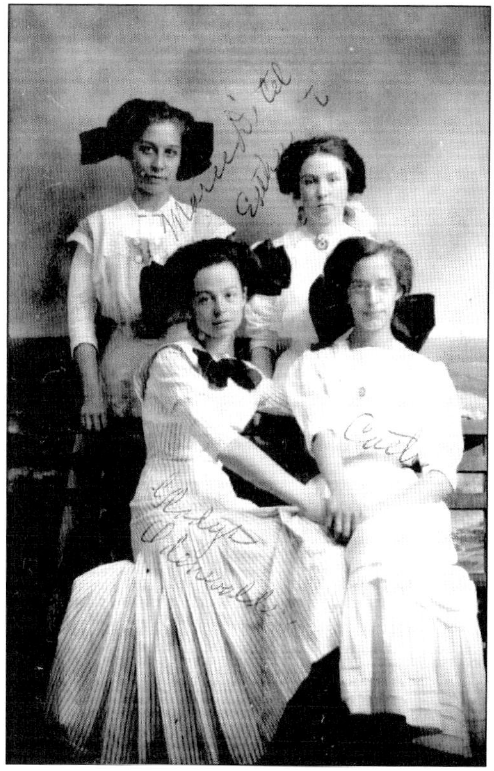

FOUR FRIENDS. Lovely in their cotton summer dresses and fashionable hair bows, four friends pose for a charming photograph about 1912. These young ladies were on the brink of a changing world. During the next decades it would be possible for them to vote, drive, fly, listen to radio, watch television, and witness two world wars. Seen here, from left to right, are the following: (first row) Gladys Odenwalder and Catherine Bosch; (second row) Marie Diestel and Esther T. Scott. (Bosch Collection.)

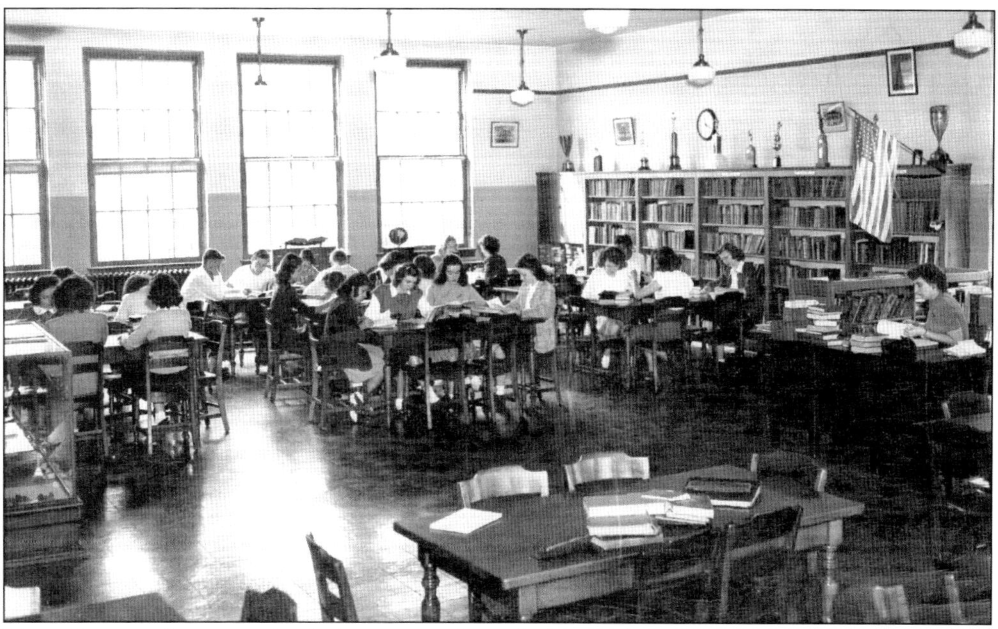

HIGH SCHOOL LIBRARY. Sunlight streams through the windows as studious teenagers pore over their books and papers at Highland Falls High School around 1944. Trophies line the bookshelf beside the 48-star flag. Their principal was Prof. James I. O'Neill, a lifelong town resident who was a civic-minded, talented, and devoted educator. A new high school would be named for him in 1976. (THHS Archives.)

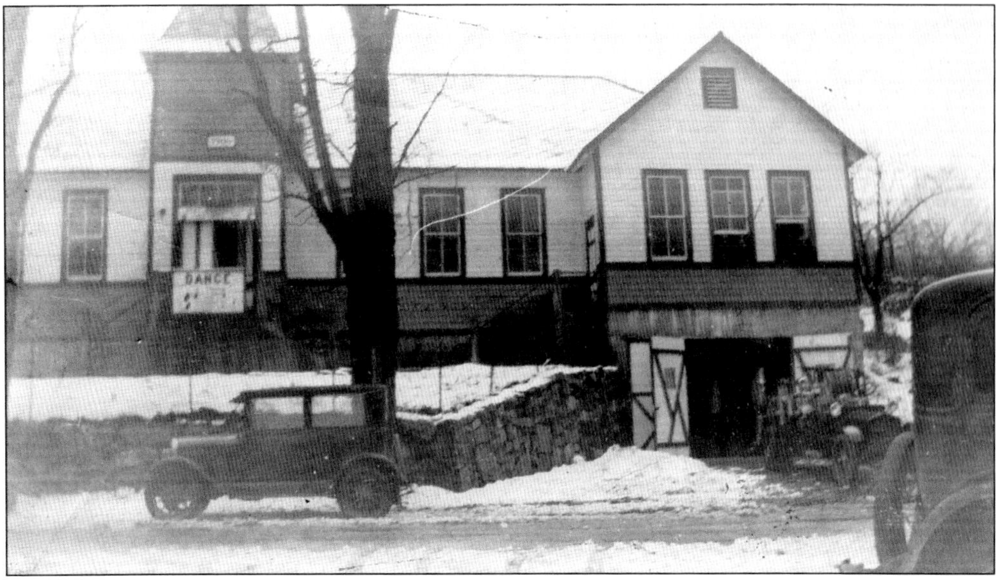

FORT MONTGOMERY SCHOOL. Built in 1900, the Fort Montgomery School served the elementary-age population of the hamlet. In 1930, a larger brick school was built to accommodate the growing population, and this structure was reborn as the Fort Montgomery Firehouse. It burned down in 1960 and was replaced with a sturdy concrete block building. (Fort Montgomery Fire Department Archives.)

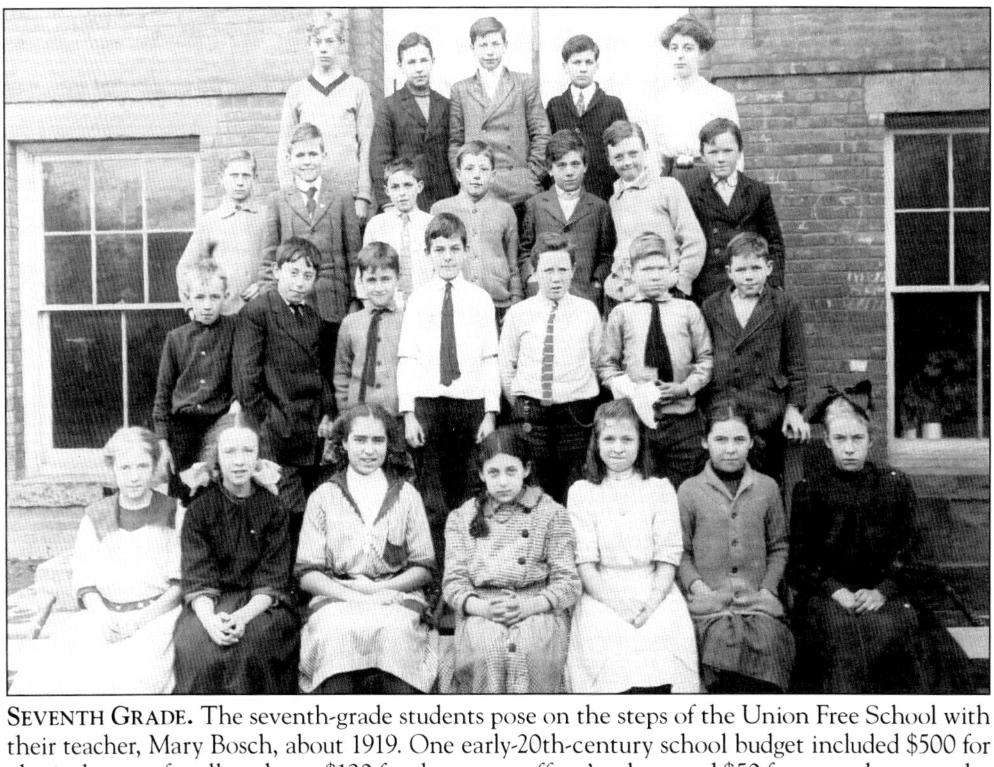

SEVENTH GRADE. The seventh-grade students pose on the steps of the Union Free School with their teacher, Mary Bosch, about 1919. One early-20th-century school budget included $500 for physical exams for all students, $120 for the truant officer's salary, and $50 for an outhouse at the Fort Montgomery School. (Bosch Collection.)

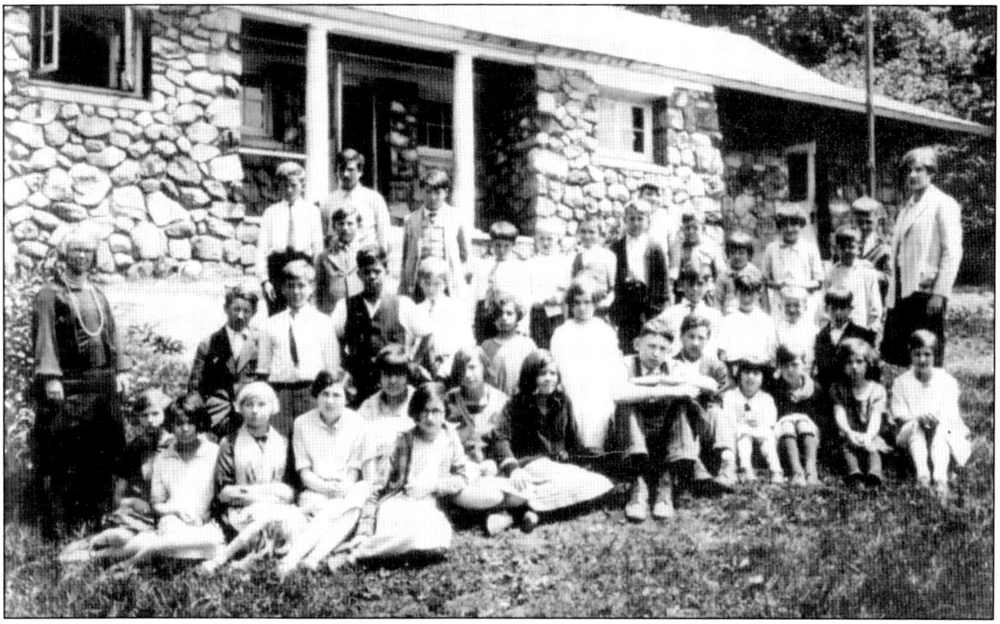

FOREST OF DEAN SCHOOL, C. 1928. Serving mining families of the Forest of Dean, this one-room school was divided by a sliding door to separate lower and upper grades. Although the school had electricity, many homes had only kerosene light at the time. Vince Julian (back row, fifth from left) recalls, "When it was time to do homework, the one closest to the lamp was the lucky one." The building is now federal property. (Julian Collection.)

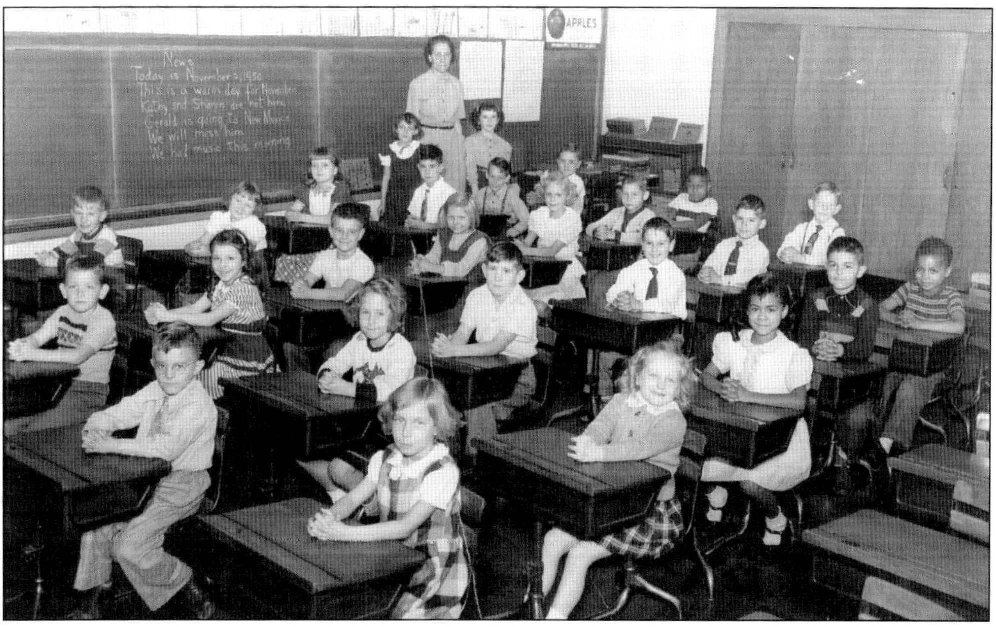

SECOND GRADE. A class of 26 second-graders demonstrates its best behavior at the Highland Falls School in 1950. Teacher Frances Frates is still remembered by longtime residents. She was so admired and respected for her dedication to children, that upon her retirement after 40 years of teaching, the community presented her with a brand-new 1954 Plymouth sedan as a gift. (Burns Collection.)

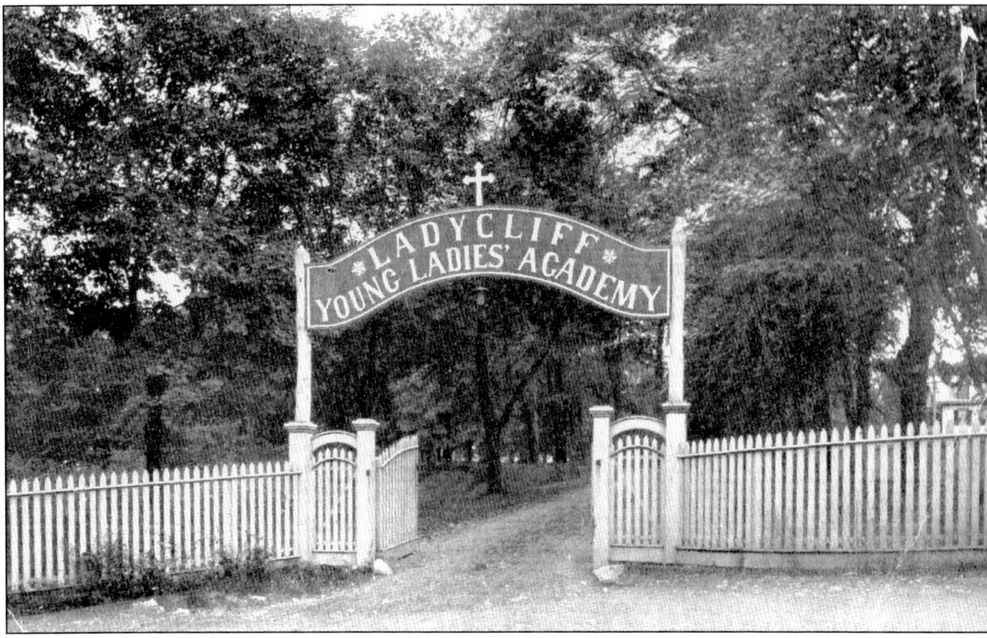

LADYCLIFF. In 1899, the Franciscan Sisters purchased the Cozzens' Hotel and its impressive grounds to use for a school. Ladycliff Academy opened in 1900 as a coeducational elementary school. It later became a girls' high school and, from 1935 onward, a college for women. For many years, the main entrance was on the south side of Station Road at the top of the hill. (Gunza Collection.)

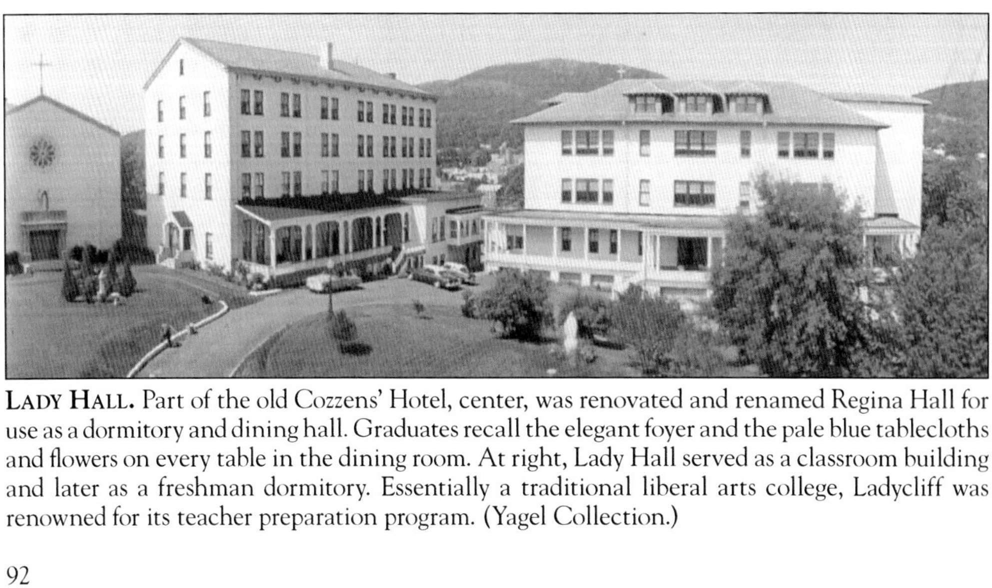

LADY HALL. Part of the old Cozzens' Hotel, center, was renovated and renamed Regina Hall for use as a dormitory and dining hall. Graduates recall the elegant foyer and the pale blue tablecloths and flowers on every table in the dining room. At right, Lady Hall served as a classroom building and later as a freshman dormitory. Essentially a traditional liberal arts college, Ladycliff was renowned for its teacher preparation program. (Yagel Collection.)

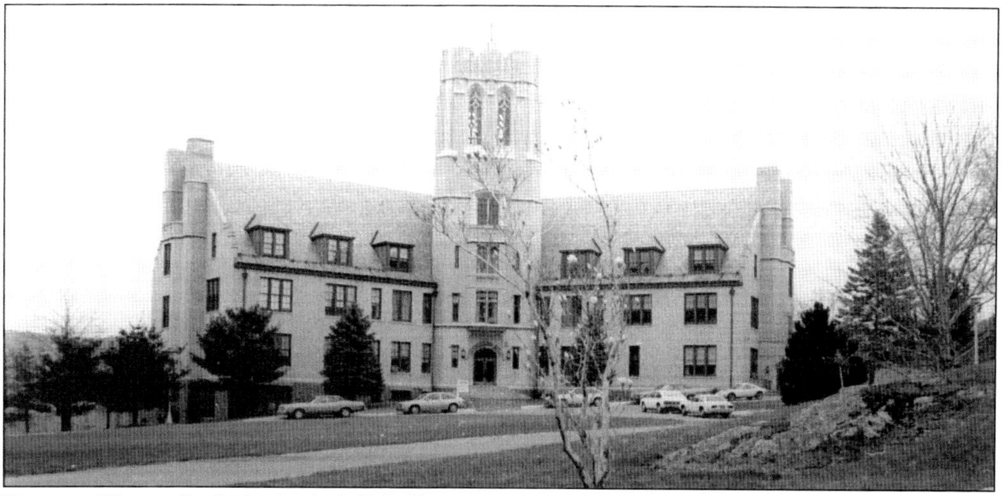

ROSARY HALL. Built for Ladycliff College in 1934, Rosary Hall was designed as a learning center. It housed a swimming pool on the lowest floor, science laboratories, classrooms, and art studios on upper floors, and a vast library overlooking the Hudson on the first floor. As a Ladycliff undergraduate, the author was often distracted by the magnificent view! Still a place of learning, this grand edifice is now the West Point Museum. (Gunza Collection.)

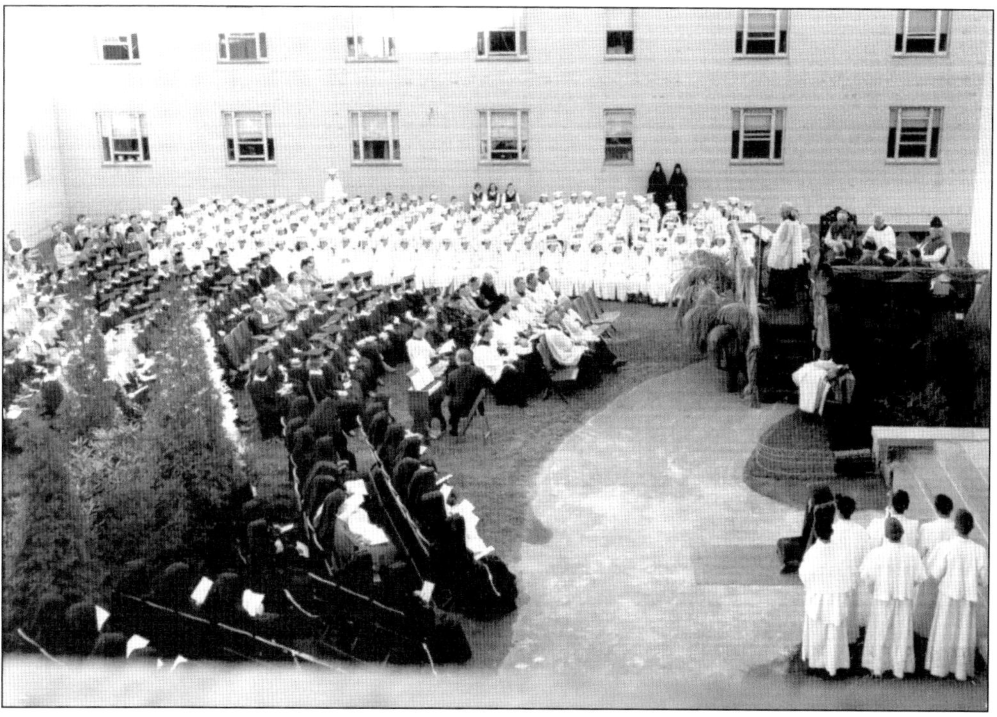

LADYCLIFF CHAPEL DEDICATION. The dedication of the new chapel facade at Ladycliff occurred in 1955. Faculty and clergy are seated in front of the students, who are formally dressed in caps and gowns. The young women of Ladycliff Academy (high school) wear white. Ladycliff College students are in black. Traditional academic attire was worn at all special events until the early 1970s. (Graber Collection.)

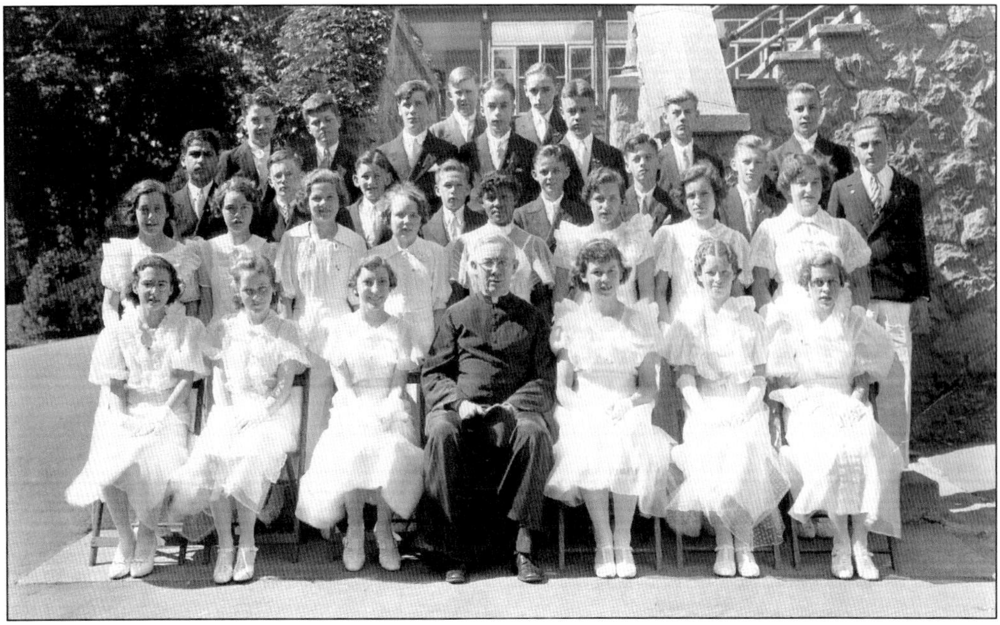

SACRED HEART GRADUATION, 1936. With help from funds raised by the annual Lawn Fetes, the cornerstone of Sacred Heart School was laid in 1930. General contractor Leo Graber completed the building, with its revolutionary intercom speaker system, at a cost of $85,000. Sacred Heart's eighth-grade class had its formal graduation portrait taken on the church steps with Father Langton, the pastor, six years later. (Murphy Collection.)

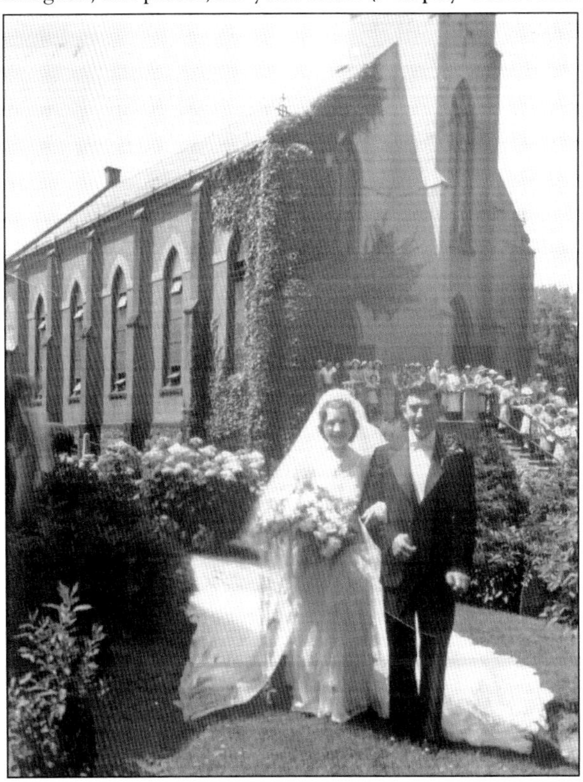

WEDDING. Jenny and Lorenzo Dapra, two of the many Italian immigrants who came to the Highlands, pose after their 1938 wedding at Sacred Heart Church. Lorenzo was recruited from his native village to build the New York City subway. When his work was finished, he learned that the military academy needed stonemasons so he migrated up the Hudson. After their marriage, they resided on Center Street in Highland Falls. (Dapra Collection.)

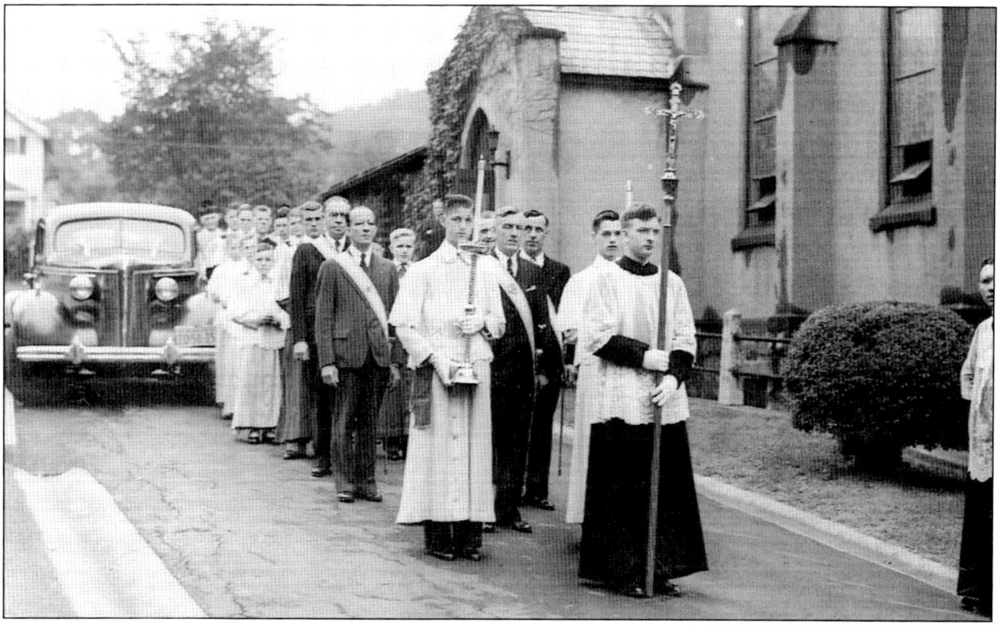

PROCESSION. Immediately behind the cross bearer, altar boys Frank Murphy (left) and Marty Maher, in ceremonial garb and perfectly shined shoes, lead a procession of the Knights of Columbus past the side entrance of Sacred Heart Church around 1938. The house on Church Street can no longer be seen from this spot because of the 1958 addition to Sacred Heart School. (Murphy Collection.)

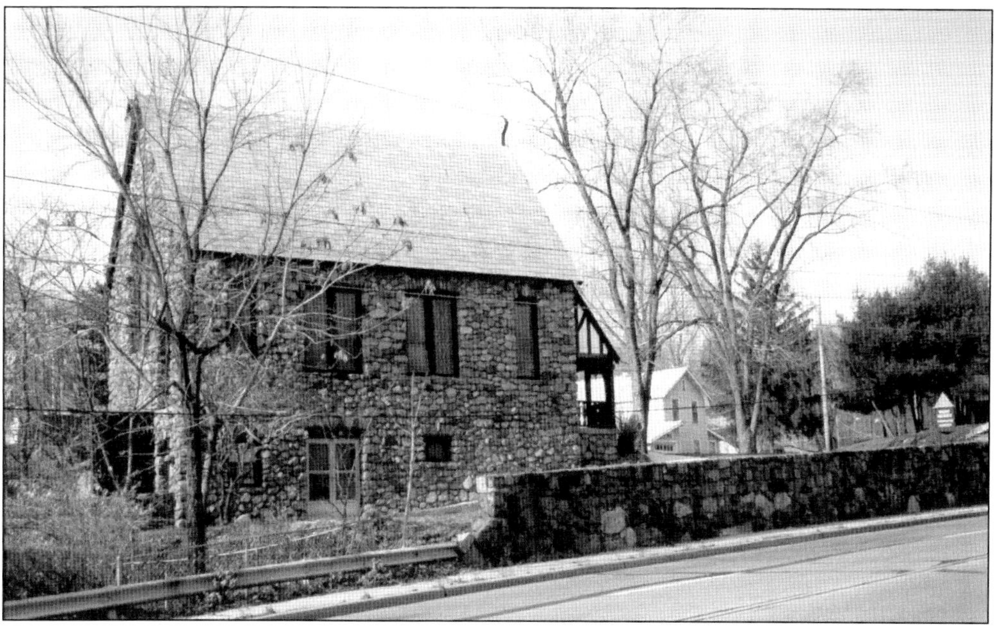

ST. MARK'S EPISCOPAL CHURCH. The congregation of St. Mark's Episcopal Church held its first service in 1914 at the home of a parishioner. About nine years later, their lovely stone church was completed on land donated by Edward Gee. Stained-glass windows no longer needed at the Cadet Chapel were acquired by town historian Donald Clark and installed at St. Mark's. The church bell was a gift of Lady Frances Pell Archer-Shee. (Sibley Collection.)

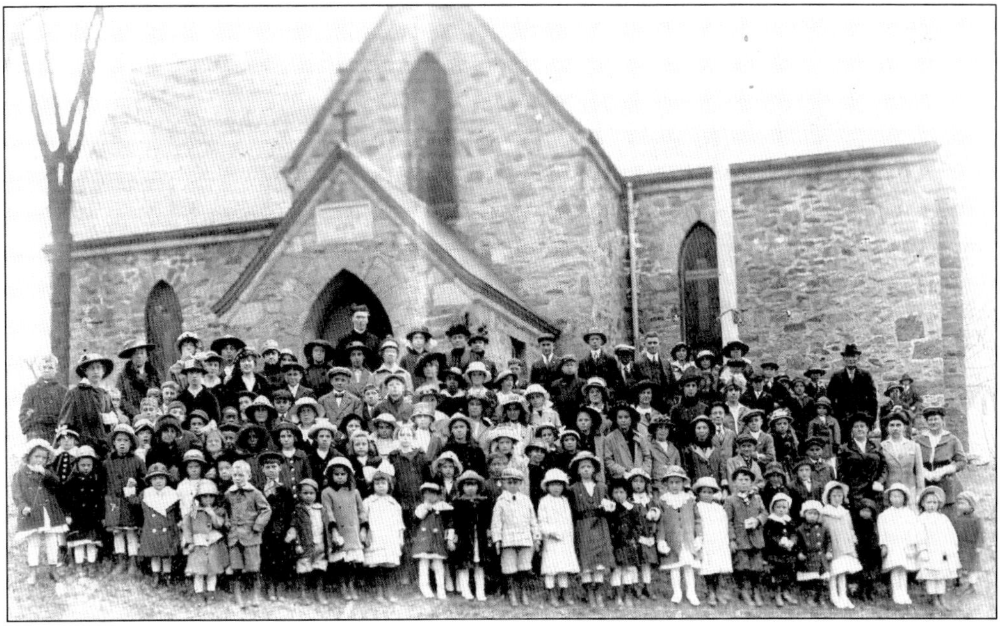

CHURCH OF THE HOLY INNOCENTS C. 1910. Parishioners gather in front of the Church of the Holy Innocents in Highland Falls. Artist Robert Weir designed the church and made a substantial monetary gift by donating the commission from his painting on the ceiling of the Capitol Rotunda in Washington. Originally built in the form of a cross, the church sits on a gently sloping hill that is popular with winter sleigh riders. (Wallace Collection.)

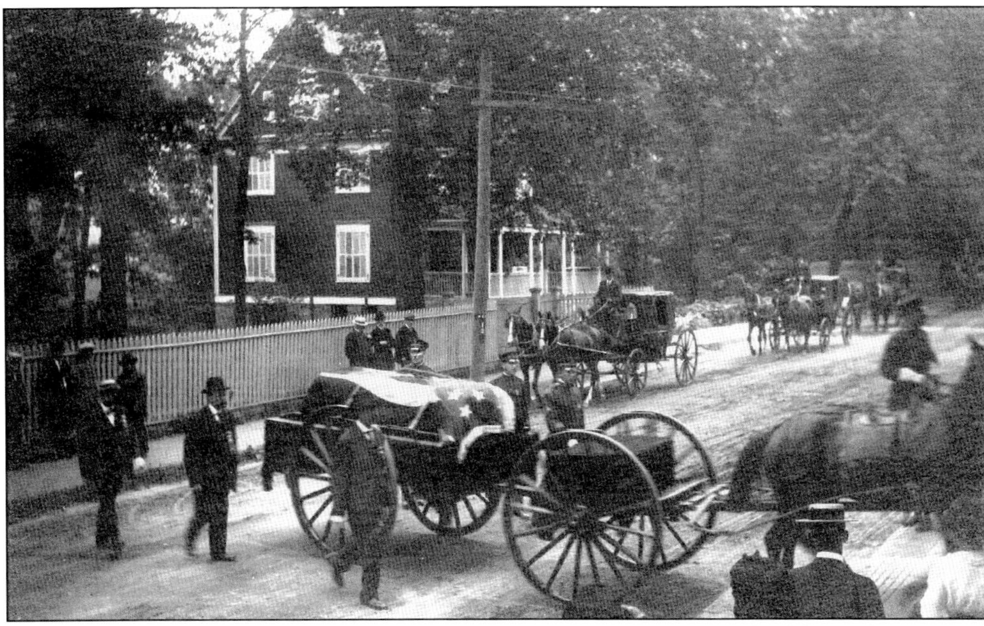

FUNERAL PROCESSION. Henry Bock's funeral procession enters the Church of the Holy Innocents grounds in July 1915. The flag-draped coffin reminded mourners that Bock, a German immigrant, had served in the United States Army. It was one of the largest funerals ever attended in town history. Later at the cemetery, following an old tradition, fellow members of the United Spanish-American War Veterans passed his grave and dropped a small American flag. (Wallace Collection.)

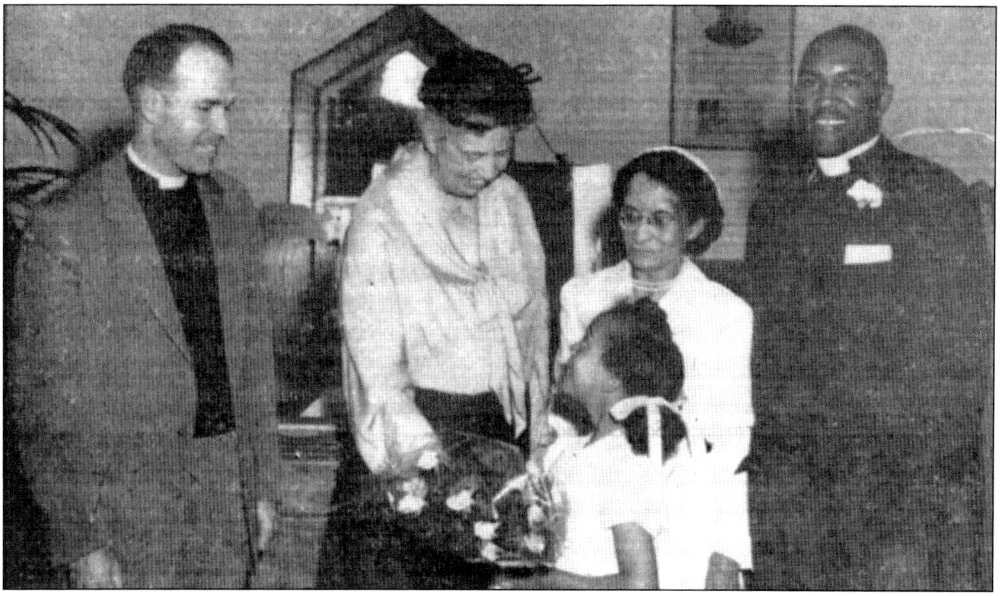

ELEANOR ROOSEVELT. In 1954, the African Methodist Episcopal Zion Church invited Eleanor Roosevelt to speak. She accepted, asking only that a person "of good standing in the community" be sent to drive her to Highland Falls. Arriving on Mothers' Day, she was greeted by Reverend Gripe (left), Armead Johnson, and Reverend McKinney (right) and presented with flowers by Jeanette Cosby. Roosevelt spoke eloquently on the role of women in achieving world peace. (News of the Highlands.)

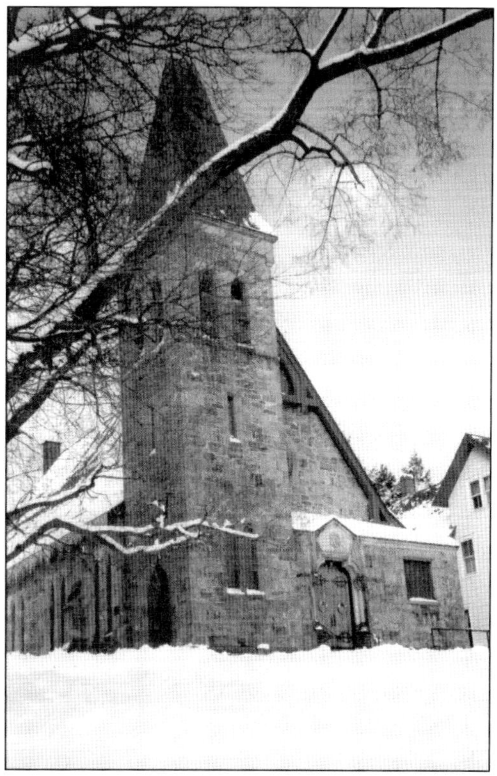

UNITED CHURCH OF THE HIGHLANDS. This sturdy stone church standing on Main Street in Highland Falls began its life as the First Presbyterian Church in 1868. Writer E. P. Roe was an early pastor. On Sundays in the early 1900s, Presbyterian cadets would march down in formation to attend services. A merger with the Methodist parish occurred in 1976, resulting in it being renamed the United Church of the Highlands. (Sibley Collection.)

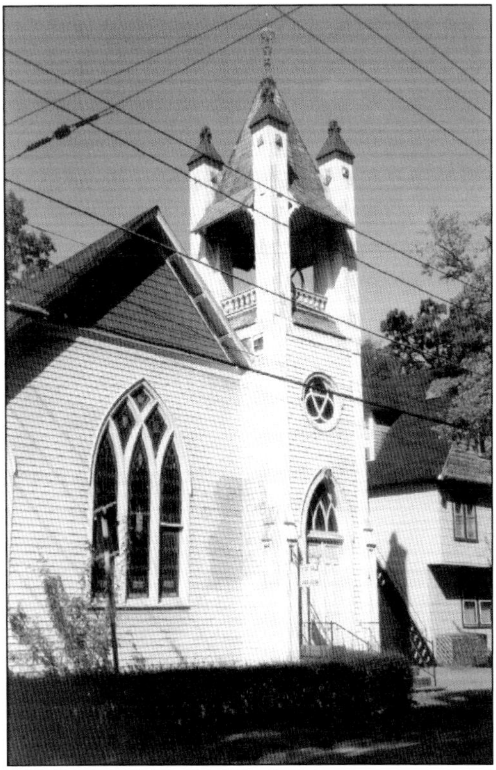

ST. MARK'S BAPTIST CHURCH. In Highland Falls, at the corner of Walnut Avenue and Main Street, is this imposing white church. Built in 1900 as a Methodist parish, it is now home to the congregation of St. Mark's Baptist Church. (Sibley Collection.)

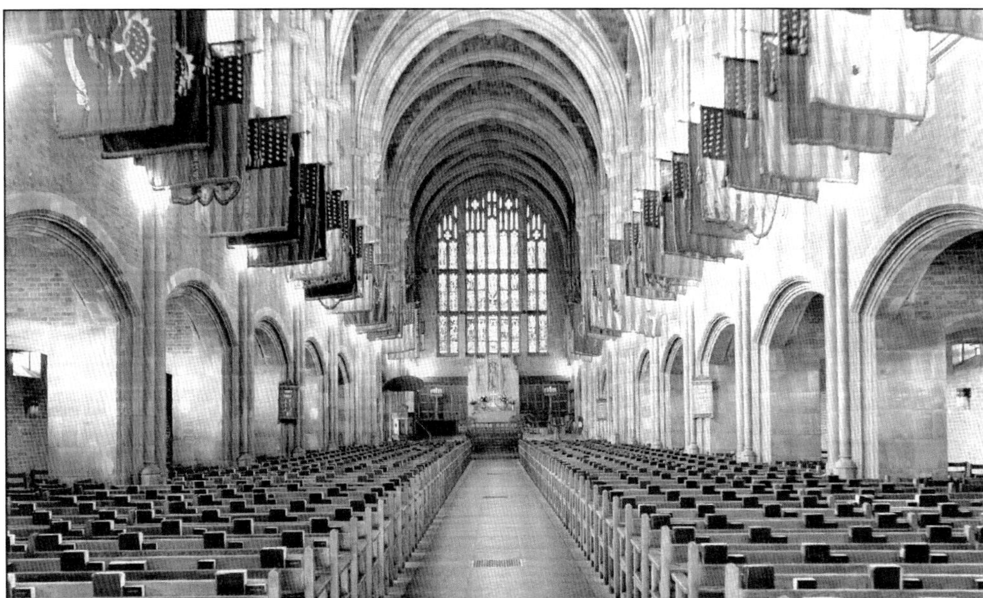

CADET CHAPEL. Completed in 1910, West Point's Cadet Chapel was constructed in the Gothic Revival style during an early-20th-century expansion of the military academy. The stone was quarried from a hill behind the superintendent's house. The world's largest church organ enhanced music at services. The great sanctuary window is inscribed with the motto of the academy: "Duty, Honor, Country." (Bosch Collection.)

Eight

SERVICE

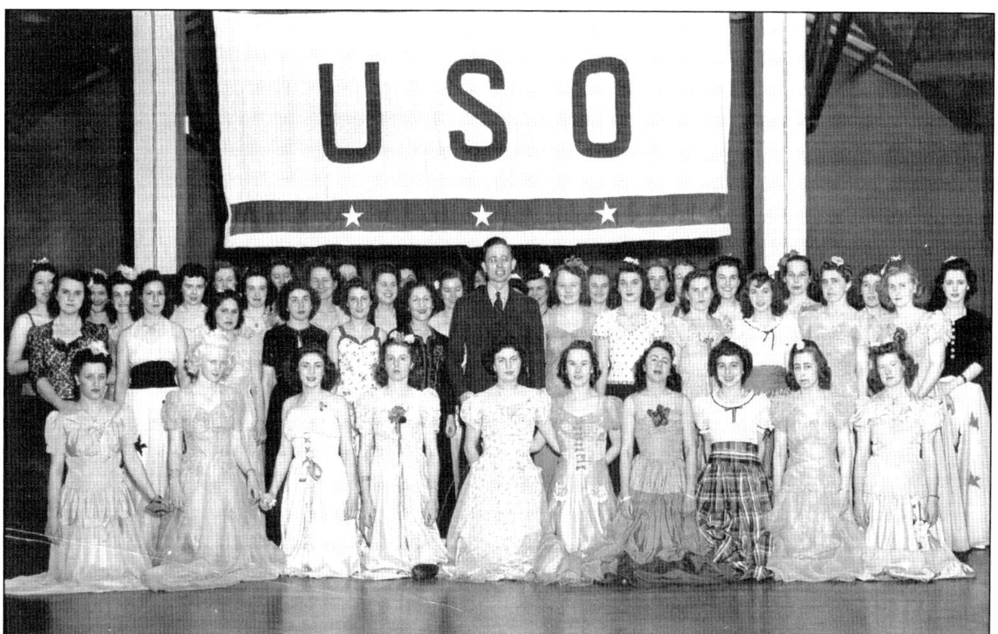

UNITED SERVICE ORGANIZATIONS. Members of the local United Service Organizations (USO) pose in their finery at a Saturday night dance in 1943, part of a program to provide support and morale-enhancing programs for servicemen at home and abroad. "Almost every unmarried girl in town belonged to the USO," according to Phyllis Murphy (second row, sixth from right). "We would bring a sandwich for ourselves and one to share with a fellow." (Murphy Collection.)

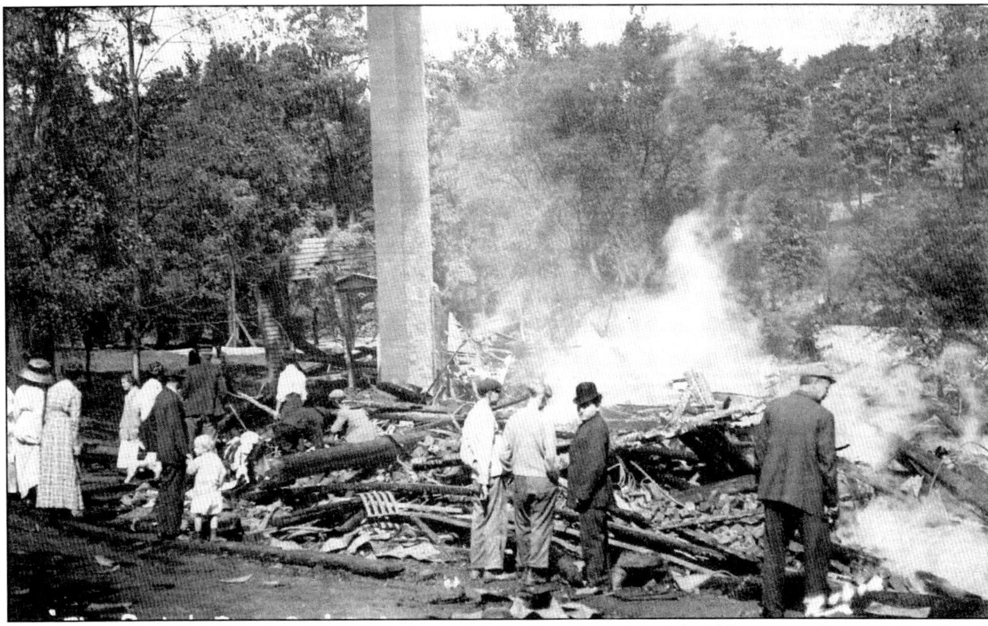

HOTEL FIRE. Fire was a constant danger in an age of wooden buildings and open fireplaces. In 1911, a fire began at the Rocks, a magnificent seven-story hotel situated on a cliff above the Hudson River in Highland Falls. Four local fire departments were joined by the West Point Company and cadet volunteers, but their efforts could not save the structure, which burned to the ground in two hours. (Gunza Collection.)

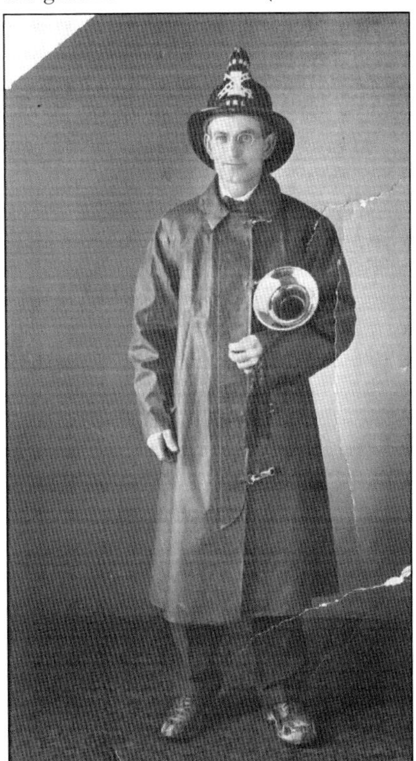

FIREMAN, C. 1919. Arthur Van Voorhis poses in his turnout gear as a member of the Bald Rock Hook and Ladder Company of Highland Falls, one of five companies in the village. The others were Goodsell Hook and Ladder and Goodsell Hose on Main Street, North End Hose in Cozzens Avenue, and Prospect Hill Hose Company on West Street. Van Voorhis carries a fireman's trumpet, an instrument like a megaphone used to shout orders at the scene of a fire. (Storms Collection.)

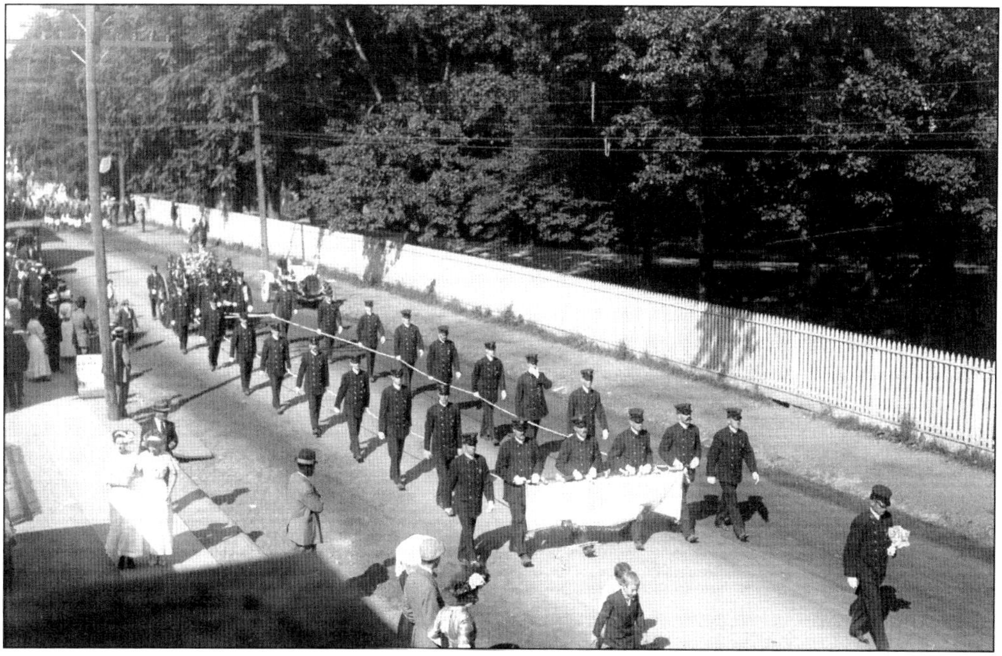

GOODSELL HOSE, 1917. Goodsell Hose firefighters march in formation, followed by their pumper. After securing the hose to a water source, members of the company manually pumped the water to extinguish the fire. Organized in 1895, the 15-man department was led by Joseph Stephens. (Bosch Collection.)

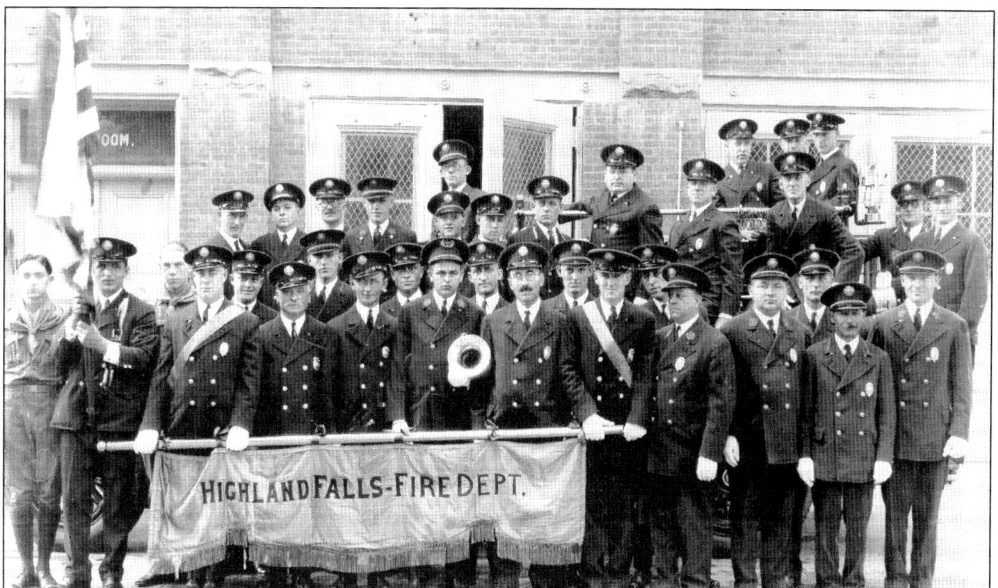

HIGHLAND FALLS FIRE DEPARTMENT. Since its organization in 1922 from five smaller companies, the Highland Falls Volunteer Fire Department has stood ready to assist the community. Early on, its lone vehicle was a Model T chassis with a pump, hose, and ladders. Fire alarm calls were made by ringing a bell atop the firehouse or by striking a curved piece of train rail with a sledgehammer. In 1926, members bought a fire siren for the village. (Gunza Collection.)

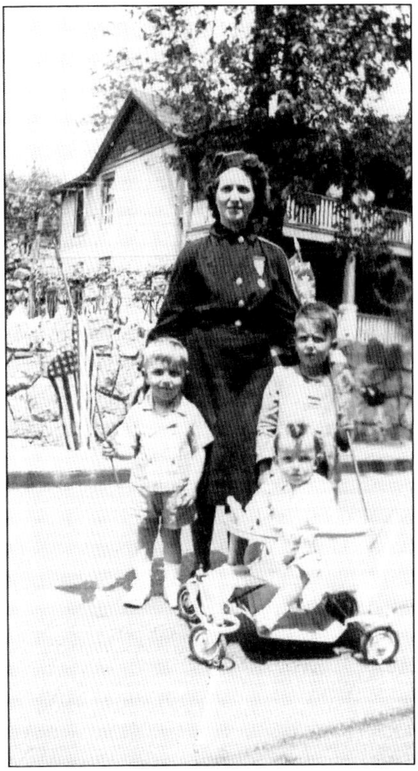

Fire Department Auxiliary. Dressed in the Highland Falls Fire Department Auxiliary uniform, Jenny Dapra stands near her Center Street home with her three sons. As explained in its anniversary program, the auxiliary was "organized to aid the department. They have given inestimable service in times of trying conditions and adverse circumstances." An active Fort Montgomery Fire Department Auxiliary has also provided exemplary service to the community. (Dapra Collection.)

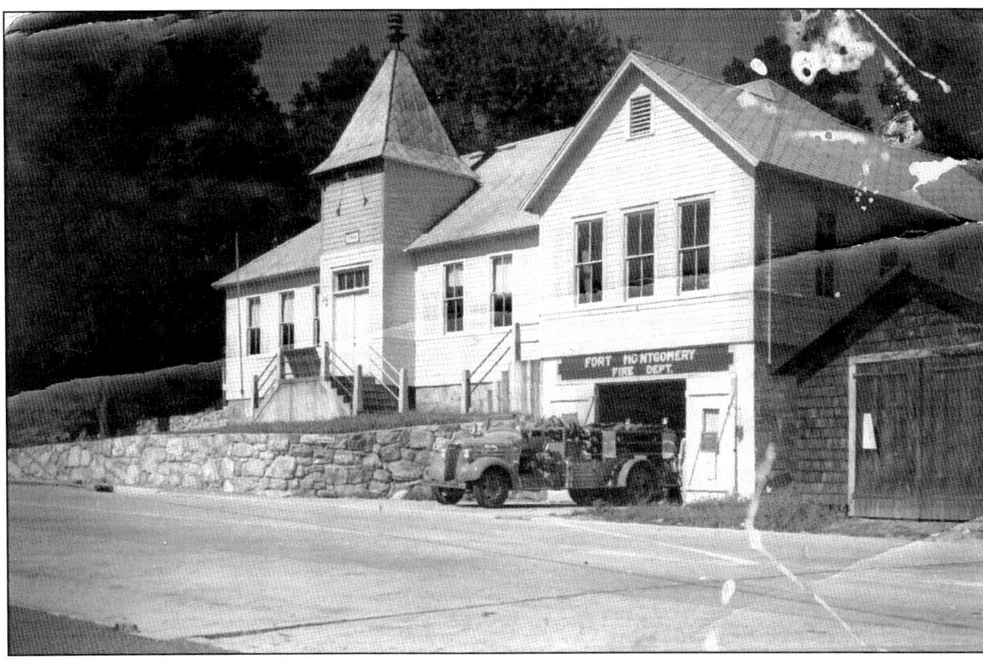

Fort Montgomery Firehouse. When a new school was built in Fort Montgomery in the early 1930s, the old school was converted into the two-bay Fort Montgomery Firehouse. In this 1933 view, the department's first truck, a Ford, is parked in the driveway. Many organizations held events here, making it a true community center. (Fort Montgomery Fire Department Archives.)

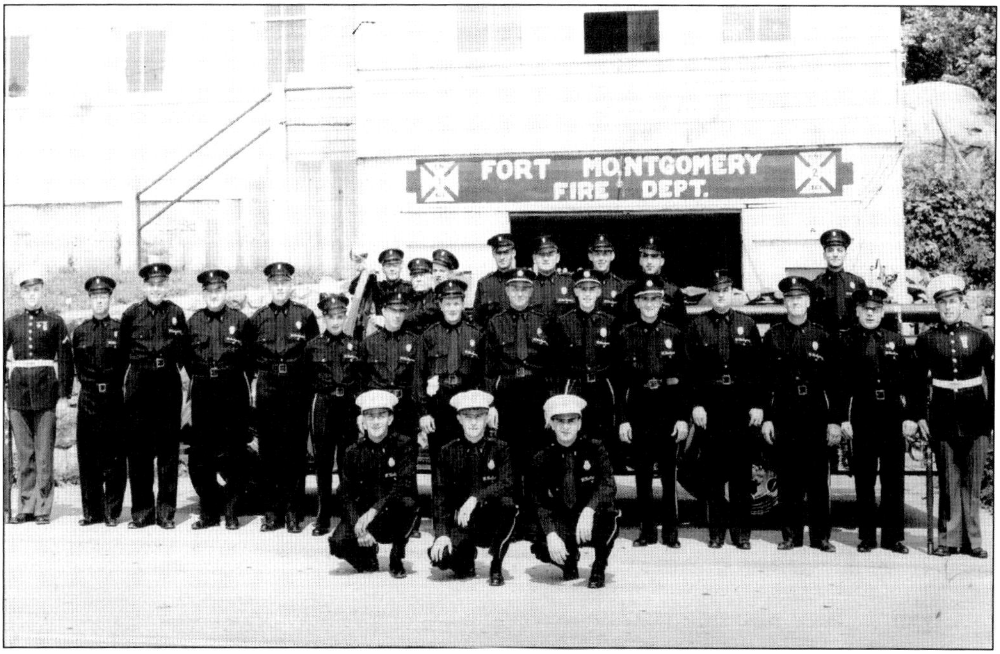

FORT MONTGOMERY FIRE DEPARTMENT. Formed in 1932, the Fort Montgomery Fire Department started its history of community service with two vehicles: a second-hand Ford fire truck and a GMC converted into a chemical truck. In this 1937 photograph, members pose in front of their first firehouse. Barely visible behind them is their third truck, a new pumper. (Gunza Collection.)

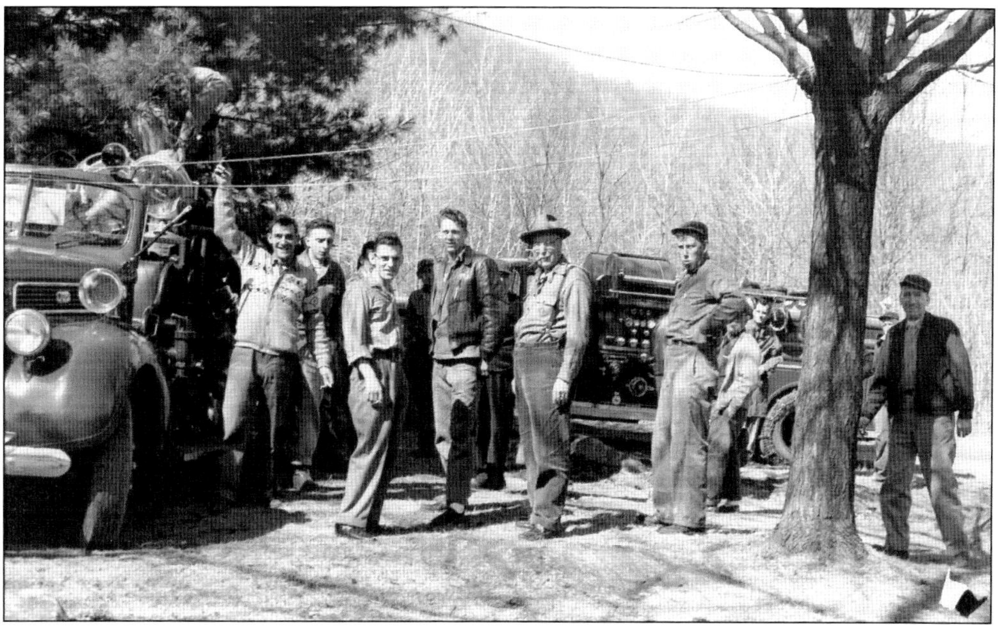

FIRE CALL. Members of the Fort Montgomery Volunteer Fire Department rest after putting out a fire on Mine Road. Throughout the Town of Highlands, volunteers who respond to an emergency drop work and chores to come to the aid of the community. Pictured here, standing in front, from left to right, are Jack Galu, Lou Discenza, Thomas W. W. Armstrong, Stan Konopko, William Doherty, Charles Bailey, and James Forrester. (Fort Montgomery Fire Department Archives.)

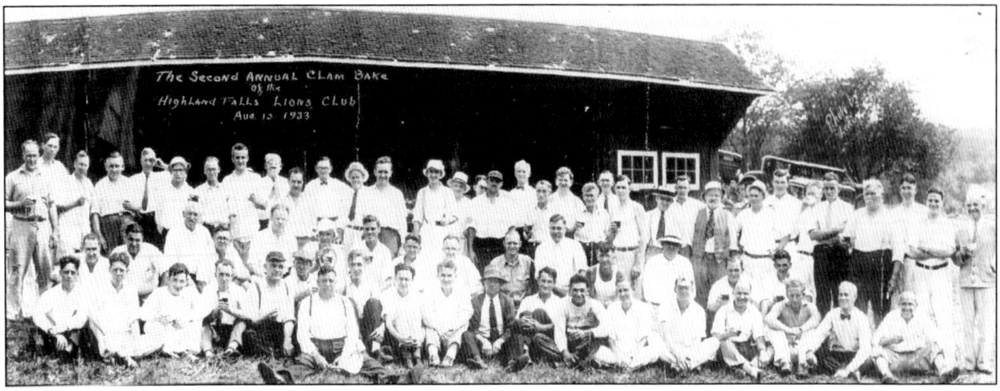

LIONS CLUB CLAMBAKE. More than 40 members of the Highland Falls Lions Club attended the annual clambake at Round Pond in August 1932. The *News of the Highlands* reported that the festivities included a swatball game in which Paul Mahan was the "Babe Ruth" of the day. The reporter jokingly added that there was "much clowning . . . with no casualties." (Kopald Collection.)

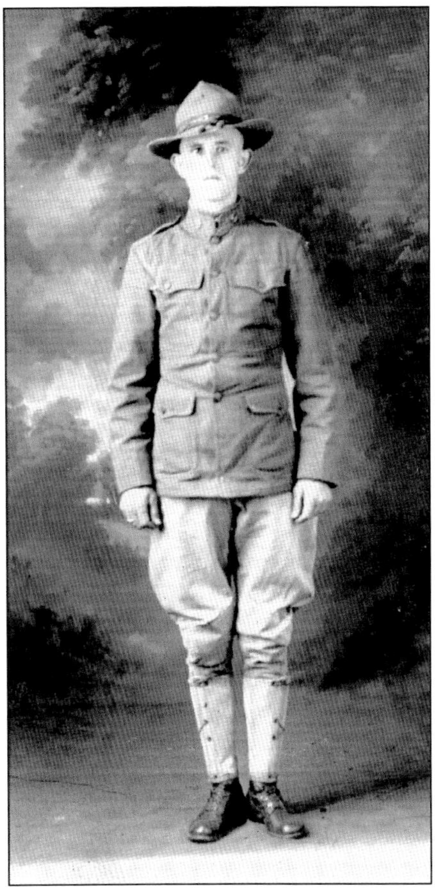

CHARLES GRABER, 1918. Born and raised in Highland Falls, Charles Graber stands in his World War I army uniform, a wool tunic and trousers and felt hat. When fully equipped, he would carry a blanket roll, small shovel, canteen, and rifle. He was one of many doughboys and sailors from the Town of Highlands who served in the Great War. Afterward he joined his father's construction firm, which built Sacred Heart School. (Graber Collection.)

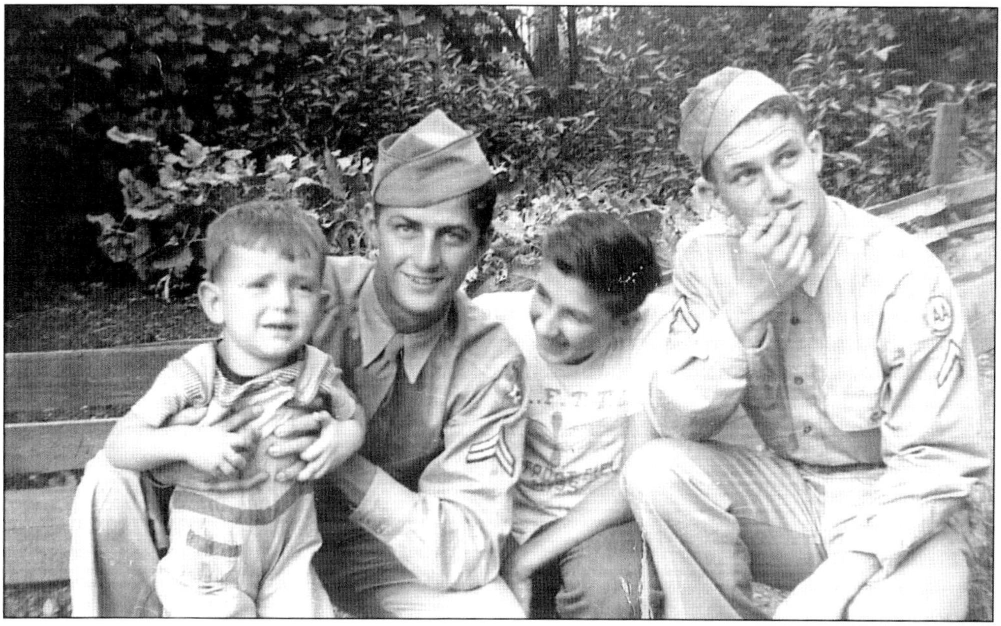

FRIENDS, 1943. On leave after army training, childhood friends Frank Murphy and Charles Durning sit with local boys George Bock and Thomas Murphy. Both soldiers later participated in the Battle of the Bulge. After World War II, Frank Murphy returned home to raise a family in Highland Falls. Charles Durning moved away to pursue a distinguished acting career. He has won a Tony, four Emmys, and two Academy Award nominations. (Murphy Collection.)

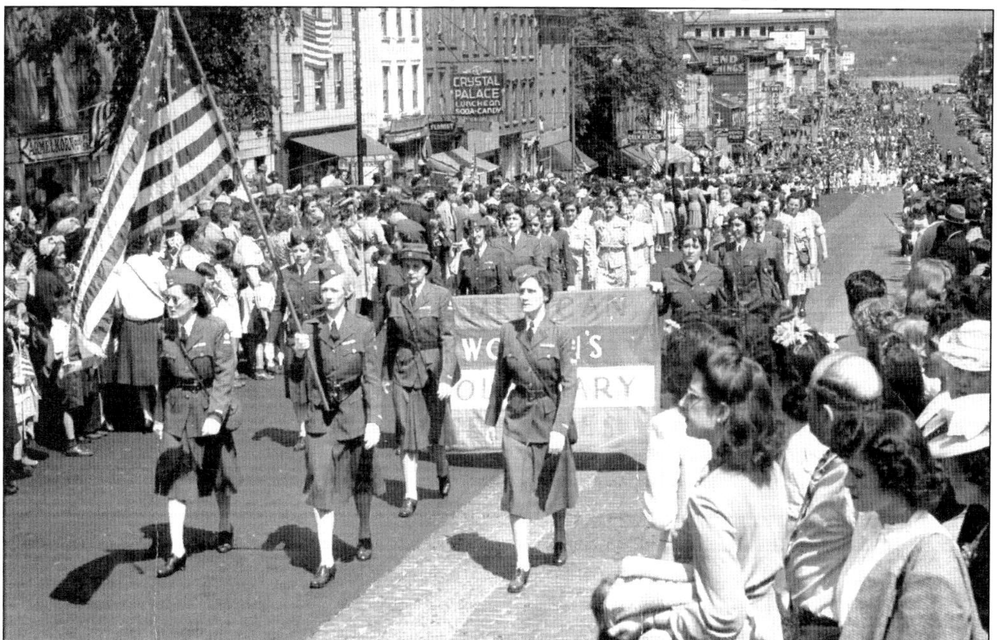

SUZIE SWIM, 1944. Parading in Newburgh as a member of the American Women's Voluntary Services is Suzie Rose Swim, to the left behind the flag bearer. During the Depression and World War II, she served as social worker for the Town of Highlands and is still remembered for her compassion and assistance to those in need. (Yagel Collection.)

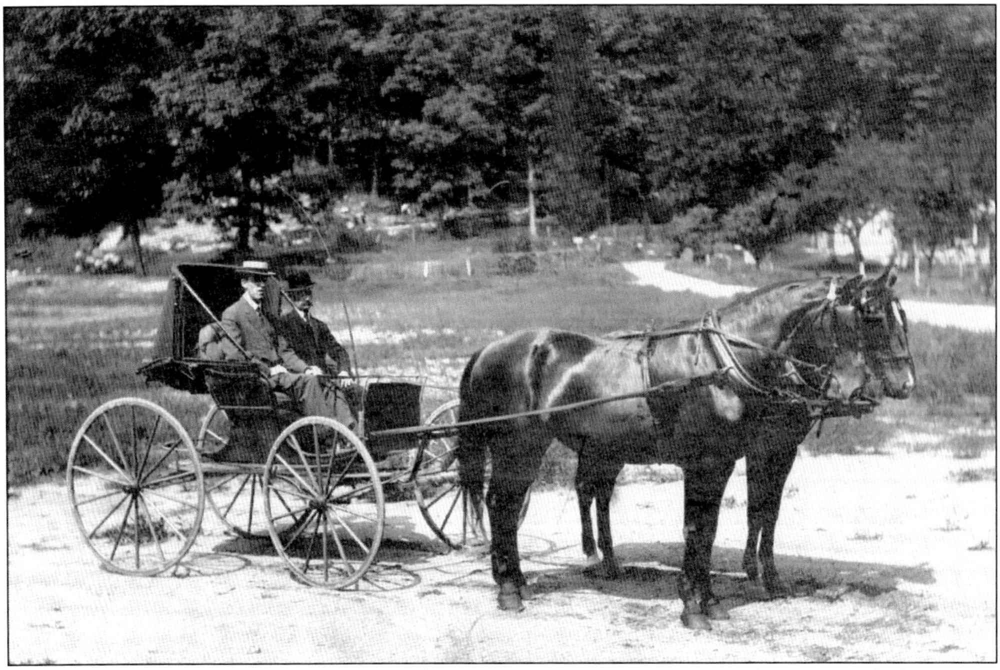

DR. MCMENAMIN, 1908. Admired for his competence, generosity, and civic-mindedness, Dr. Joseph McMenamin practiced medicine in the Town of Highlands from 1904 to 1944. Here, he holds the reins of his buggy as he rides with a friend at Roe Park. "House call" had a literal meaning in those days. In 1906, the *News of the Highlands* reported that Dr. McMenamin performed appendectomies in the homes of Daniel Weyant and Wesley Conley "with satisfactory results." (Highland Falls Library Archives.)

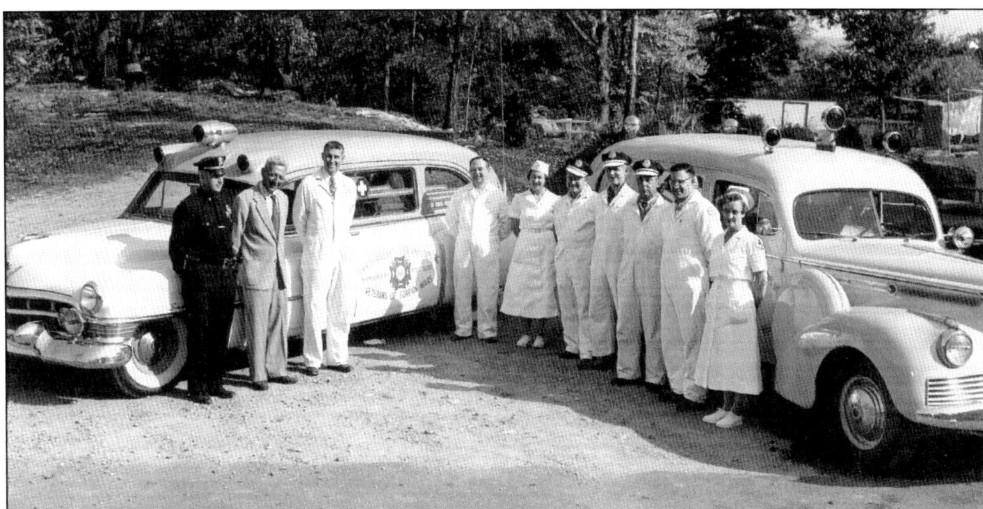

AMBULANCE CORPS. The Town of Highlands Ambulance Corps stands proudly in front of two ambulances about 1957. Corps members had succeeded in acquiring two used vehicles under the sponsorship of the Veterans of Foreign Wars. Gathered here, from left to right, are chief of police Murton Church, Mayor Lorentz Graber, Wendell Tonneson, Joseph Zint, Pearl Christolon, Henry Knapp, Henry Cox, unidentified, Vince Julian, and Edith Brogi. (Graber Collection.)

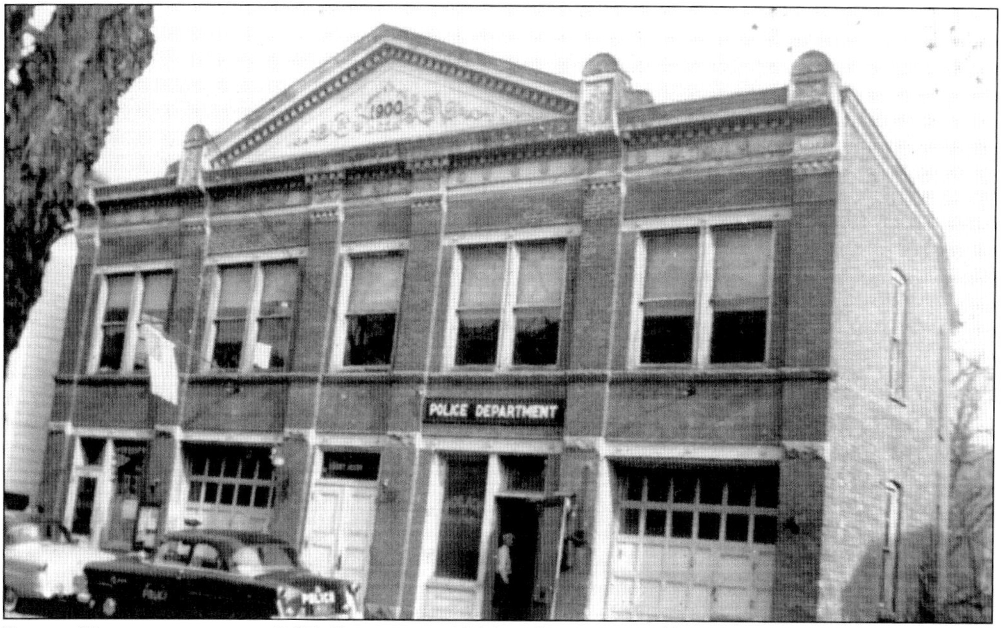

POLICE DEPARTMENT, C. 1955. Starting in 1906 with just one village policeman (Bernard Kelly), the combined force of the Village of Highland Falls and Town of Highlands Police Departments has grown to 36 highly trained officers. Town hall was the former headquarters. West Point is protected by military police, while Bear Mountain is protected by the Palisades Interstate Park Police, a division of the Office of Parks, Recreation, and Historic Preservation New York State Park Police. (Weyant Collection.)

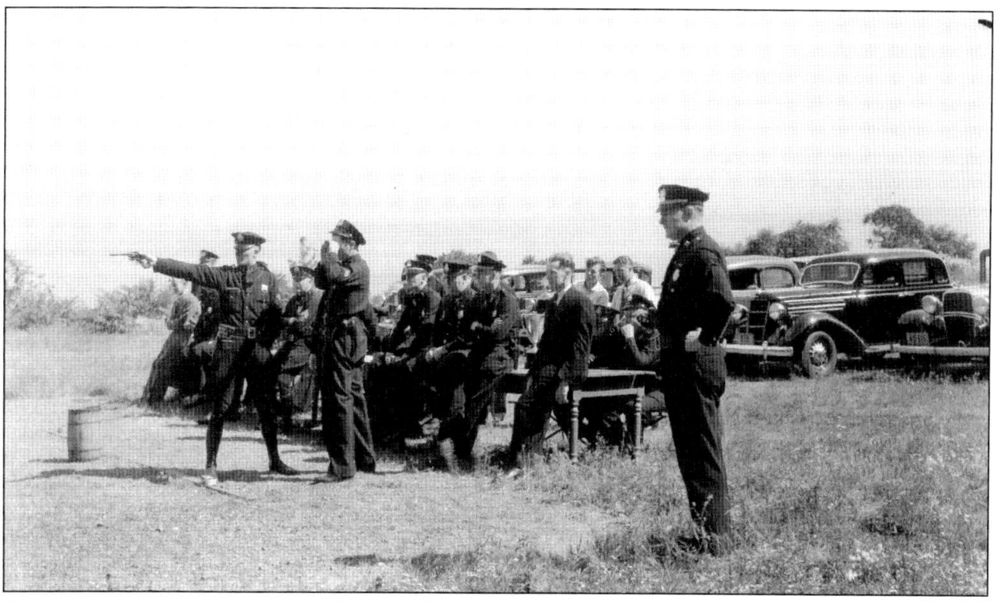

PALISADES INTERSTATE PARK POLICE. By the time of this 1930s photograph, the Palisades Interstate Park Police Department had grown from one part-time law enforcement official in 1905 to a full-time staff of professionals. Here, officers engage in shooting practice under the watchful eye of their supervisors. Known as excellent marksmen, the park police had an award-winning pistol team. (Wallace Collection.)

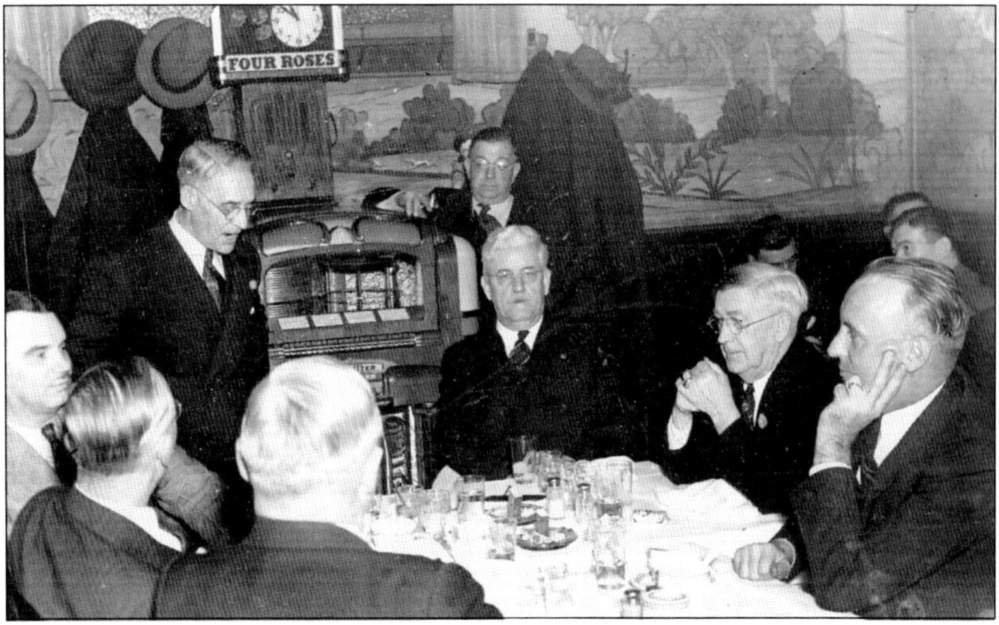

TOWN LEADERS, 1937. With fedoras and topcoats as a backdrop, Mayor James Davis addresses town leaders at Benny Haven's Restaurant. Davis led Highland Falls throughout the Depression. Economic hardships were not as severe in the Highlands as in the rest of the country because of the various opportunities for work. The military academy remained in operation, munitions facility on nearby Iona Island needed staffing, and the Civilian Conservation Corps had several camps in the vacinity. (Baker Collection.)

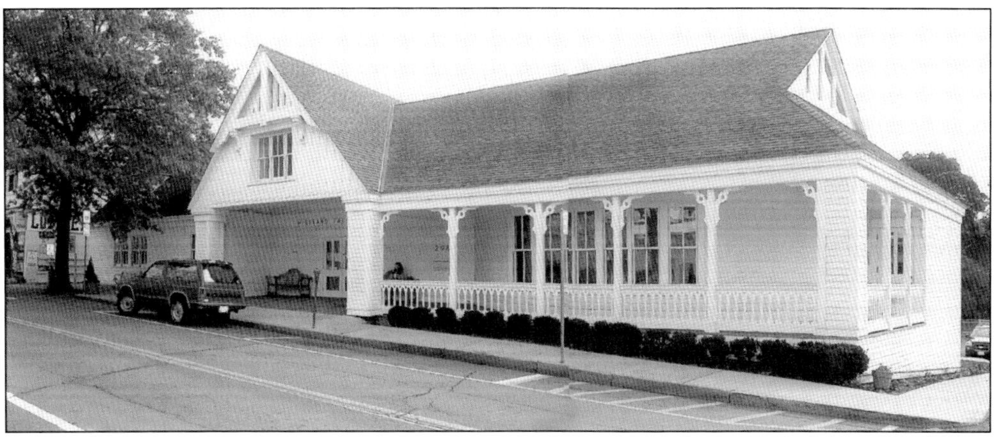

HIGHLAND FALLS LIBRARY. The award-winning architecture of the Highland Falls Library has enhanced Main Street since 2001. A library has existed continuously on this property, a gift of Frances Tracy Morgan, since 1883 when the Highland Falls Library and Reading Rooms first opened to the public. Originally, the building included a reading room and a game room primarily for men and boys. Ladies were only allowed to attend on Saturday evenings. (Highland Falls Library.)

Nine

RECREATION

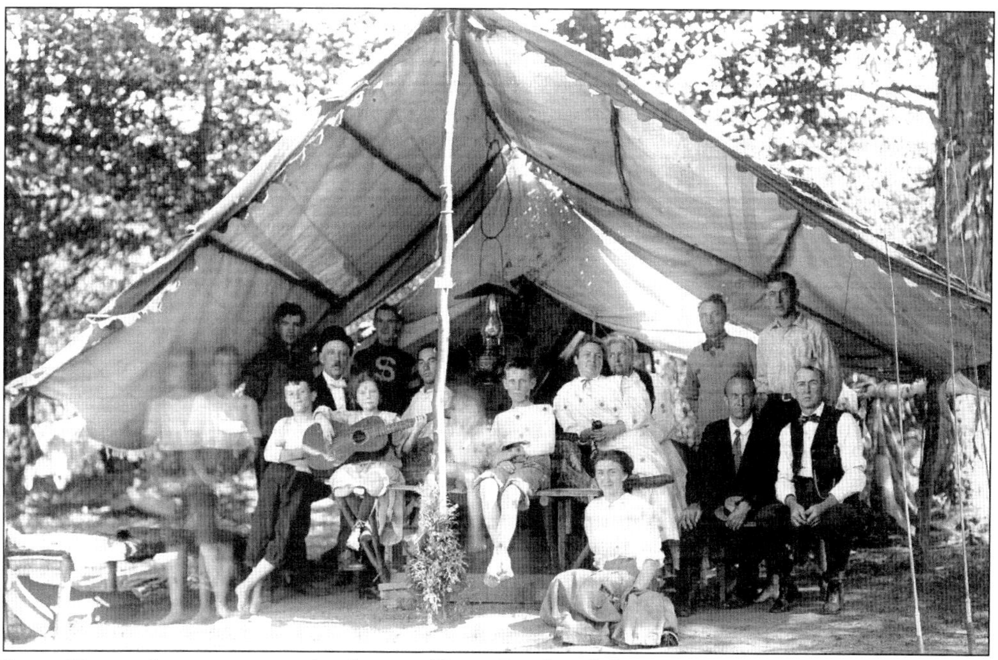

LONG POND. A century ago, the shores of Long Pond and the surrounding lakes were filled with small cabins and tents during the summer months. Harris Scott's camp, pictured here in 1919, is a good example. Although overnight camping is no longer permitted, summer still brings parents and delighted children to swim and dig in the sand. (Yagel Collection.)

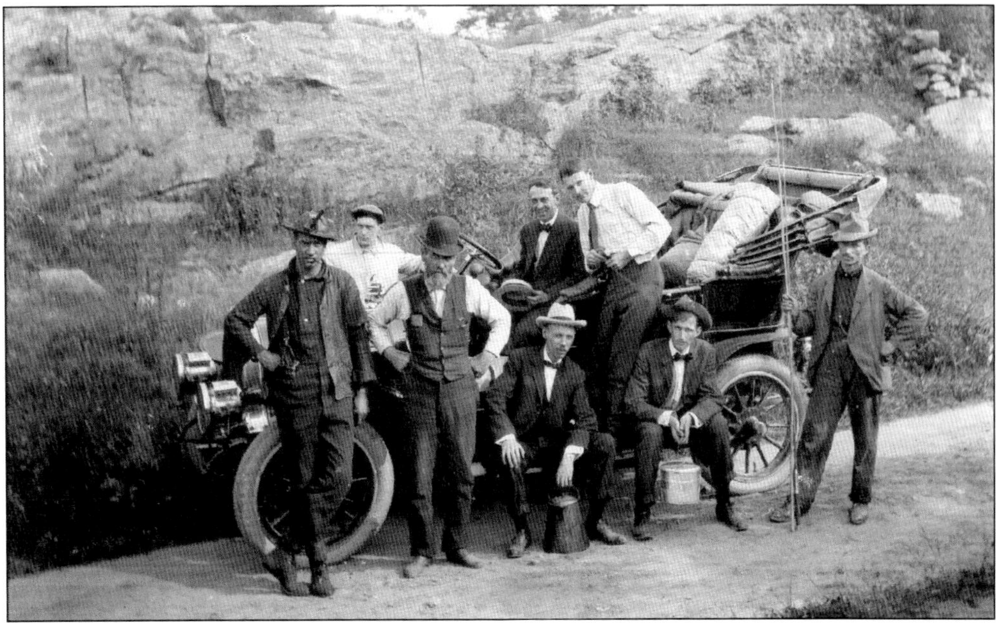

AUTOCAMPING. "Gypsying," or autocamping, was born with the automobile. After packing the car with food, blankets, clothes, repair kits, and other necessities, motorists found a spot along the road and set up camp. Highlands writer-photographer William Howell recorded this camping trip to the Forest of Dean in 1907. He can be seen third from right pulling a string tied to his camera shutter, capturing this moment with friends. (PIPC Archives.)

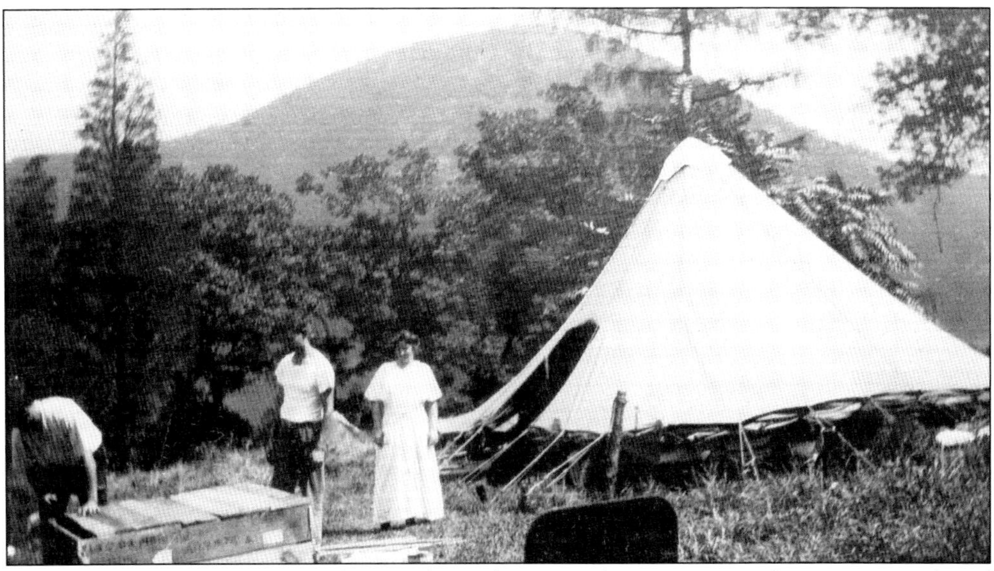

TENTING TONIGHT. Annie and Samuel Smith pause after setting up their tent as a friend unpacks a box of supplies. In the early 1900s, campers often brought their tents with them on the trains of the West Shore Line from New York City. The Smiths owned this piece of land in Fort Montgomery but later had to sell it, as the property was needed for the approach road to the Bear Mountain Bridge. (Burley Collection.)

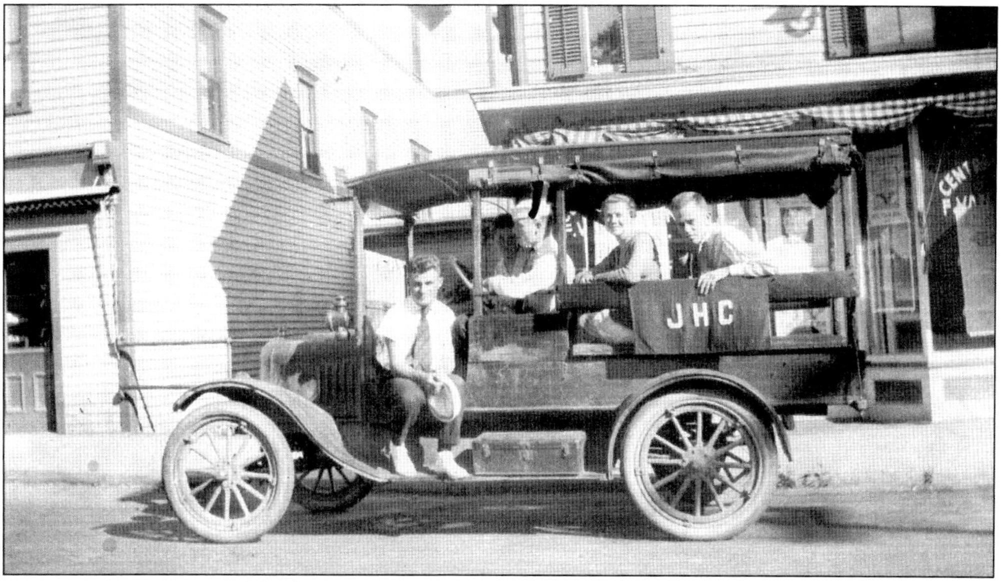

CAMP, C. 1922. One of the best-known camps in Fort Montgomery was the Juliette Hollenback Camp on Mine Road. Sponsored by Willoughby House in Brooklyn, it consisted of small cabins and tents, as well as a common building housing a recreation room and library. Prospective campers applied by mail for a two-week stay. This jitney transported campers from the railroad station or steamboat dock. (THHS Archives.)

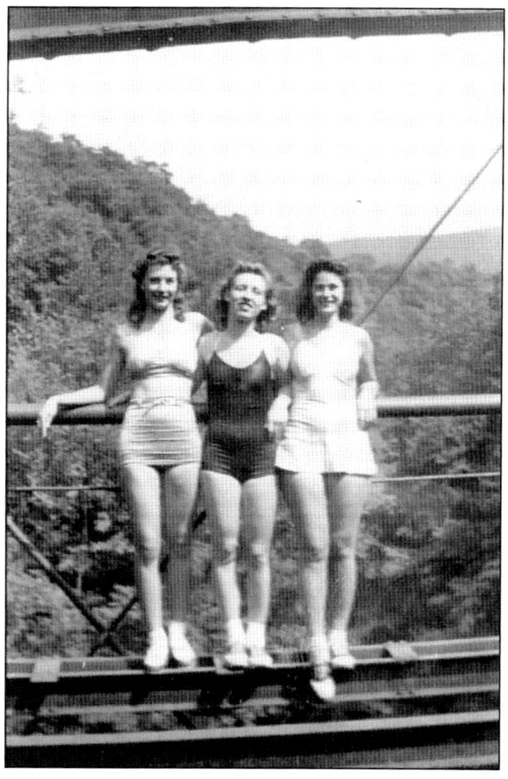

BRIDGE BEAUTIES, C. 1938. Three bathing beauties—from left to right, Ruth Ruscelli (née Williams), Winnie Steinmetz (née Martin), and Anne Burley (née Smith)—pose on the old bridge over the Popolopen Dam at Hell Hole. For several years the metal structure of this old bridge remained in place, although the wooden roadbed had been demolished. It was a popular, though dangerous, place to climb. (Burley Collection.)

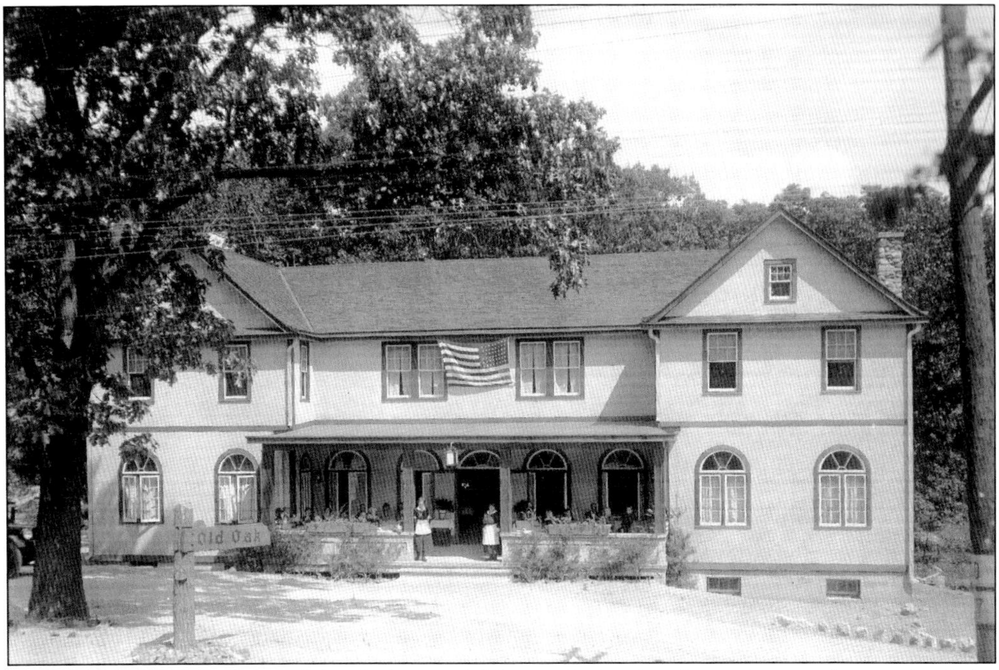

OLD OAK INN. Members of the Cobey and Morganthaler families relax on the porch of the Old Oak Inn on a pleasant day in 1925. Uniformed waitresses stand ready to serve them. With its restaurant, ballroom, and ideal Fort Montgomery location, the Old Oak was popular with travelers and locals alike. (Scott Collection.)

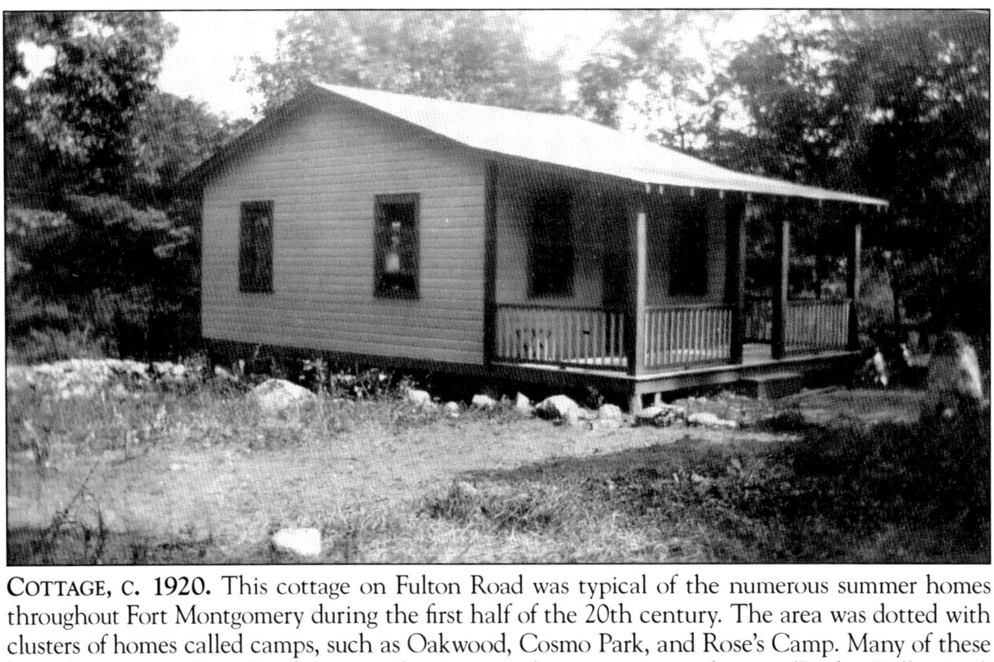

COTTAGE, C. 1920. This cottage on Fulton Road was typical of the numerous summer homes throughout Fort Montgomery during the first half of the 20th century. The area was dotted with clusters of homes called camps, such as Oakwood, Cosmo Park, and Rose's Camp. Many of these bungalows were enlarged and renovated, existing today as permanent homes. (Burley Collection.)

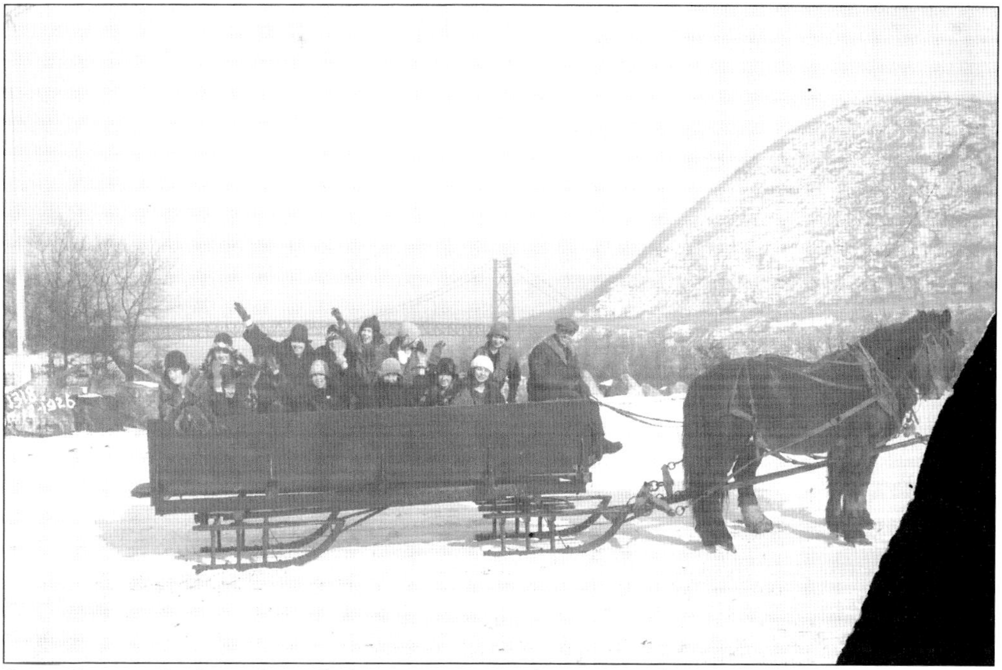

OPEN SLEIGH. Dashing through the snow in a two-horse open sleigh, a party of exuberant ladies enjoys some fresh winter air in 1926. Looking north, this view reveals the Bear Mountain Bridge in the background, with Anthony's Nose to the east. (THHS Archives.)

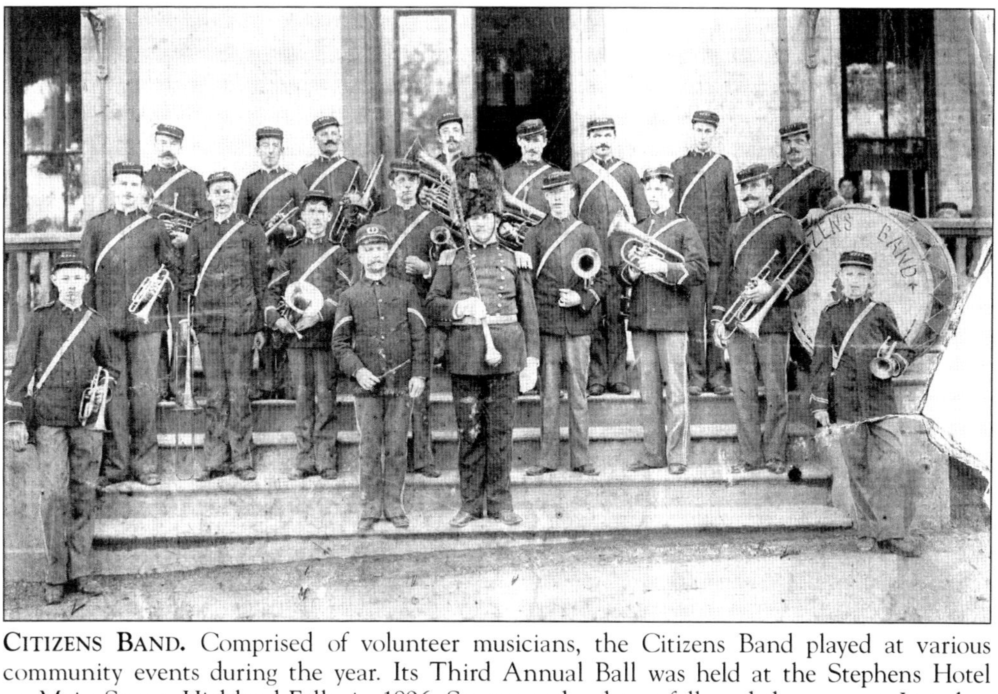

CITIZENS BAND. Comprised of volunteer musicians, the Citizens Band played at various community events during the year. Its Third Annual Ball was held at the Stephens Hotel on Main Street, Highland Falls, in 1896. Supper and a dance followed the concert. Listed as "Committee of Arrangements" members were W. Stewart, Carr Mount, Henry Ellen, Joseph Farrell, O. Bock, F. LaForge, C. Vollmer, and F. Yagel. (THHS Archives.)

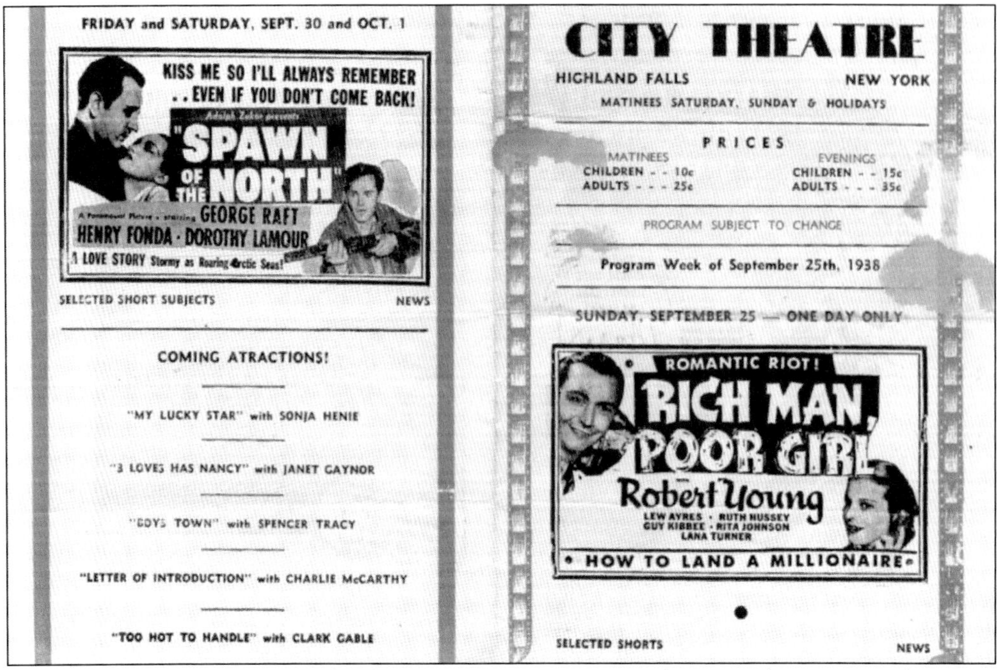

FRIDAY and SATURDAY, SEPT. 30 and OCT. 1

KISS ME SO I'LL ALWAYS REMEMBER
..EVEN IF YOU DON'T COME BACK!
"SPAWN OF THE NORTH"
GEORGE RAFT
HENRY FONDA · DOROTHY LAMOUR
A LOVE STORY Stormy as Roaring Arctic Seas!

SELECTED SHORT SUBJECTS NEWS

COMING ATRACTIONS!

"MY LUCKY STAR" with SONJA HENIE

"3 LOVES HAS NANCY" with JANET GAYNOR

"BOYS TOWN" with SPENCER TRACY

"LETTER OF INTRODUCTION" with CHARLIE McCARTHY

"TOO HOT TO HANDLE" with CLARK GABLE

CITY THEATRE
HIGHLAND FALLS NEW YORK
MATINEES SATURDAY, SUNDAY & HOLIDAYS

PRICES

MATINEES	EVENINGS
CHILDREN - - 10c	CHILDREN - - 15c
ADULTS - - - 25c	ADULTS - - - 35c

PROGRAM SUBJECT TO CHANGE

Program Week of September 25th, 1938

SUNDAY, SEPTEMBER 25 — ONE DAY ONLY

ROMANTIC RIOT!
RICH MAN, POOR GIRL
Robert Young
LEW AYRES · RUTH HUSSEY
GUY KIBBEE · RITA JOHNSON
LANA TURNER
• HOW TO LAND A MILLIONAIRE •

SELECTED SHORTS NEWS

CITY THEATRE, 1938. Destined to become a town institution, the City Theatre opened in 1914. Over time it converted from short silent films to full-length silent movies and to talkies. Before television, people flocked to the theater, which advertised its change of programs three times a week, to see their favorite stars and to watch newsreels of current events. After a 55-year run, the City Theatre closed in 1969. (Gunza Collection.)

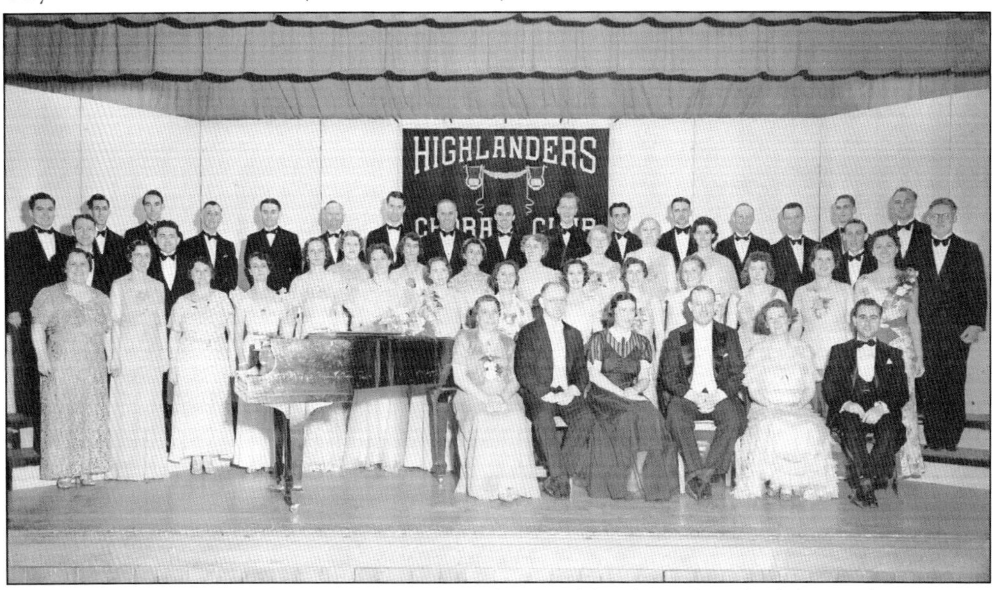

HIGHLANDERS. Known for exceptional musicality, Highlanders Choral Club members pose in April 1938 at their Fifth Annual Spring Concert. Six months of weekly practices had paid off. In a review of the show, the *News of the Highlands* called it "a stirring triumph which brought glory to the organization." As customary, following the concert the group had a banquet and party at the Bear Mountain Inn. (Bosch Collection.)

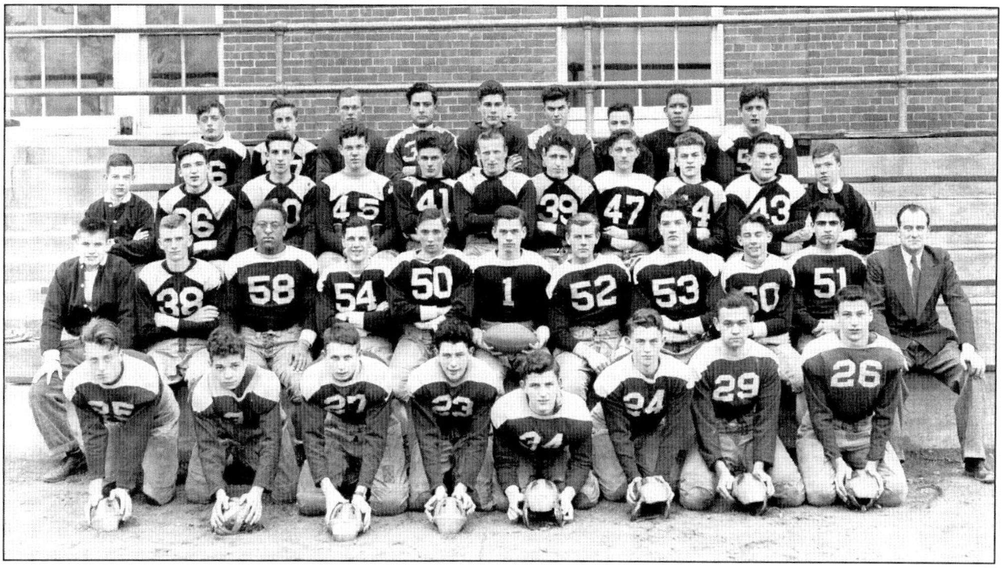

RAIDER FOOTBALL. Known as the Red Raiders, the 1940 Highland Falls High School football team was a formidable squad. Like the school's student body, it was composed of teens from Fort Montgomery, Highland Falls, Bear Mountain, and West Point. Guided by rookie coach Waldo Wood and captained by Marty Maher, the team included "Slugger" Murphy, "Jiggs" Congigliere, "Moon" McIntyre, "Socko" Vanzetta, and future actor Charles Durning. (Murphy Collection.)

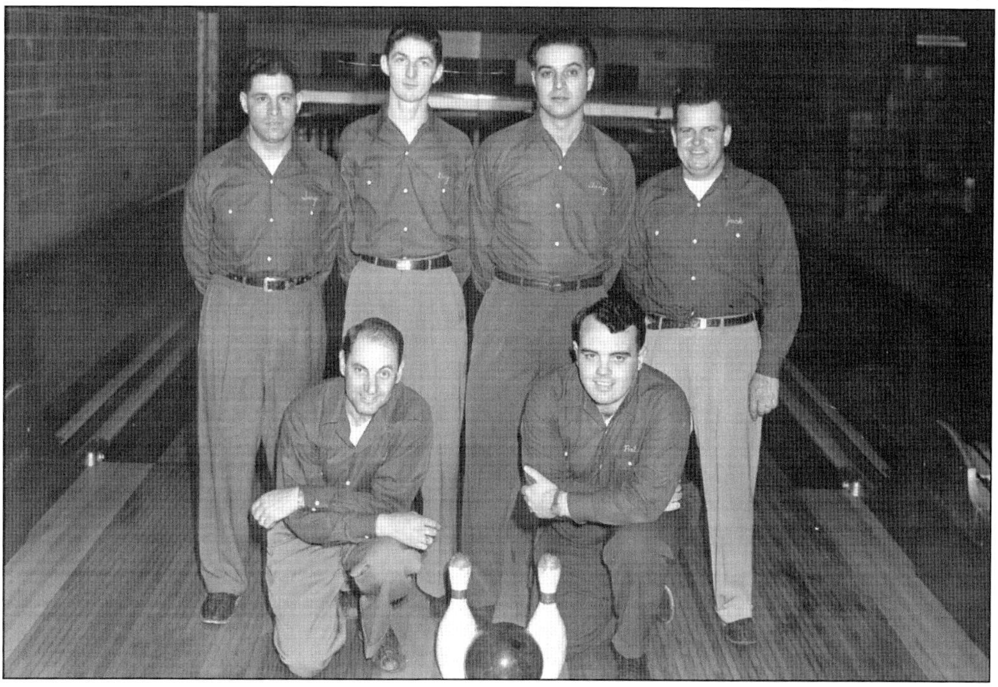

BOWLING TEAM. From the 1930s through the 1970s, the nationwide popularity of bowling was evident in Highland Falls and Fort Montgomery. Several men's and women's teams played and socialized at Brogi's Bowling Alley off Main Street. Private businesses such as Bavaro's Cleaners, Contour Beauty Salon, and Hogan's Funeral Home sponsored the teams. Pictured here in 1960 are six local kingpins with no time to spare. (Murphy Collection.)

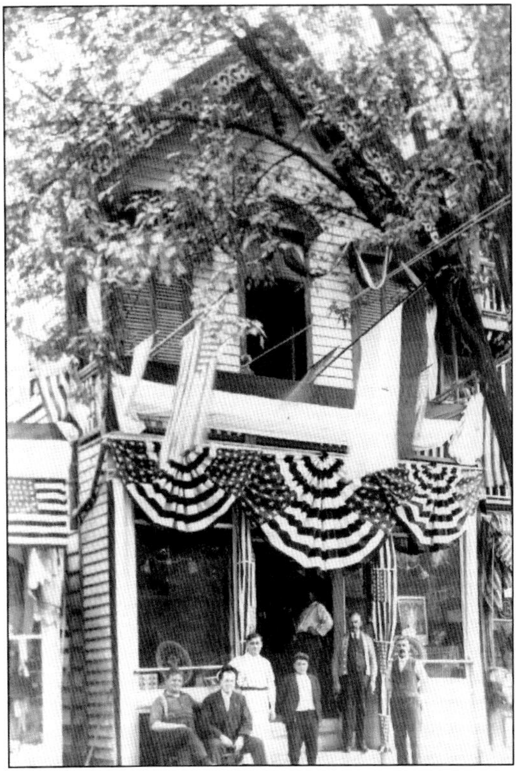

Hubner Saloon. Although the buildings remain, many of the businesses in the Town of Highlands have changed through the years. John Hubner, second from right, stands on the steps of his Main Street saloon in 1912. Later in the century Edward Rose Sr. operated the space as the Radio Bar. The building on the left is Goldsmith's Store, which eventually became B. Rose Hardware. (Gunza Collection.)

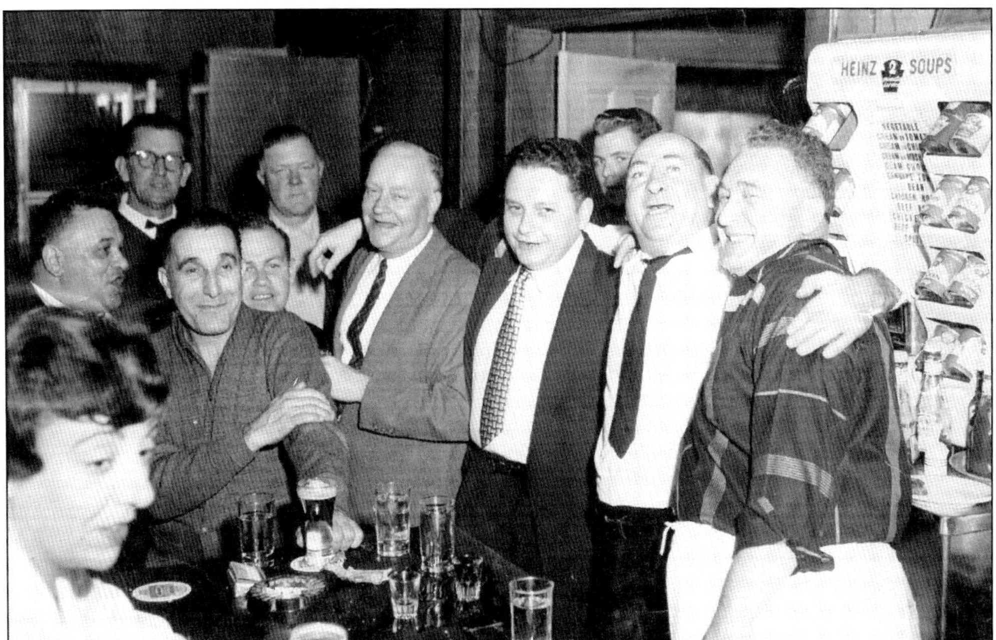

The Hilltop. One of several lively pubs in Highland Falls, the Hilltop was housed in a former firehouse perched on a hill overlooking the center of the village. Surrounded by a group of friends, John Pozo (third from right) and Charles Zint (second from right) serenade some lucky fellow customers in 1958. (Pozo Collection.)

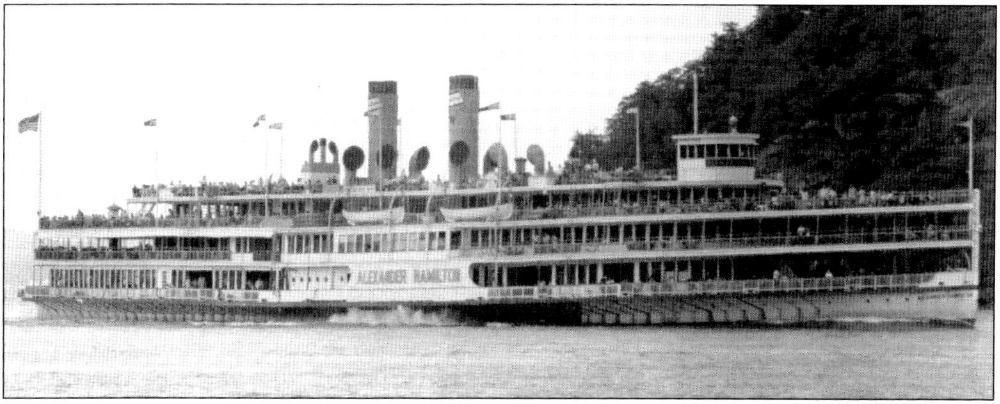

ALEXANDER HAMILTON. Launched in 1924, the *Alexander Hamilton* made its final voyage from Manhattan to Bear Mountain in September 1971. The trip marked the end of the great era of steamboat service on the Hudson. The older steamboat was replaced by a more modern diesel-powered vessel called simply the *Dayliner.* (Photograph by Fred Brennan, Gunza Collection.)

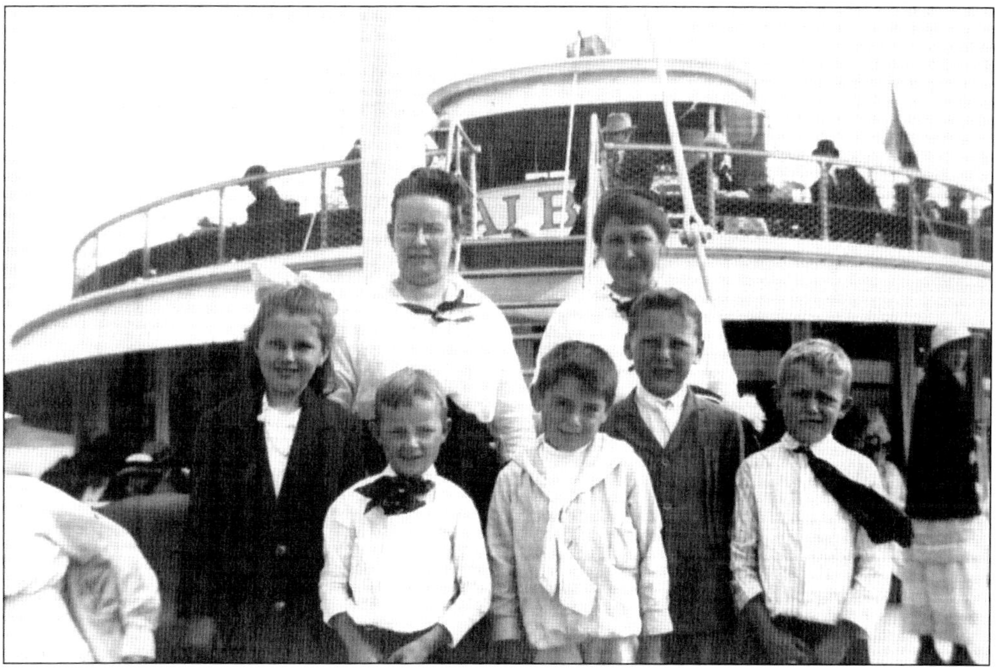

STEAMBOAT *ALBANY*, 1910. Famous for their speed and elegant appointments, the white steamers of the Hudson River Day Line were a common sight from 1863 to 1948. During the height of their popularity, the Day Line vessels serviced every landing from New York City to Troy. Aboard the *Albany* are members of the Graber and Oberle families. A popular excursion was to take the boat to Newburgh and then the trolley to Orange Lake. (Graber Collection.)

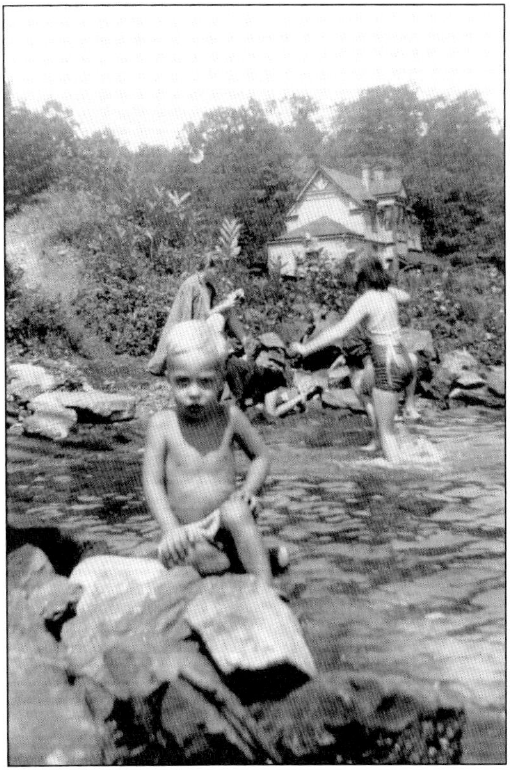

River Swim. Bruce Thomson and his mother, Eva, enjoy a dip in the Hudson River not far from their summer residence in Fort Montgomery in 1941. The elegant Victorian railroad station can be seen in the background. The Town of Highlands became a permanent home to many individuals who, motivated by happy summer memories as children, returned to settle here as adults. (Thomson Collection.)

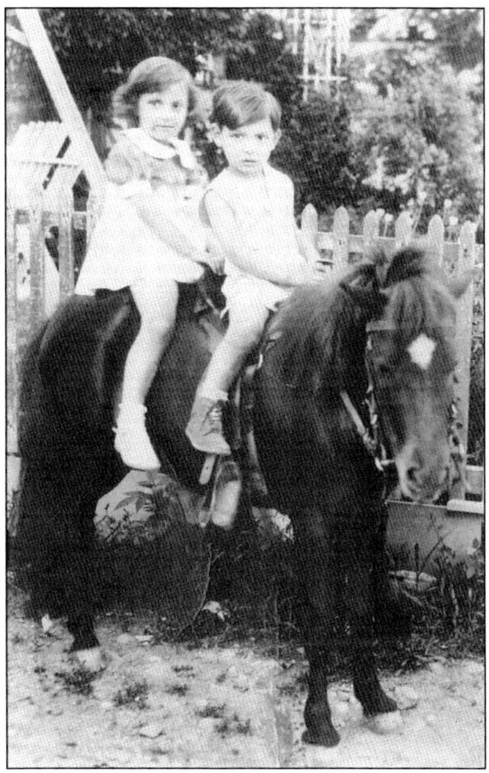

Pony Ride. The joy of a pony ride is a universal childhood experience. A generation ago, a farmer offering rides for 5¢ or 10¢ was an occasional visitor to the community. Many children eagerly took advantage of the opportunity. It was a good time for parents to capture a memory for the scrapbook. Antoinette and Rocco Galu tried out their equestrian skills at the top of Schneider Avenue in 1937. (Galu Collection.)

Ten

HOMETOWN, USA

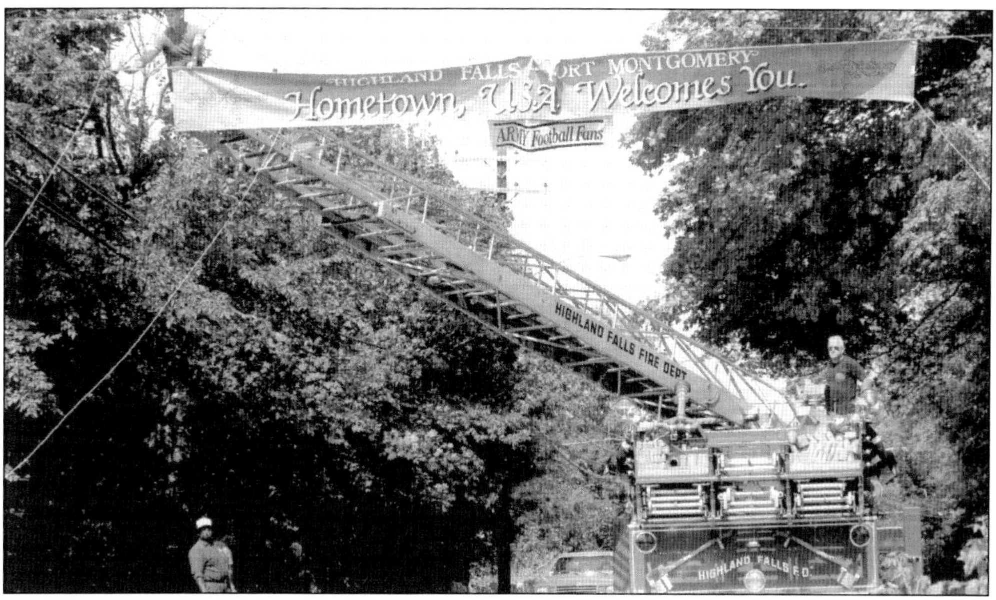

HOMETOWN, USA. The nickname "Hometown, USA" has been associated with the Town of Highlands since 1981, when it welcomed the American hostages home from Iran. To its residents, though, it has always been Hometown, USA, with its patriotic history, Main Street, and celebrations of community life. Here, Sam Bass (on the ladder), Neil Brown (standing below), and John Gunza (standing on the truck) of the Highland Falls Fire Department display a welcome sign to Army Football fans. (Gunza Collection; photograph by News of the Highlands.)

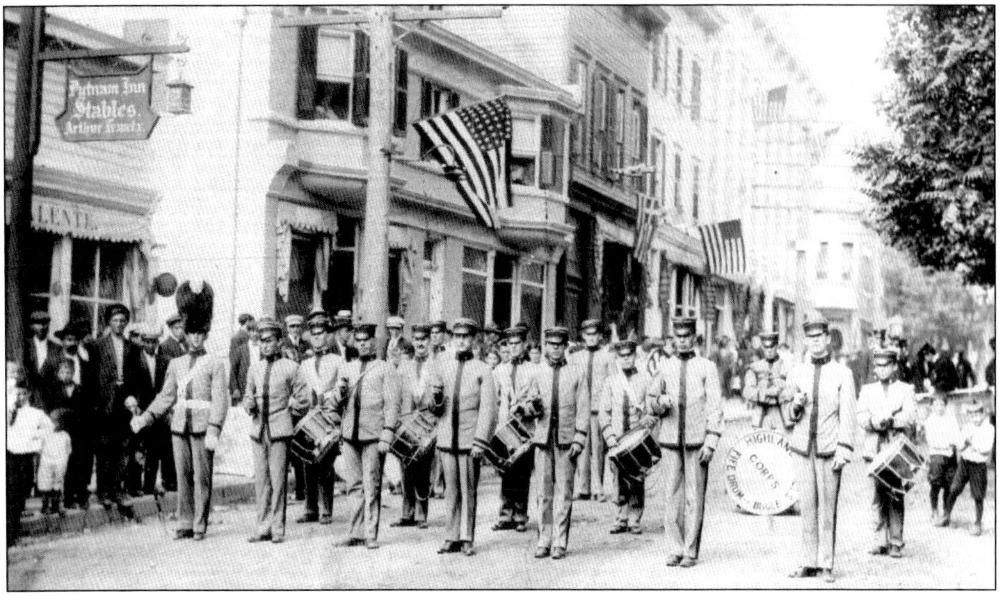

HUDSON-FULTON CELEBRATION. The Highland Falls Bugle Corps parades down Main Street for the Hudson-Fulton Celebration of 1909. The international commemoration included local parades and an elaborate naval and airship parade from Manhattan to Troy. Dirigibles and hot-air balloons soared high above the river. Wilbur Wright flew his own plane. Among the committee of prominent organizers were residents John Bigelow, J. P. Morgan, Charles F. Roe, and Herbert Satterlee. (Gunza Collection.)

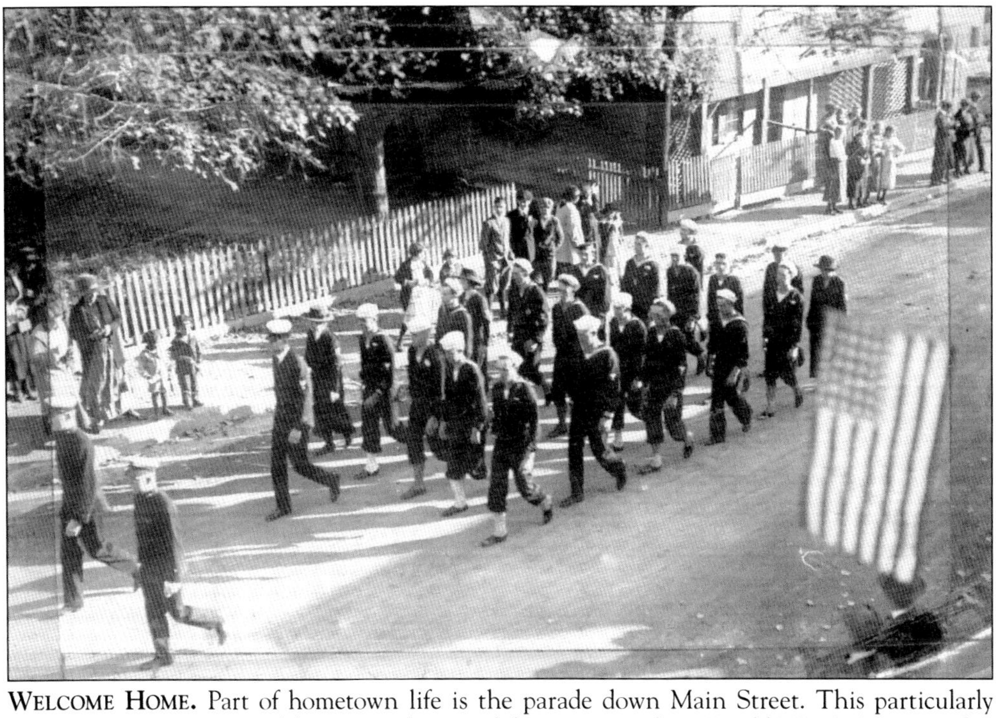

WELCOME HOME. Part of hometown life is the parade down Main Street. This particularly poignant view is a 1919 celebration in honor of the returnees from World War I. A 48-star flag hangs proudly over this group of uniformed sailors and naval officers. (THHS Archives.)

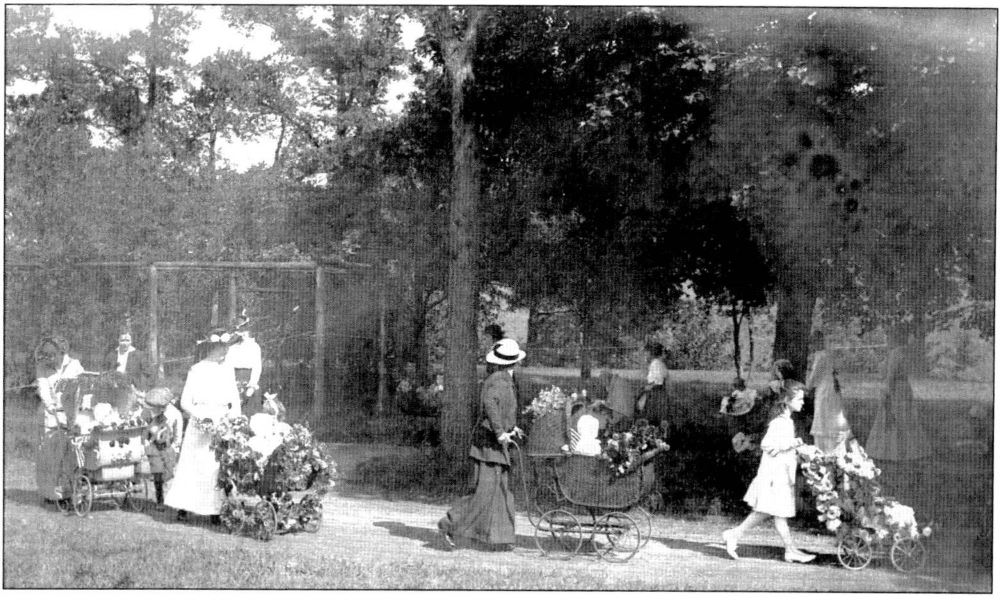

BABY PARADE. The Highland Fling of 1915 was a library fund-raiser organized by Jenny Bigelow Tracy. Held on the estate of Herbert Satterlee, the event featured foot races, pony rides, a fortuneteller, a cake competition, a sled-dog demonstration, tennis matches, and a baby parade. "Great care had been taken decorating the carriages," Tracy wrote afterward. "With the little tots in all their glory it was a very attractive feature." (Sidamon-Eristoff Collection.)

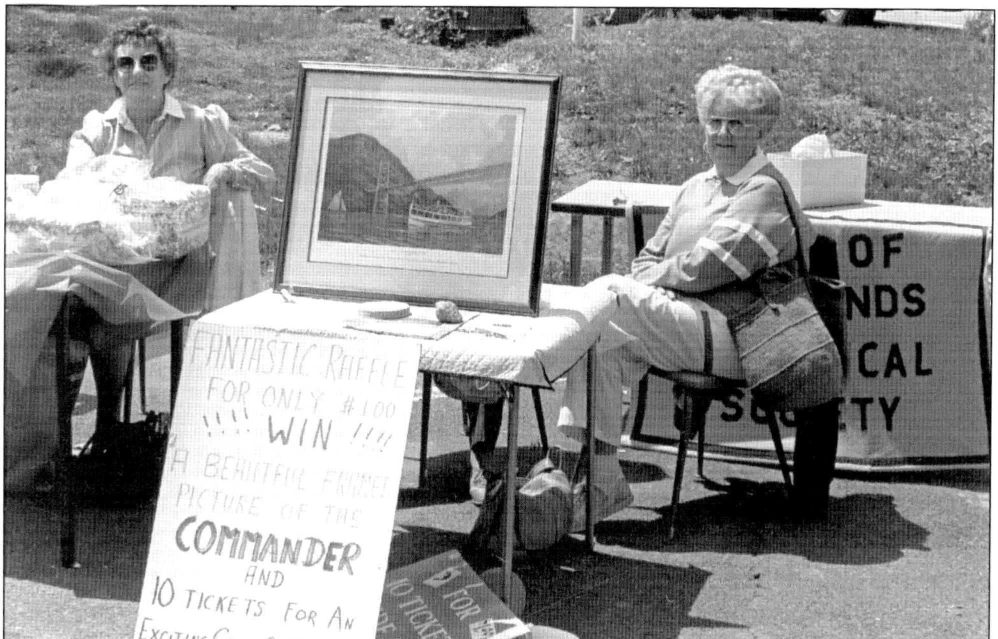

RAFFLE. The raffle is an ever-present form of hometown fund-raising. Here, Rosemary Gannon (left) and Catherine "Dolly" Baker sell chances for the benefit of the historical society at the Fall Foliage Festival. Volunteers have raised thousands of dollars for churches and other nonprofits by raffling off quilts, baskets of goodies, artwork, tickets, and sums of money. The supervised all-night bash after high school graduation ends with the raffle of a car. (Baker Collection.)

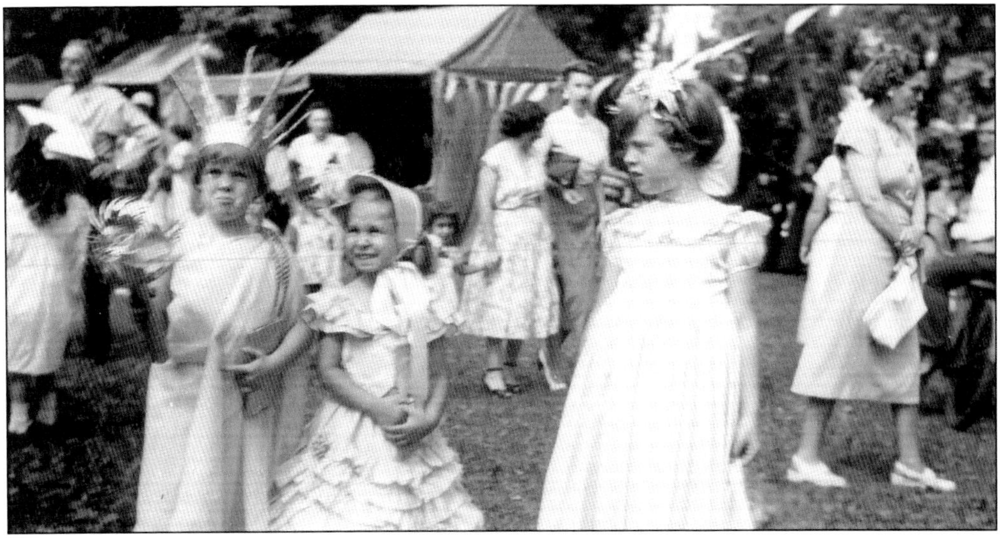

LAWN FETE. Colorful canvas booths with games, food, raffles, and prizes were part of the annual Lawn Fete sponsored by Sacred Heart Church. Begun in 1919 as a fund-raiser, it became a summer tradition that continues today. Originally held on Ladycliff's grounds, it moved to the churchyard and then to Main Street. This 1950 photograph shows, from left to right, Marcia Graber, Carol Fabritius, and Valerie Graber in costume for the festivities. (Graber Collection.)

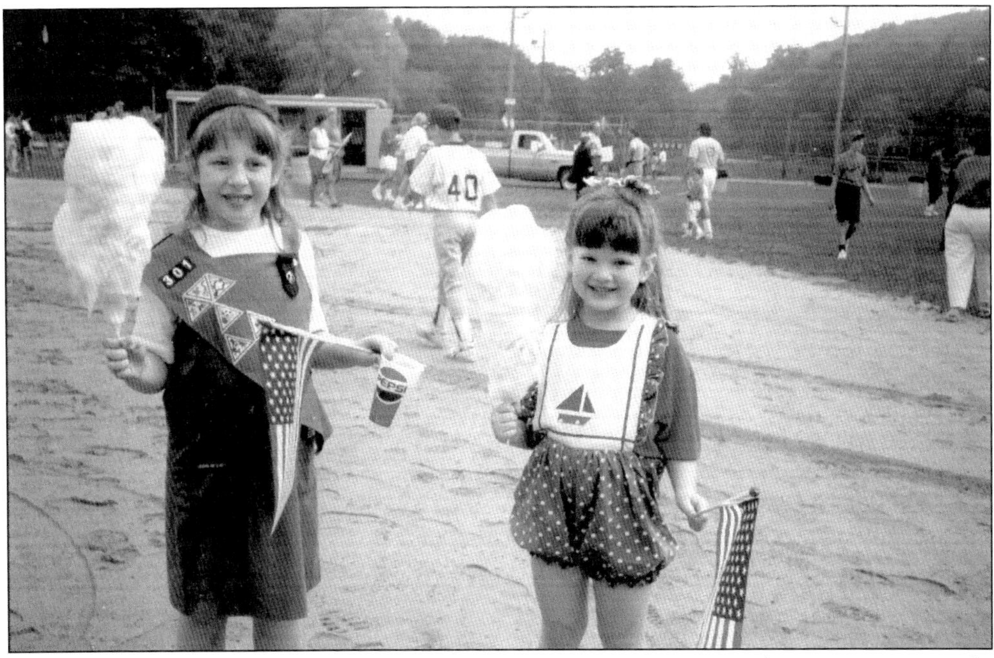

INDEPENDENCE DAY. The Fourth of July is a favorite community event. After an exciting parade, residents like Veronica (left) and Juliet Coffey enjoy treats sold by volunteer organizations at Roe Park. As the day progresses, people gather at the park, a tradition dating back to the early 1900s. The field fills with people playing, strolling, dancing the Electric Slide, and watching the competition to climb the greased pole. The day ends with spectacular fireworks. (Coffey Collection.)

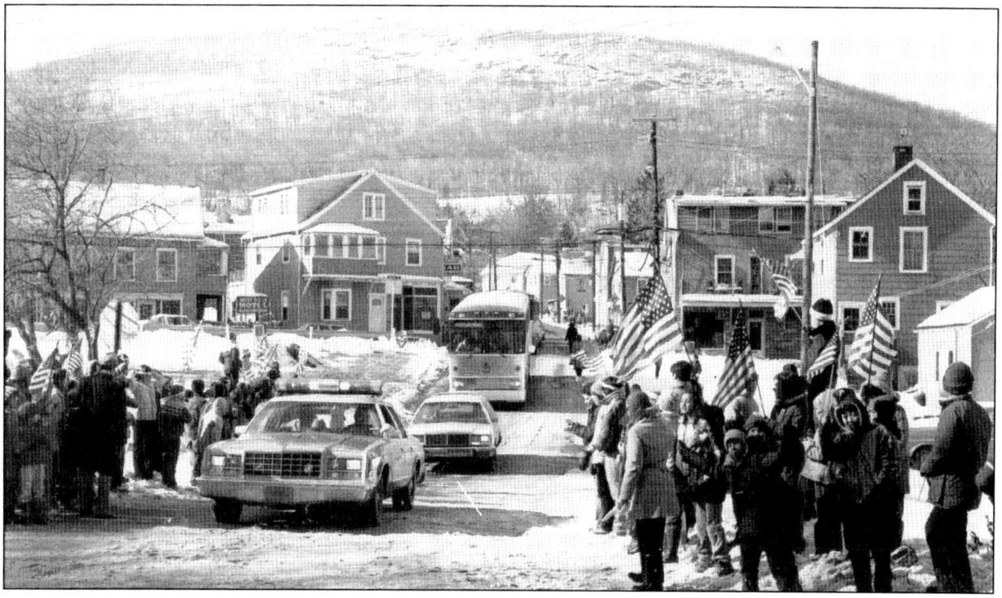

HOSTAGES RETURN. On January 25, 1981, the 52 American hostages who had been kidnapped and kept captive in Iran for 444 days were returned to the United States. After landing at Stewart Airport, the hostages were reunited with their families and bused to West Point, to enjoy some quiet time out of the public eye. Along the way, the buses came through Highland Falls, where bells from the churches rang 444 times. Boats on the Hudson sounded their horns. The town had taken upon itself the symbolic responsibility of representing all the hostages' hometowns. Residents had decorated every object in sight with yellow ribbons and American flags. In these photographs, the buses are shown traveling east down Mountain Avenue, then north to West Point, with crowds shouting joyful cheers of welcome. (Above, Gunza Collection, photograph by News of the Highlands; below, Storms Collection, photograph by Joseph V. Gill.)

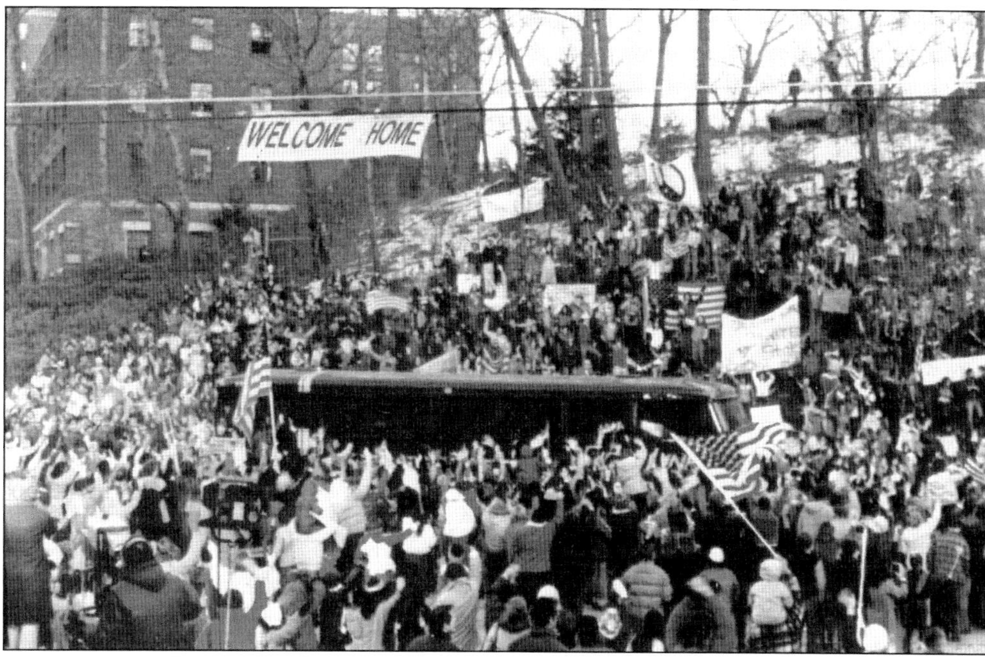

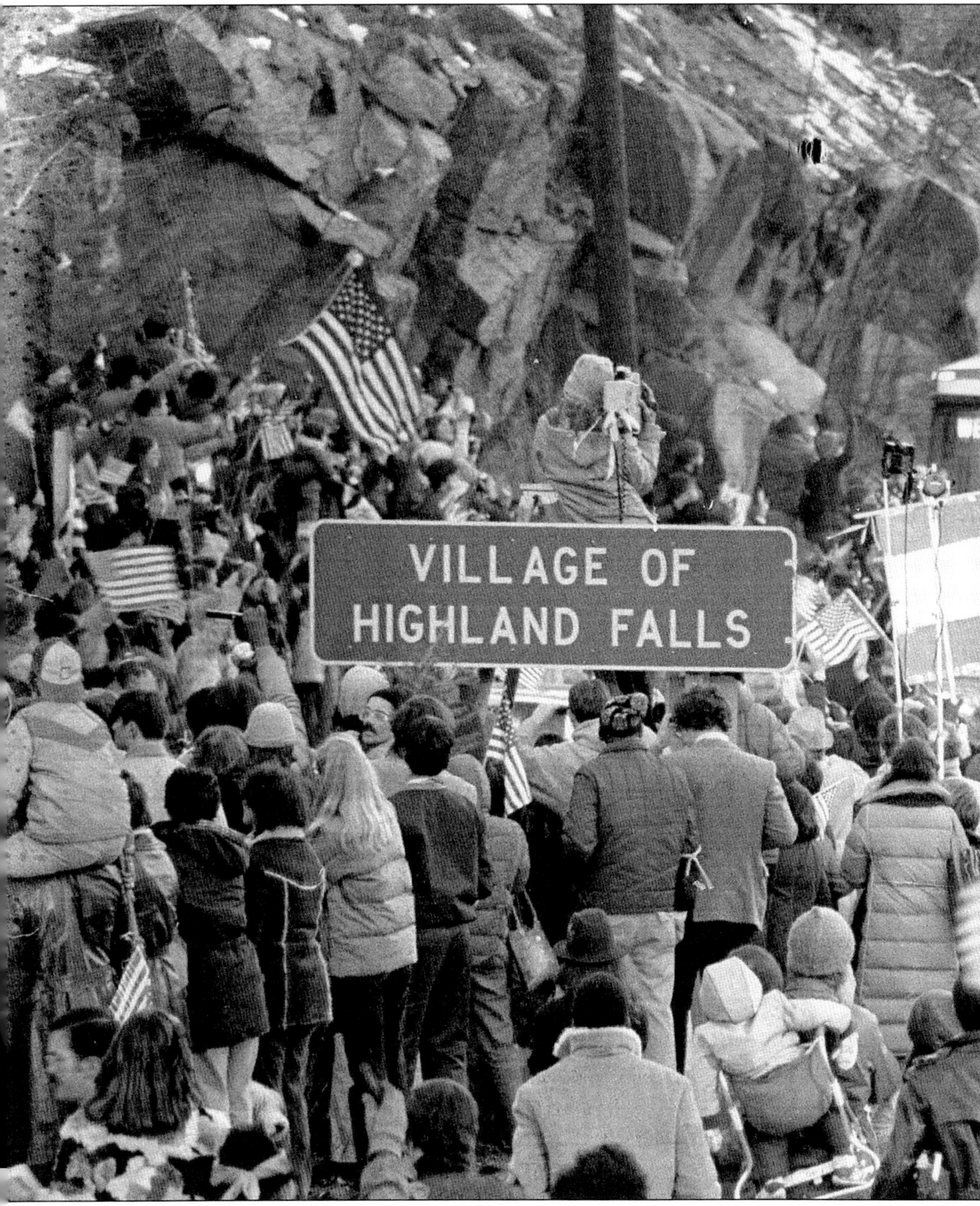

GRATEFUL AMERICANS. Upon their arrival, Lieutenant General Goodpastor, superintendent of the military academy, greeted the returnees: "Our Fellow Americans, with happy and thankful hearts we welcome you. . . . You are free. You are safe. You are home." Two days later, the following letter was received by the *News of the Highlands*: "This is an open letter to the patriotic citizens of Highland Falls. Thank you all from the bottom of my heart for turning out by the

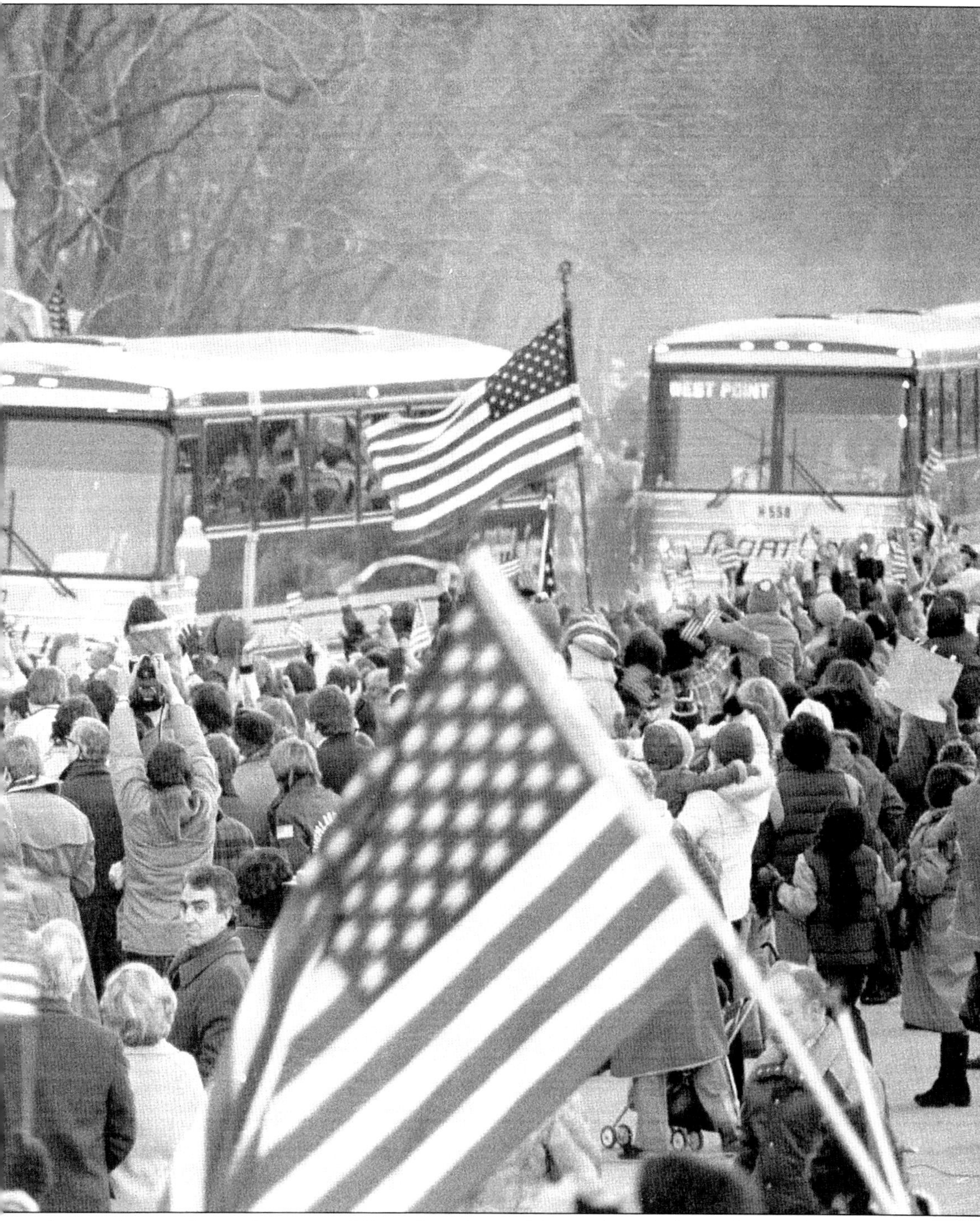

thousands to welcome home our fellow Americans. I know I speak for millions when I say that . . . we watched the news coverage and prayed that you would give the hostages the homecoming they deserved. Not only did you turn out by the thousands but there were flags, yellow ribbons and signs everywhere. It was tremendous! Thank you for representing America so well." It was signed "A Grateful American." (Associated Press.)

ACKNOWLEDGMENTS

This book is dedicated to my husband, Kevin Coffey. His collaboration, loving support, visual mind, and sense of humor made writing this book a joy. The encouragement of my daughters, Veronica and Juliet Coffey, added to the excitement of my research.

It takes a village—in this case a town—to assemble a photographic history like this.

I have been blessed with tremendous cooperation from citizens whose roots and affection for this community are deep and strong. John and June Gunza, Peter Carroll, Anne Sidamon-Eristoff, Michael and Chris Graber, Robert Scott, James and Georgia Wallace, and Arthur and Helen Yagel graciously shared their extensive knowledge of the community and their expansive collections of postcards, photographs, and documents. Suzanne Brahm, director of the Highland Falls Library, was instrumental with scholarly assistance. Town of Highlands historian Stella Bailey allowed me access to photographs at the historical society (THHS). Catherine Baker, John and Helen Bosch, Joann Brown, Thomas and Anne Burley, Carla Burns, George and Elaine Dapra, Helen Feldman, Mabel Galu, Mary Therese Hansen, Ned and Regina Kopald, Joseph and Katherine McCormick, Richard and Shirley Rose, George Sibley, James and Vivian Thomson, Vince and Louise Julian, Frank and Phyllis Murphy, Betty Storms, Frank and Lila Wallace, Bryan Weyant, and David and Georgianna Woodward shared memories and loaned me special images of their lives.

Michael Bosch, Leslie Leo, Casey Madrick, Richard Parry, June Patterson, Michael Pozo, Rev. Judith Sibley, Albert Schaut, Susan Smith, Rev. Steven Snavely, Jean Talman, *News of the Highlands* editor Fred Brennan, and *Cornwall Local* editor Joseph Gill made time in their busy workdays to answer my questions and provide photographs.

Additional details were obtained in telephone or personal interviews with Mary Lou Bullotta, William desRosiers, Roxanne Donnery, Joseph D'Onofrio, Col. James Johnson, Hattie LeBleu, Edward Lenik, Garry and Doris Lent, Edward Rose Jr., Violet Rosner, and David Weyant.

Special thanks go to Elaine McConnell and the entire staff at the Special Collections and Archives Division of the United States Military Academy (USMA) Library, Barbara Thomas of the Palisades Interstate Park Commission (PIPC) Trailside Museums and Zoo, Los Angeles Dodgers team historian Mark Langill, Regalle Asuncion of the Associated Press, Richard deKoster and Faith Herbert of the Constitution Island Association, and Marguerite Lavin of the Museum of the City of New York. Photographic credits that appear at the end of the captions name either the individuals sharing their images or the collections from which the images came.

The preparation of this book was made easier by the graceful inspiration of Mary and Stuart Clark. I am likewise indebted to my sister Jill Rose, who is always ready with her help and support. Pamela Salmon aided me with her unfailing encouragement.

Reflecting on gratitude, I add a last acknowledgment. During one research interview, a resident, recalling his life spent in the Town of Highlands commented, "I'm thankful I could raise my family here." Indeed, so am I.

Ronnie Clark Coffey
June 6, 2006

BIBLIOGRAPHY

Beach, Lewis. *Cornwall*. Newburgh, NY: E. M. Ruttenber and Sons, 1873.

Binneweiss, Robert O. *Palisades: 100,000 Acres in 100 Years*. New York: Fordham University Press, 2001.

Brunner, Sister M. Gabriel. *Highland Falls during the Jacksonian Era*: 1970.

Carr, William and Richard J. Koke. *Twin Forts of the Popolopen*. Bear Mountain, NY: Bear Mountain Trailside Museums, 1937.

Clark, Donald. "History of the Town of Highlands." *Orange County Times Past* II:IX. Warwick, NY: Salisbury-Hill Publishing Company, 1997.

Clark, Donald F. *Fort Montgomery and Fort Clinton*. Fort Montgomery, NY: Town of Highlands, 1952.

Cole, Mark. "Buffalo Soldier Recalls Days at West Point." *Pointer View* 43, no. 4 (January 30, 1987): 10.

Daly, Kathleen and Angel D'Arpa. *Ninety Years in the Highlands*. Highland Falls, NY: Sacred Heart Church, 1960.

Eager, Samuel Esq. *History of Orange County*. Newburgh, NY: S. T. Callahan, 1846.

Fischer, Charles L., ed. *The Most Advantageous Situation in the Highlands*. Albany, NY: New York State Museum, 2004.

Foreman, Sidney. *A Hudson Highlands Social History*. Fort Montgomery, NY: 1983.

Howell, William Thompson. *The Hudson Highlands*. New York: Walking News, 1982.

Hudson River Restoration. *Hudson River Sloops*. Hastings-on-Hudson, NY: Morgan and Morgan Publishers, 1970.

Koke, Richard. *Who Was Mrs. Pell?* Bear Mountain, NY: Palisades Interstate Park Commission Press, 2002.

Lenik, Edward. *Max Schrabish, Rockshelter Archaeologist*. Wayne, NJ: Wayne Township Historical Commission, 1998.

Logan, Emilie Louise. *West Point, Gibraltar of the Hudson*. West Point, NY: West Point Hotel, 1918.

Maher, Sgt. Marty. *Bringing up the Brass*. Revised Edition. Quechee, VT: Vermont Heritage Press, 2002.

Myles, William J. *Harriman Trails*. New York: New York–New Jersey Trail Conference, 1991.

News of the Highlands. Volumes I-LXXXXI, 1893–1981.

1909 Hudson-Fulton Celebration: The Fourth Annual Report on the Hudson Celebration Commission to the Legislature of the State of New York. Albany, NY: 1910.

Ransom, James M. *Vanishing Ironworks of the Ramapos*. New Brunswick, NJ: Rutgers University Press, 1966.

Ringwald, Donald C. *Hudson River Day Line*. Berkeley, CA: Howell-North Books, 1965.

Salomon, Julian Harris. *Indians of the Lower Hudson Region: The Munsee*. New City, NY: Historical Society of Rockland County, 1982.

Sanders, Katherine. *The Story of the Battle of Fort Montgomery*. Highland Falls, NY: Highland Falls Public Library, 1969.

Sergent, Mary Elizabeth. *They Lie Forgotten*. Middletown, NY: Prior King Press, 1986.